Public Sector Management

Fourth Edition

Norman Flynn

FINANCIAL TIMES

Prentice Hall

An imprint of **Pearson Education**

Harlow, England · London · New York · Reading, Massachusetts · San Francisco · Toronto · Don Mills, Ontario · Sydney
Tokyo · Singapore · Hong Kong · Seoul · Taipei · Cape Town · Madrid · Mexico City · Amsterdam · Munich · Paris · Milan

Pearson Education Limited
Edinburgh Gate
Harlow
Essex CM20 2JE

and Associated Companies throughout the world

Visit us on the World Wide Web at:
www.pearsoneduc.com

First published in 1990 under the
Harvester Wheatsheaf imprint

© Harvester Wheatsheaf 1990
© Prentice Hall UK Limited 1993, 1997
© Pearson Education Limited 2002

ISBN 0273–64634–6

British Library Cataloguing-in-Publication Data
A catalogue record for this book is available from the British Library

10 9 8 7 6 5 4 3 2 1
05 04 03 02

Typeset in $^{10}/_{12}$pt Janson by 35
Printed in Great Britain by Henry Ling Ltd, at the Dorset Press, Dorchester, Dorset

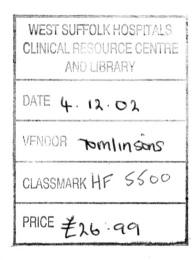

Dedication

This book is dedicated to the memory of Kieron Walsh

Contents

Acknowledgements

Personal Acknowledgements

This book has grown out of the experience of teaching, researching and consulting and therefore owes a lot to all the colleagues, students, clients and research informants along the way. Special thanks are due to Carole Ballardie, Richard Common, Michael Connolly, Ashley Dowlen, Michael Flynn, Peter Hall, Dominic Hurley, Veronica James, Andrew Likierman, Stephanie Macauley, Elizabeth Mellon, Clive Miller, Janet Newman, Sandra Nutley, Alice Perkins, Andrew Puddephatt, Ellie Scrivens, John Stewart, (late) Kieron Walsh, Stuart Wilks-Heeg.

Publisher's Acknowledgements

We are grateful to the following for permission to reproduce copyright material:

Figure 1.1 after Figure in Employment in the Public and Private Sectors in *Economic Trends*, No. 547, June (MacGregor, D., 1999); Figures 1.2, 4.3, 4.4 and 4.5 from *Social Trends*, 31 (ONS, 2001); Table 1.3 from *Public Spending and Statistical Analyses 2000* (HM Treasury, 2000); Table 1.4 after Table in Office of National Statistics, November (ONS, 2000); Table 1.5 after Table in *Public Spending Statistical Analyses 2000*, Cm 4601 (HM Treasury, 2000); Figures 3.1, 3.2 and 3.3 after Figures in *Comprehensive Spending Review* (HM Treasury, 2000); Figure 3.4 after Chart in *Budget March 2001* (HM Treasury, 2001); Table 3.4 after Table in *Comprehensive Spending Review* (HM Treasury, 2000); Figure 4.1 from *Modernising Local Government Finance: A Green Paper*, September (DETR, 2000); Table 4.1 after Table in *The Changing Welfare State* (Department of Social Security, 2000); Figure 4.2 from *Modernising Social Services: Social Services Inspectorate 9th Annual Report* (Social Services Inspectorate, 2000); Table 4.2 after Table in *Modernising Social Services: Social Services Inspectorate 9th Annual Report*, Appendix A (Social Services Inspectorate, 2000); Table 4.3 after Table in *Social Trends*, 31 (ONS, 2001); Table 4.5 after Table in *Our Future Homes, Opportunity, Choice, Responsibility*, Cm 2901 (Department of the Environment and Welsh Office, 1995); Figures 4.6 and 4.7 after Figures in *Social Trends*, 31 (ONS, 2001); Table 4.7 after Table in *Social Trends*, 31 (ONS, 2001); Figure 7.3 after Figure in *Making a Difference: Effective Implementation of Cross-Cutting Policy, A Scottish Executive Policy Unit Review*, June (Hogg, K., 2000); Figure 10.2 after Figure in *NHS Performance Indicators* (Department of Health, 2000); Table 11.1 after Table in *Economic Trends*, No. 565, HMSO (2000), Figures 13.1 and 13.2 from *The Annual Report of Her Majesty's Chief Inspector of Schools*, February (Department for Education and Employment, 2001); Table 13.2 after Table in *MORI, Consumer Focus for Public Services, People's Panel, Wave 5* (Cabinet Office, 2000); Figure 13.3 from *Compendium of Health Statistics* (Office of Health Economics, 1995); Table 13.3 after Table in *The Annual Report of Her Majesty's Chief Inspector of Schools*, February (Department for Education and Employment, 2001); Figure 13.4 after Figure in *Compendium of Health Statistics, 12th Edition* (Office of Health Economics, 2000), all Crown copyright. Crown copyright material is reproduced under Class Licence Number C01W0000039 with the permission of the Controller of HMSO and the Queen's Printer for Scotland; Table 7.1 from Capita Profile, figures for 2000, in *Hoover's Company Profiles*, reprinted by permission of Hoover's, Inc.; Figures 7.4 and 7.5 from Capita Group plc unpublished presentation, reprinted by permission of The Capita Group plc; Figure 9.1 from A spectrum of consumer/citizen control in *Public Money and Management*, July–September, Blackwell Publishers (Skelcher, C. K., 1993); Tables 11.2 and 11.3 after Tables in *Britain at Work: As depicted in the 1998 Workplace Employee Relations Survey*, Routledge (Cully, M. *et al.*, 1999).

We are indebted to HMSO for the reproduction of an extract from HM Inspector of Prison's report on Wandsworth, published October 1999.

While every effort has been made to trace the owners of copyright material, in a few cases this has proved impossible and we take this opportunity to offer our apologies to any copyright holders whose rights we have unwittingly infringed.

Part

1

Introduction

This is a book about management in the public sector in the United Kingdom. Successive governments have restructured, reformed, privatized, reorganized and modernized public services so that managers and workers are uncertain about what will happen next and unsure about what is expected of them. This book helps anyone who is working in or studying the public sector to understand and cope with the recent changes, and places them in the context of the development of the welfare state.

What is the public sector?

The scope of the public sector has changed since the 1980s. There has been a programme of privatization which has transferred virtually all the nationalized industries into private ownership, along with the public utilities. The privatized industries are now no different from other companies in the private sector. In the case of the utilities and telecommunications, the public sector is still involved in the industries as a regulator, especially of price movements.

In other areas, the boundary between the public and private sectors has changed as activities have remained under public control but been contracted out to companies. The policy of compulsory competitive tendering in local government transferred work on a whole range of activities to contractors. Contracting out in the National Health Service (NHS) increased the involvement of companies in ancillary services, such as cleaning and catering, while the Private Finance Initiative (PFI) involves the private sector in designing, building, financing and operating hospitals which are leased to the NHS, and in schools, military establishments and highways. In the Civil Service, market testing, 'strategic contracting' and partnerships have involved companies in running computer systems, security, laboratories and a whole range of activities previously done by state employees. While the services carried out by these companies are still financed by taxation, and they therefore remain as public services, the ways of managing them through contracts rather than through employment contracts with individuals are different and require new skills.

As well as these transactions across the boundary between the public and private sectors there is still a large public sector in which services are provided by state employees, who number 5 million. About 20% of the economy consists of public services and a further 20% of GDP is taken up by transfers of pensions, benefits and subsidies.

What is management?

Management in the public sector means many different things. First, there is a distinction between administration and management, the former involving the orderly arrangement of resources to follow previously defined procedures and rules, the latter involving discretion in the management of resources to achieve a set of objectives. In practice, both activities occur in public services: many activities require administration rather than management, and many managers are engaged in both. The distinction may in any case be more a matter of language than practice. After all, the most 'managerial' qualification which people take is the MBA, or Master of Business Administration.

Management, in the sense of exercising some discretion, requires that managers think and act to find the best ways of achieving some target or objective, using other people's skills. In this sense, the managers become distinct from the various professions in the public sector, such as teachers, doctors, nurses, social workers, engineers, lawyers and accountants, who use their own professional skills and knowledge to produce results. The distinction between a manager and a professional has been promoted by those who believe in management and by the professionals, who like to remain different from managers. Professionals keep their knowledge and skills within the profession and look after the resources put at their disposal using their own ideas about how to work.

In this sense management is 'the management', or a group of people who are separate from those doing the work, whether of a professional, technical or manual kind. 'The management' has some formal authority as well as a set of activities, such as budgeting, performance measurement, setting up organizational arrangements, which they perform to direct and control the others. While such managers may previously have been technicians, workers or professionals, once they are put into a managerial position they behave as a manager.

To be able to do this, and to keep themselves in a position of authority over the others, they have to acquire a set of techniques, skills and language which give their claim to authority some legitimacy. Managers develop or learn them as a way of keeping in control. The techniques include strategic planning, budgeting, project management, marketing, personnel management, performance management, quality procedures and the whole apparatus of contracting. The language is sometimes only understood by a select few, although often there is a normal word which would be a good substitute. For example, 'delayering' would be understood by most people as sacking middle management, 'downsizing' as sacking management and workers, 'business process re-engineering' as doing things differently, 'quality circles' as groups of workers discussing how to do things better, 'network organization' as a group of subcontractors, and 'mission statement' as understanding what they are supposed to do.

In the public sector, politicians also claim a legitimacy to manage. After all, if they are elected to positions of authority and are held accountable for the money spent on public services, they have a right to influence how they are run. The distinction between policy and management is not always clear. Managers, as well as professionals, will have views about what are the most effective services and therefore which should be provided. At the same time, politicians will have views about the best way to manage, either from their experience or from beliefs about management which they have developed or acquired though politics.

Ideas about management are not technical and free of values. Many of the main ideas about how organizations should be run are based on beliefs about people's motivation, how they relate to each other, the use of authority, and the extent to which people can be trusted. In other words, management itself can be ideological. Indeed 'managerialism' or the pursuit of a particular set of management ideas has itself been described as an ideology.

In many cases where activities have been contracted out to the private sector, the management activity of public sector managers does not consist of directly managing resources. Rather, the task is how to specify services and make sure that contractors provide them in accordance with the specification. For many this has meant that they have to get new skills, in contract writing, negotiating and supervising another organization's work.

Change and the search for a mode of control

There is no doubt that the way in which the public sector is managed has changed, not only in the United Kingdom but also in other countries faced with similar issues of rising demand for and expectations of services, governments nervous of the level of public expenditure, and the development of different ways of managing in the private sector. Not all governments have approached the issue in the same way as the United Kingdom, although all have had similar aims — which are to try to increase the efficiency with which public money is spent while maintaining political support.

Management was once seen as the solution to the problem that the professionals were in charge of public services and could not be brought under political control. In this version of management, the targets, incentives and controls of a top-down approach to management, known in the 1950s as Management By Objectives, were imposed in a range of services. Ministers set big targets and sent them down though the hierarchy, where they were translated into more and more explicit individual targets.

The other problem that politicians detected in public services was that they were bureaucracies, run according to set rules and procedures and not susceptible to change. Management was one solution to this problem, asking people to be managers rather than administrators. The other solution was the market, according to a belief that competition would apply pressure on cost and quality of public services.

When neither management nor markets turned out to be the complete solution to the problems of professional rule and bureaucracy, other modes of control were sought. These included a bigger role for auditors and inspectors, greater use of collaborative working and a focus on policy outcomes.

All of these solutions have been pursued at the same time. Collaboration is required at the same time as competition. Audit and inspection of management processes and work practices are imposed at the same time as the requirement to meet efficiency targets.

The structure of the book

This book is in two parts. Part One is concerned with the institutional, political, financial and policy environment in which managers work and how the environment affects them. Part Two deals with the main aspects of management practice in the public sector and the search for alternative modes of control. It ends with an assessment of how successful the changes have been and speculates on the future.

Chapter 1 describes the public sector, its scale and institutions. It shows that the privatization programme has made the public sector smaller by transferring nationalized industries and public utilities to private ownership but that the Civil Service, local government and the National Health Service are still recognizable and relatively stable in numbers employed and money spent. There have been changes in boundaries, functions and methods of control but the institutions themselves would be recognized as similar by someone who had seen them at any time during the past fifty years.

Chapter 2 starts by looking back over that period at the development of the public sector. It shows that, while the Second World War and the post-war reconstruction were very significant, many of the institutions of the welfare state had been formed before the war. While there was a long period in which no very radical change was made to the size and functions of the state, this did not mean that there was a complete consensus: there were always those who wanted to reduce the scope of the welfare state. It also argues that there was not as explicit or strong an agreement between the state, the employers and the trade unions about the economy and welfare provision as there was in other countries.

Similarly, it is possible to exaggerate the extent to which the election of the Conservative government under Margaret Thatcher in 1979 was a sudden, radical change from a previously consensual approach to these matters. While the post-1979 government spoke of 'rolling back the frontiers of the state', the previous Labour government had started the process of trying to reduce spending and the Thatcher government concentrated mainly on privatization of nationalized industries and the sale of council houses, rather than reducing the scale of the welfare state institutions. The governments under John Major's leadership were in some ways more radical, using processes which had been established under the Thatcher governments to tighten central control over the welfare state and introducing an ideology of management that had real effect. It argues that the Blair government, despite its talk of a 'Third Way', shared many characteristics with the Conservative administrations it succeeded.

Chapter 3 deals with public expenditure. It describes where the money comes from and what it is spent on. It then makes distinctions between types of expenditure, capital and current and services and transfers, which are important in understanding how spending changes are achieved. Budgeting and spending control in the main sectors are described, together with their implications for managers. It argues that one change introduced by the Labour government is a change in the attitude towards public spending, ending a period in which the aspiration (although not the achievement) was to cut spending.

Chapter 4 is concerned with the effects of changes in social policy on management. The purpose is to identify the changes in recent years, which have meant that managers have had to change their behaviour. There were six themes apparent in the long period of Conservative rule: from equality of treatment to different treatment of different people; from universal services to selection and more rationing; the promotion of a 'mixed economy' of provision of services by public, private and voluntary sectors; some increase in choice for users of services; the development of stronger central policy control while allowing more local managerial autonomy and accountability; and changes in funding regimes towards performance or competition. The chapter asks how many of these themes the Labour government continued and whether new themes emerged, and finds an eclectic mixture of attitudes and policies.

Part Two looks at how governments and managers have changed how the public sector is run. The introduction sets out the framework of analysis, the search for modes of control to replace or supplement rule by professionals and rule by bureaucracy.

Chapter 5 examines the nature of the markets that have been put in place. It first looks at the arguments in favour of markets and shows that there are political limits to a market solution. When it describes the markets in health, local government and the Civil Service it shows that they have been used for different purposes in different places and the structures of the markets vary. In the main, markets have been used as a way of controlling costs, rather than improving consumer choice. The chapter also looks at how managers respond to the markets in which they find themselves. It argues that the degree of competition determines how much change managers have to make but that the minimum effect is that they have to be very clear about exactly what it is they do and how much it costs. A strong element of competition leads to uncertainty and fragmentation. The introduction of markets has also promoted the growth of public service companies, based both in the United Kingdom and elsewhere.

Chapter 6 is about the contractual relationships which have developed in the markets. It shows that just as the form of the markets varies, so do the relationships. In some cases, where contracts are essentially internal, they look more like budgets and operational plans than contracts. It looks at the elements of the contractual relationship and how they have developed in the public sector. It concludes that when we look in detail at the contractual arrangements they often reflect a hierarchical relationship rather than what we would define as a market. The Labour government recognized this, especially in the NHS, and reverted to administrative control instead of a market approach. The chapter also examines the big contracts between the government and various suppliers of information and communications technology and asks why such big overspends and failures were possible.

Chapter 7 looks at the response of managers to the request that organizations should collaborate more with each other. It finds that there are different degrees of collaboration and that the behaviours required vary according to how close collaboration needs to be. It concludes that it is possible to identify those factors that encourage or inhibit collaboration.

Chapter 8 looks at the use of audit and inspection as a mode of control. It shows that the role of audit and inspection has changed and that inspectors are laying down specific ways of managing. It also shows that the results of inspection vary according to sector. Some departments have greater powers to intervene in the management of their institutions than others. The extreme case is prisons, where the management arrangements seem to give the Home Office little control over what happens in prisons despite inspections. Schools, on the other hand, are susceptible to intervention.

In Chapter 9, the relationship between the state and the users of services is examined. It argues that people have a variety of relationships with the state, some of which are equivalent to a customer–supplier relationship, and some which are custodial and unwelcome. People also have a relationship derived from citizenship rather than consumption. These complications make 'customer orientation' a difficult thing for managers. The chapter sets out some ideas on how a service-user and citizen orientation might be developed.

Chapter 10 turns to performance measurement and management. Managers have increasingly been asked to account not just for the money they have spent but also how effectively they have spent it and to what result. The chapter defines economy, productive efficiency, allocative efficiency, effectiveness and equity. It argues that a distinction needs to be made between measuring the effects of policy and measuring managerial effectiveness. Choices about what services to provide and for whom are often more important to the people than how efficiently they are managed. Performance measurement should be distinguished from policy evaluation.

Chapter 11 turns to the management of people. It shows that there are two main approaches: people can be told what to do in detail and controlled tightly, or they can be given autonomy to work in their own way, using their skills and knowledge. The arrangements that have been put in place in recent years have a tendency towards the former. The chapter then looks at how people are paid and finds that there is an increase in the use of personal contracts and performance-related pay and a decrease in the use of automatic increments for everyone. Pay bargaining has been localized in the NHS and the Civil Service, although the problem of disparities caused by local bargaining in local government has caused it to turn back to national bargaining.

Chapter 12 is about managing money. It looks at the relationship between the mode of management control and the style of financial management. It shows that the national budget process is moving towards trying to generate a more effective use of the money provided and describes the recent changes in financial management and accounting.

Chapter 13 deals with two questions: Can we assess the effect of all these changes? What is likely to happen in the future? Nobody has carried out an evaluation of the managerial changes, so the answers to the first question are only indicative. However, three answers emerge: the Civil Service has not reduced running costs significantly, other than by shedding functions. Even where Civil Service staff numbers have been reduced, costs have not come down proportionately as the jobs have largely been transferred to the private sector. The NHS seems to have become more efficient, increasing hospital output by twice as much as the increase in cost, in real terms. In school education, improvement of which has recently been a government priority, we see small but discernible increases in standards.

As to the future, the chapter considers the influences on public sector management, including the macro- and micro-economic conditions, political conditions and attitudes, 'events' that provoke change, and the institutional arrangements. It concludes that if managers are to influence the way in which the public sector is managed they have to understand the context in which they operate and be prepared to demonstrate that their methods work. If not, they will have their ways of working determined for them.

1

THE PUBLIC SECTOR IN THE UNITED KINGDOM

Introduction

This chapter defines the public sector. What is private and what is public varies between countries and with time within countries. We start by asking whether users of services or workers are concerned about whether the organizations providing services are in public or private ownership, and conclude that people are probably more concerned with quality and accessibility of services as users, and income and security as workers, than with the ownership of the assets. In any case, the distinctions are no longer very clear. Private companies using state-owned assets are providing public services. The state is leasing assets owned and managed by private companies. Workers in the state sector may be employed on casual or temporary contracts and be badly paid.

One characteristic makes the management of public services different in principle from managing private services: the fact that they are not usually sold to people at a price that yields a profit and are not withheld from people who cannot afford them. While even this definition is not inclusive of all public services it is the most important in thinking about the differences in the way in which they are run. In private services, marketing is designed to attract customers. Strategies of market segmentation are designed to distinguish between types of customer and offer them different services at different prices. Good service is offered to persuade people to come back. In the public sector, the problem is often one of rationing, not marketing; considerations of equity require that all service users are treated similarly, and pricing, where it is done, is not normally to maximize profit. The whole purpose of public services is not to make money but to collectively provide protection, help, restraint, education, recreation and care outside market relationships.

The United Kingdom has been through a period of transferring industries and assets from state ownership to private ownership. The scale of privatization, the reasons for it and some of the effects are then briefly looked at. The main results have been to raise a large amount of revenue for the government and reduce employment in the privatized companies.

The chapter then describes the scale and scope of the remaining public sector, including the Civil Service, local government, the NHS and 'quangos' or quasi-non-governmental organizations, with which the rest of the book is concerned.

It concludes by asking whether the United Kingdom is different from other countries. On one dimension, spending on social protection, the United Kingdom is close to the European average. A main difference is that the UK state is more centralized than that of most other countries, despite the genuine devolution in Scotland and to a lesser extent Wales.

What is a public service? The boundary between the public and private sectors

A premise of this book is that managing public services is not the same as managing services in the private sector. It is important to be clear about what the differences and similarities are, so that good ideas and ways of working from both sectors can be applied in the public sector.

A public view

A public opinion survey commissioned by the Trades Union Congress during the last Conservative government's term of office[1] produced answers which surprised people working in public services. The respondents made no distinction between services provided to the public by public institutions and those provided by companies. Banks were linked in people's minds with hospitals and social security. This was not a result of ignorance but of concern: people were concerned with good service not with the ownership of the facilities or the employment contracts of the service providers. Who knows or cares whether the staff at their local leisure centre are employed by the local authority or a leisure management company? Or that their income tax or council tax form is processed on a computer operated by a private sector employee? Or, more obscurely, that the hospital in which they are being treated is owned by a developer and leased for 60 years, serviced, to the NHS Trust?

The exceptions were the public utilities, especially gas and water, where opinion surveys showed that people resented the combination of higher charges, poor service and the publicity given to the very large salary increases for senior management. This seemed not to be an objection in principle to privatization but to the practice of a few people getting rich at the public's expense. This reaction also produced a majority against the privatization of the railways and the Post Office. The catastrophic record of track maintenance following the privatization of the railway and its division into many separate operating companies shows that public opinion was probably correct.

At the same time, surveys have shown that citizens do not have a clear idea about the distribution of functions among the institutions of the state. 'The social' refers to social security and social services; few people have a clear idea about the distribution of functions between the tiers of local government, where these still exist. This makes accountability to the public difficult and is a contributor to the low levels of participation in local elections.

The employees' view

Employees may have a different opinion. Surely a 'proper job' is more likely to be found in the Civil Service or other public services than in a company which has a short-term contract with the government or local authority. Traditionally jobs with local authorities were considered secure if not very well paid. People who preferred security or were at a stage in their life where security was most important could find stable employment, usually with provision for an occupational pension. Now there is great variation. If you are a casual cleaner, employed on a weekly contract with an office cleaning company, then your terms and conditions of employment are probably much worse than a previous position in which cleaners were employed directly, with sick pay and holiday pay. The change from public to private is not just a matter of benefits and pay, it is also a question of affiliation to the institution. In the cases of both hospital and school cleaners, there was often a rapport between the cleaners and the patients and children, benefiting both sides in the relationship: a (usually) friendly representative of an otherwise daunting institution getting satisfaction from personal contact in an otherwise tedious job. Once cleaning is contracted out, staff are moved from one site to another with no time to stop and say hello, so both sides lose those benefits.

If you are a home carer, working as a self-employed person for a homecare agency, you are probably earning the minimum wage and in a less secure job than when you used to be employed by the social services department. Contracting out low-paid jobs such as these has resulted in lower pay, fewer benefits and less security, especially for women workers.

However, if you are a clerical worker on a short-term contract with the Benefits Agency, you may well have less security than if you had been employed as a programmer by a company running one of the Benefits Agency's computer applications. Certainly if you are employed as a leisure centre worker by a leisure company with a three-year contract with a local authority, you are probably better off than a casual worker taken on by the same authority. In an extreme case, that of management consultants working for companies contracted to the government, the benefits are much higher than those of a civil servant, as the numerous civil servants who made the transition discovered. People resigned from government departments, under policies of staff reductions, joined a consulting firm and were hired back at three to four times their cost and paid twice their previous salary.

In other words, security is not a necessary result of working for public authorities any more; nor is it necessarily the case that employment in companies contracted to the public sector is less secure than a public sector job. The unskilled and low-paid, whether in the clerical or manual operations, are increasingly insecure with both employers.

Public goods and public services

There are four elements to the distinction between private and public services. The first is that certain things are 'public goods'. One feature of such goods and services is that they produce 'externalities', or benefits that accrue to people other than those who benefit directly. For example, education is said to benefit everyone living in a society of skilled and educated people. The other feature is that people cannot be excluded from certain benefits. Everyone benefits from clean air or street lighting. Because no one can be excluded, people should pay for such services collectively rather than individually. Even those politicians who believe that the state should do the minimum possible are normally willing to concede that these categories of services should be carried out by the public sector. Some people believe that no services are better provided by government and that even clean air is best achieved by property rights in air.

As a *justification* for the public sector, the 'public goods' argument suggests that the public sector should provide services where the market fails to do so, and the goods or services are required collectively, a decision made through the political process. As an *explanation* of what is public and what is private it is less convincing, since different services are in the public and private sectors in different societies and at different stages of development. Examples of the differences include the extensive provision of education through religious organizations but financed by the state in the Netherlands, the private provision of ambulances and fire protection in Denmark, and public ownership of airlines in various countries. History and politics have more convincing explanations than a theory about public goods. Britain went through a period in which the ruling Conservative Party had an instinctive suspicion of public provision and preference for markets and the private sector. The Labour Party abandoned its belief in state ownership as part of its modernization programme and claims to be pragmatic in its approach to what should be private and what should be public.

The second distinction is how services are financed. Services are public services if they are financed mainly by taxation, rather than by direct payments by individual customers. One characteristic of some public services is that they are not available for sale and people cannot necessarily have more if they pay more. Even those services which are 'commercial', in the sense that money is exchanged at the point of consumption, are still public services in the sense that they are controlled through the political process, and accountability for service delivery is through politicians to the public rather than to shareholders.

The distinction is no longer absolute. People who receive homecare, for example, may pay for extra hours beyond those which they are assessed as needing. Although it is not legal, school children who do not pay for school visits may be left at school. Some services which are public are subject to charging: leisure facilities and car parks are normally charged for at cost or close to it. The NHS has charged for drugs since 1952, and in 1995 patients paid about 10% of the cost of drugs to the NHS.[2] NHS Trusts have private wings in which patients who pay may receive quicker treatment and better facilities than NHS patients. A high proportion of public services are 'free', at least at the point at which they are used: most of education and health, social security, criminal justice.

A third difference is who owns the facilities and by whom the service providers are employed. Traditionally public services were provided by public employees in public buildings. Again, such a distinction is not absolute, after a period of contracting out and privatization. Take public transport. In the United Kingdom outside London, bus transport is privately owned and deregulated. But there are still public service features. Everyone benefits from there being a public transport system, even car users, whose freedom to drive is enhanced by having passengers on buses. In London, buses are privately owned, but the routes are regulated by London Transport Buses and some routes are subsidized. Or take refuse collection. Where private companies have won the right to collect rubbish, their employees are not public employees, the vehicles may or may not be owned by the local authorities, but the details of the service are determined by the local authority.

The main defining characteristic is whether goods and services are sold only to people who pay for them and whether anyone with money can access them while other people are excluded. For people running and providing the services this distinction is important. In a business, the task is to attract customers, persuade them to pay a price that produces a profit, and satisfy them enough to persuade them to remain customers. Public services have to attract people to use them, but they also have to enforce eligibility criteria where scarce resources have to be rationed in a way which does not apply in the private sector; scarce services are rationed by price. In the public sector, resources are rarely deliberately rationed by price. Prescription charges for drugs may deter poor people from taking medication, but there are safeguards to try to ensure that people in need do not have to pay and are not deterred. Nor do the managers and workers of public services have to satisfy people enough to persuade them to return. In those cases where the service is a monopoly, the service users have no choice. Even if they have a choice, it is not always the case that attracting more service users creates benefits for the organization or its workers: often it just means more work. The motivation for satisfying customers is not to persuade them to return and generate more profit, but the value of public service.

It is really this last feature, the lack of a direct connection between ability to pay and access to the service and the fact that there is not always a direct

Table 1.1 Privatization proceeds, 1979–96, £ million

1979–81	578	1988–9	7069
1981–2	493	1989–90	4225
1982–3	455	1990–1	5347
1983–4	1139	1991–2	7952
1984–5	2050	1992–3	8184
1985–6	2706	1993–4	5460
1986–7	4458	1994–5	6300
1987–8	5140	1995–6	2500

Source: HM Treasury (February 1995) *Public Expenditure: Statistical Supplement to the Financial Statement and Budget Report 1995–96*, Cm 2821. London: HM Treasury; and HM Treasury (March 1996) *Public Expenditure, Statistical Analyses 1996–97*, Cm 3201. London: HM Treasury

benefit from attracting customers, that makes management in the public sector distinct: marketing to generate sales is mostly irrelevant, unless artificial markets are created. Customer satisfaction as expressed by repeat business is not a relevant measure of success, and nor is profitability. Motivations for good service are not themselves based on profit.

If these differences did not exist, then managing in the private and public sectors would be identical. Of course there are similarities: people's motivations in both sectors may have no connection with the well-being of the organization or its customers; services in both sectors need to be designed and managed in similar ways; and organizations have to be created to support the service process. Underlying these techniques, however, are the important differences in values and definitions of success.

Privatization

The Conservative governments from 1979 reduced the scale of the public sector through a series of privatizations, initially the sale of nationalized industries, such as Cable and Wireless and British Aerospace (1981). Then came oil (British Petroleum first shares in 1983) and telecommunications (British Telecom 1984). The utilities were privatized in the late 1980s (gas 1986, water 1989 and electricity 1990). Revenues from privatization since the mid-1990s have mainly come from the sale of the remaining government shares in businesses such as British Telecom. 1996/7 privatizations raised a further £10 billion, in an effort to maintain the flow of revenue at the levels attained before 1995/6. The scale of the privatizations under the Conservatives is shown in Table 1.1.

The main form of privatization has been the flotation of the company on the stock market. British Telecom, Gas and Steel, together with the water and electricity supply industries, were all sold in this way. Other privatizations were by 'trade sale', where businesses were sold to existing companies, including Royal Ordnance, National Bus Company, British Rail areas and British Coal. Some were sold to management and employee buyouts, including National Freight Corporation, parts of British Leyland, parts of British Coal and some of the research laboratories, e.g. the Laboratory of the Government Chemist.

Apart from these 'denationalizations', privatization has been achieved in other ways. Contracting out has been pursued in local authorities, the National Health Service and central government. In these cases, the state retains the function but has the work carried out by contractors. Sometimes the contracting out process is carried out by organizing a competition between the existing employees and private companies, in a tendering process. In other cases, there is a competition without a bid from the in-house employees. In yet other cases, there is no competition, rather a negotiation between the government department and a preferred supplier. In central government, the competition policy was stated in a White Paper in 1991, *Competing for Quality*. Departments and agencies were expected to subject a proportion of their work either to 'market testing', i.e. inviting a competition between the private sector and the in-house teams to bid for existing work, or to what was known as 'strategic contracting', i.e. an invitation to outside firms to tender for work without an in-house bid. The Labour government slightly changed this policy for the Civil Service through its Better Quality Services initiative and a new office to oversee procurement, but continued with the outsourcing programme.

Another form of privatization was the Private Finance Initiative, which was announced in 1992, under which private companies were invited to design, build, finance and operate facilities which would then be leased to public authorities. The initiative was to include roads, hospitals, computer facilities and anything else which the private sector was willing to supply. PFI is discussed in more detail in Chapter 12.

Privatization was the main cause of the shrinking scale of employment in the public sector. Figure 1.1 shows trends in employment in the main parts of the public sector from 1981 to 1998. The overall numbers fell from over 7 million at the beginning of the period to around 5 million at the end, a reduction of more than 2 million. Of those reductions, 1,355,000 were in the nationalized industries. Local government lost 321,000, mainly because of the transfer of outsourced jobs, education lost 250,000, almost all because schools and colleges were redefined as private when they became corporate bodies. The Civil Service shrank by 200,000 and the armed forces by 114,000. Only the sale of nationalized industries involved the state withdrawing from activities because of a political view about the role of the state. The reduction of the scale of the armed forces was the result of the end of the Cold War. The other reductions involved contracting out or the redefinition of the sector.

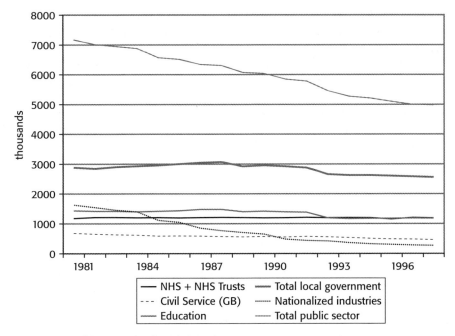

Figure 1.1   Public sector employment trends
Source: HMSO (June 1999) *Economic Trends* No. 547, 25–38

Why privatization?

Although privatization was not in the manifesto of the Conservative Party for the 1979 general election, by 1981 it had become a central part of the policies of the Thatcher governments. As the privatizations proceeded, they became part of the political campaign to revitalize the British economy by reducing the scale of the state, reducing taxation and returning decisions about investment from politicians to managers and owners of companies.

There were also fiscal reasons to continue with the privatization programme. The annual revenues raised from privatization rose to £7 billion at their peak, contributing to total public spending of around £250 billion, and allowing government to keep down the standard rate of income tax, a politically sensitive figure for a government committed to reducing taxation but forced by economic circumstances to raise it. Revenues from privatization became an important element in the budget.

Privatization also became a cause which symbolized Prime Minister Thatcher's project and united the right wing of the Conservative Party after her replacement. In November 1994, an economist in a London stockbrokers[3] said: 'Privatization projects are becoming less and less important in what they contribute to government spending. It's far more important in a political context'. These two aspects of politics — an ideological aversion to state ownership and a desire to keep taxation down — coincided to make privatization attractive.

Increased efficiency was an argument for the early privatizations: governments claimed that British Airways could not have been so successful in public ownership, nor could British Steel have reduced capacity and increased efficiency so quickly. In later years the economic argument switched from the inherent efficiency of the private sector to the availability of private funds for capital investment. Subsequent failures of privatized companies such as Corus (previously British Steel) were only minor political embarrassments.

Price and regulation

The utilities have regulators which set pricing rules and in some cases detailed plans for the companies which now run the industries. The electricity regulator was criticized in 1995 for being too strict a regulator of price, depressing electricity shares by 17% soon after the government had disposed of a block of its shares in the industry. In the case of gas, the regulator imposed, in May 1996, a price regime of RPI – 5% — which reduced the British Gas share price by 10%. These examples illustrate the degree of influence the regulators have on the profitability of the industries. While no longer under public ownership, the utilities are under the influence of governments through the regulators.

Mergers and acquisitions

There has been a trend towards utilities merging with each other within their areas, the electricity and water companies especially. There has also been a lot of take-over activity in the sector. We are seeing the development of global utility companies, such as Lyonnaise des Eaux, which are operating in the United Kingdom in the same way as in their other countries. Similarly, British Rail franchises and businesses have been partly bought by multinational companies. Politicians of all parties take some pride in the fact that UK utility companies are now successfully operating in other countries.

Jobs

All the privatizations have resulted in job losses, as companies sought to increase efficiency. Examples include British Telecom, which lost 90,000 jobs after privatization (20 per cent of the total); Midlands Electricity, which went from 7700 before privatization in 1990 to 4100 in 1995; National Power, which reduced from 11,000 to 4500; PowerGen from 10,000 to 3000, part of a reduction of over 40,000 jobs in the electricity industry; and Yorkshire Water, which reduced from 7000 to 2900 after privatization. When the Wisconsin Transportation Company bought Royal Mail trains and the Royal

Train and the British Rail freight companies it announced that it wanted to reduce the staff from 8000 to 5000. When Stagecoach bought South West Trains it shed 1000 of 4000 jobs.

The future of privatization

While privatization proceeds amount to 1.5–2% of government spending, they are significant in their impact on the tax level and the level of government borrowing. Privatization is not a central part of Labour's ideology. Although it abandoned its commitment to public ownership as a principle its stance became neutral with respect to ownership of assets. Sale of public assets would therefore be acceptable if it could be justified on grounds of efficiency. Unfortunately the easy targets in manufacturing and service industries had already been sold by the time the Party got back into power in 1997. When it wanted to raise funds through privatization it had to sell more difficult 'businesses' in a climate of public opinion that was less in favour of the process than it had been.

The institutions of the state

Despite the privatizations, the public sector is still a very significant part of the economy. It employs about 5 million people out of a workforce of 27 million and spends about 40% of GDP, if we include the payment of pensions and benefits, or about 20% if we exclude them. The main institutions are the local authorities, still the largest public sector employer, the Civil Service, including both its policy aspects and its service delivery functions, and the National Health Service, similarly divided into people who decide what should be done and people who do it. In addition to these institutions there are other public bodies with different statutory forms and different status, many set up to have relatively autonomous routine management, such as school boards, hospital trusts and various entities which are run by people appointed by ministers, whether in England or the devolved administrations.

Devolved government

Constitutional change was an important part of the Labour government's agenda, including changes in the membership of the House of Lords, trying to change the institutions of government in Northern Ireland and creating national assemblies in Scotland and Wales. Scotland and Wales have different devolution arrangements, more powers being devolved to Scotland.

Scotland has a parliament, and a Scottish Executive consisting of ministers drawn from members of the Scottish Parliament. The Scottish Consolidated Fund has about £18 billion. Scotland also has nine executive agencies, including the Scottish Prison Service and Student Awards Agency. While the

Table 1.2   Local government in the United Kingdom

England
46 Unitary authorities in urban areas
36 Metropolitan district councils
32 London boroughs and the Corporation of the City of London
34 County councils in rural areas
238 District councils in rural areas plus parish and town councils

Wales
22 Unitary authorities

Scotland
32 Unitary authorities

Northern Ireland
26 District councils
9 Area Boards for Health and Social Services

Act of Union is still in place, Scotland has developed distinctive policies since the parliament was established in 1999, especially in education, where Scottish universities do not change fees for home undergraduates, and health and social care funding.

Wales has the National Assembly for Wales and a cabinet. The functions on which it can make policy are:

- Agriculture
- Ancient monuments and historic buildings
- Culture
- Economic development
- Education and training
- The environment
- Health and health services
- Highways
- Housing
- Industry
- Local government
- Social services
- Sport and leisure
- Tourism
- Town and country planning
- Transport and roads
- The Welsh language

Wales has only two executive agencies, for historic monuments and European funding.

Both countries have had significant powers and responsibilities devolved to them and are developing distinctive policies and ways of working.

Local authorities

The structure of local government was changed by the Local Government Review, implemented between 1995 and 1998. The distribution of authorities is set out in Table 1.2.

Table 1.3 Current and capital expenditure by local authorities 1999–2000, Great Britain, £million

	Current	Capital
Education and Employment	21,962	1262
Health	9629	147
DETR main programmes	8706	2126
Home Office	9659	239
Legal departments	336	30
Trade and Industry	170	2
Agriculture, Fisheries and Food	41	−6
Culture, Media and Sport	1562	342
Social Security	11,751	
Scotland	6192	579
Wales	2641	475
Northern Ireland	229	60
Total	72,900	5300

Source: HM Treasury (2000) *Public Spending Statistical Analyses 2000*, Table 6.2. London: HM Treasury

In those areas of England which do not have unitary authorities, the main functions of county councils are education and social services, main roads, strategic planning. District councils are responsible for housing, local planning, refuse collection and council tax collection. The parish and town councils do not have many service functions but are important as representative bodies. In Wales and Scotland and the metropolitan and urban areas of England the unitary authorities are responsible for all local authority services. Expenditure by service, defined according to the responsible central government department, is shown in Table 1.3.

Civil Service and the agencies

Table 1.4 shows where civil servants worked in 2000. The biggest employer is the Ministry of Defence, which has one civil servant for every two members of the armed forces. The other big employers are those that collect taxes, nearly 90,000 in the Inland Revenue and Customs and Excise, and those that distribute benefits.

The Civil Service has been divided into departments and executive agencies since 1988. The agencies were established on the principle that management of service delivery would be improved if policy formulation was separated from management. Agencies were to be given explicit performance targets and a defined framework of managerial discretion in which to operate.

About 60 per cent of civil servants work in executive agencies that deliver services on behalf of their parent department. There are 108 such agencies,

Table 1.4 Civil Service staff in post, April 2000[4]

Defence (excludes armed forces of c. 200,000)	101,940
Social Security	85,210
Inland Revenue	66,920
Prison Service	41,790
Education and Employment	37,810
Customs and Excise	22,310
Environment, Transport and Regions	17,810
Home Office	13,150
Scottish Executive	11,190
Lord Chancellor's	10,910
Agriculture, Fisheries and Food	9990
Trade and Industry	9090
Other Chancellor of the Exchequer	5820
Foreign and Commonwealth	5490
Health	5280
Security and intelligence	4520
National Assembly for Wales	2780
Others	34,710
Total	486,720

Source: Office of National Statistics, November 2000

ranging in size from the Social Security Benefits Agency with over 65,000 staff to a conference centre (Wilton Park) with 30 staff. Agency staff are part of the Civil Service but increasingly the responsibility for their management, including pay and grading, is with the agency rather than the Civil Service as a whole. Expenditure by department, including their agencies, is shown in Table 1.5.

National Health Service

The NHS has been reviewed and reorganized many times since it was founded. Organizational form has been used to solve many continuing dilemmas: what should be controlled locally and what centrally? How should local people be represented in decision making? Should the doctors be controlled by somebody other than doctors, and if so, how should this be done? How can access be organized so that people have the same chances of getting treated wherever they live? How should resources be allocated, to populations or to hospitals and other services?

The answers to these questions have been varied. There have been hierarchies of health authorities and various other bodies between the Department of Health and the patients. Local people have been represented on health authorities, although never through direct elections, and on community health councils. The two mechanisms that have been used to control the doctors

Table 1.5 Central government expenditure by department, control total and estimated outturn, 1998–99, £ million

Social Security	81,405
Health	37,376
DoE – local government, regional policy and main programmes	44,213
Defence	22,476
Scotland	14,786
Local authority self-financed expenditure	14,630
Education and Employment	13,851
Northern Ireland	8473
Home Office	7107
Wales	6992
Net payments to EC institutions	3572
Agriculture, Fisheries and Food	3315
Legal departments	2680
Trade and Industry	2585
International Development	2417
Cabinet Office	1248
Foreign and Commonwealth Office	1098
Culture, Media and Sport	846
Chancellor's Departments	2779
Control total	271,849

Source: HM Treasury (2000) *Public Spending Statistical Analyses 2000*, Cm 4601, Table 1.12. London: HM Treasury

have been some form of management through which someone other than a doctor has tried to tell them what to do, and a brief experiment with the market. Resource allocation has always struggled with the fact that hospitals and doctors have been concentrated in the cities while the population is more dispersed, and many formulas have been designed to preserve or correct that imbalance.

Currently the UK has four slightly different organizational forms for healthcare, one for each of Northern Ireland, Scotland, England and Wales. Each was based on its own White Paper or consultation paper complete with catchy title: *Fit for the Future* in Northern Ireland, *Designed to Care* in Scotland, *The New NHS, Modern, Dependable* in England and *Putting Patients First* in Wales. The structures are shown in outline in Table 1.6.

All four systems have trusts. Northern Ireland stands out because of its longstanding integration of health and social services. This is replicated to some extent in the most recent arrangements for care commissioning at local level in the other jurisdictions. England has a longer hierarchy, including a policy board and eight regional offices of the NHS Executive. The division of responsibilities between the various bodies is similar in each case. Trusts, which can be for acute services in hospitals, for integrated services, community services or mental health, enter long-term agreements with the bodies

Table 1.6 National Health Service organization

Northern Ireland	Scotland	England	Wales
Assembly Health and Social Services Executive in Northern Ireland Office	Parliament Scottish Executive	Parliament Secretary of State	Assembly Welsh Office, Health Department
		Policy board	
	Management Executive	NHS Executive	NHS Wales Directorate
		NHSE regional offices	
Health and Social Services councils	Health boards	Health authorities	Health authorities
health and social care partnerships	Local healthcare cooperatives	Primary care groups	Local care groups
	Local health groups	Community health councils	Community health councils
Trusts	Trusts	Trusts (including primary care trusts)	Trusts

responsible for commissioning services. These bodies have different names and compositions in the different places but mostly consist of general practitioners and other healthcare professionals and representatives of social services in a district. In addition there is a body (council, board or authority) whose job is public health and health policy.

About 970,000 people work for the National Health Service in the United Kingdom, including 57,000 medical and dental staff, 473,000 nursing and midwifery staff, 125,000 professional and technical, 213,000 administrative and clerical and 100,000 domestic and ancillary staff.

Quangos

Quango, or quasi-non-governmental organization, is a term used to define those public bodies which are not elected, which are technically independent but whose members are appointed either directly or indirectly by government.

The Cabinet Office defined one category of such organizations: 'A non-departmental public body is a body which has a role in the processes of national government, but is not a government department or part of one, and accordingly operates to a greater or lesser extent at arm's length from Ministers'.[5] They include 325 executive bodies, 814 advisory boards, 71 tribunals and 135 boards of visitors, among them employing about 75,000 people. As well as these, the category of quango should include NHS bodies which are not elected, school boards of governors (about 1000 grant-maintained schools, accountable to the Department for Education and Skills and the 650 boards of further and higher education colleges and universities. There are also the Learning Skills Councils, legally set up as companies contracting with the Department of Education and Employment but which are effectively public sector organizations able to spend £6 billion of public money on education and training.

These bodies do not fall into the traditional structural arrangements of public administration: they are neither part of a government department nor directly run by local government; nor are they public corporations. They have a variety of relationships with government. NHS Trusts contract with purchasers, as do LSCs with the DfES. Further and higher education boards have funding formulas and responsibilities to deliver education but not contracts. They also have a variety of members, some paid, some voluntary.

In many cases the quango is legally established as a company but carries out functions which would otherwise have been carried out by a department or by local authorities. Housing action trusts refurbish housing and estates. The use of companies for these functions has eroded local democracy in the sense that people are appointed rather than elected; it also fragments the actions taken by the state at local level since each body carries out its own mandate.

These arrangements have important implications for managers. One results from the authority and accountability of board members. Local authority members are directly elected and have a legitimacy as a result. Paid officials are accountable to them and understand where responsibility for decisions lies. Similarly the relationship between civil servants and ministers may cause occasional problems but generally people understand who is responsible for what. When working for an appointed board, the relationships are not so clear. Board members may be removed by ministers, for example, so a manager must take account of the minister's wishes as well as the board's. In some cases the boards are very part-time and have no legitimacy which comes from professional expertise. Their relationship with the managers is therefore not hierarchical, as between a company board and company managers: it can be more advisory, with the paid managers having most of the power. Some school boards have this relationship with head teachers.

Is the United Kingdom different?

If we look at expenditure on what in Europe is called 'social protection', including social security and health care, we see that the United Kingdom spends slightly less than the European Union average. Figure 1.2 shows the figures for 1997.

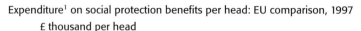

Expenditure[1] on social protection benefits per head: EU comparison, 1997

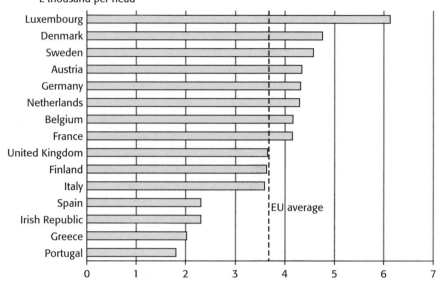

[1] Before deduction of tax, where applicable. Figures are purchasing power parities per inhabitant.

Figure 1.2 Expenditure on social protection, EU comparison, 1997
Source: Social Trends 31, 2000, p.145

The range of spending on social protection as a proportion of GDP in the EU was from 18% in the Republic of Ireland to 34% in Sweden. The figure for the United Kingdom was 27%.

One important difference between the United Kingdom and the rest of Europe and the United States of America is the degree of centralization of the public sector, with the exception of the devolved administrations. Other states have more autonomous local and provincial levels of government. In the cases of Germany, Switzerland and Austria, regional and local governments are protected by the constitution from interference by the federal or central governments, as they are in the United States of America. The protection includes the right to raise local taxation to pay for local services, although this right may be exercised by agreement among levels of government about the overall tax rates. In the extreme case, such as Switzerland, the principle of subsidiarity is put into practice: that no level of government should carry on an activity which could be done at the level below. In the United Kingdom local government can only provide services or carry out activities which are legislated for by Parliament, there being no powers of general competence.

In addition, as we shall see, there is a collection of controls which central government has over local authorities.

Simon Jenkins[6] argues that the Conservative governments' changes to the public sector were all part of a process of 'nationalization' or a reduction of local autonomy. In Chapter 4 we shall see in more detail how control has been centralized by government in all aspects of social policy. What has been decentralized is the detailed administration and management of individual units, such as schools, hospitals and colleges, within a centralized policy and financial framework. In those services which are still under the control of local authorities, the management task for officials and politicians alike is constrained by the controls and influence from government departments and their various monitoring units and inspectorates, supported by guidelines and procedures written by central government. In the NHS, control is exercised through the NHS Executive and the regional offices, supported by directives, guidance and performance information. For those services delivered through executive agencies, ministerial and departmental control is exercised through framework documents, key performance indicators and budgets agreed annually along with business and corporate plans. Of European countries, probably France is the only one that is so centrally controlled, and France has been attempting to decentralize in recent years.

Another difference seems to be one of the attitude to the role of the state and public spending. In northern Europe, governments of all political persuasions seem to regard the state as an integral part of the economy and society, whereas in southern Europe and the United States of America, it is seen only as a last resort for certain functions which cannot be carried out by individuals or companies. UK governments have for a long time tried to define the role and scale of the state, and swing between a north European and a United States approach.

Conclusions

Despite changes in the boundary between the public and private sectors, the public sector is still a significant part of the UK economy. However, the job of management is not only about running departments providing services. Many services are now managed through contracts with companies, and many are privately owned and are not managed but regulated. Even when services are provided by directly employed public servants, there are periodic competitions in many areas which mean that public sector managers have not only to manage within an environment of rationing and other special public sector characteristics but also be competitive. The other aspect of the managerial environment is that while there is decentralization of budgets and operational management, central government operates strong central control.

Further reading

Drakeford, M. (2000) *Social Policy and Privatisation*. London: Longman.

Notes and references

[1] The survey was conducted in 1994 and not published.

[2] Office of Health Economics (2001) *Compendium of Health Statistics*, 12th edn, Figure 4.17.

[3] Adam Cole of James Capel.

[4] On June 8th 2001 the government re-organized the Ministries in England. The Ministry of Agriculture, Fisheries and Food and the Department of Social Security were both abolished and their functions dispersed among other ministries. Four new departments were set up: Environment, Food and Rural Affairs; Transport, Local Government and the Regions; Work and Pensions and Education and Skills. Staff were redistributed from the abolished departments to the new ones.

[5] Cabinet Office (1995) *Public Bodies 1994*. Norwich: HMSO p.v.

[6] Jenkins, S. (1995) *Accountable to None: The Tory Nationalisation of Britain*. London: Hamish Hamilton.

2

POLITICS AND THE PUBLIC SECTOR

Introduction

In the previous chapter we saw that the public sector is still a large part of the economy, despite the privatizations of the 1980s and 1990s. Here, we begin by asking how the current public sector developed. Many of the elements of social security, health and education can be seen before the Second World War, if in somewhat different form, and subsequently the institutions of the state were strengthened as part of the post-war reconstruction during a period of state involvement in most parts of the economy, including basic industries and manufacturing. While there may have been a majority opinion in favour of the broad shape of what became known as the 'welfare state', there was not a consensus in the sense that all politicians agreed even on the proper scale and scope of the public sector. Indeed, as early as the first Conservative government after the war, there were cuts in the size of the Civil Service and the introduction of prescription charges in the NHS. Since then there were other attempts to cut public spending, notably during the Labour administration of 1974–9.

What happened when Margaret Thatcher became Prime Minister in 1979 was not, therefore, a sudden ending of a consensus. It was more that those who favoured a smaller state and lower public spending had gained a majority. This majority was more keen to carry out these policies than the previous, Labour, government although it also had tried. Implementing a radical policy of making the state smaller was not to prove easy, except in the cases of the sale of nationalized industries and council houses. Both policies were achieved by giving the people who bought them a chance of making a quick, usually large financial gain or discount on the market value. The Thatcher administrations also started a process of controlling the public sector, even if they could not reduce its size. Efforts were made to control local government and to change the way in which the health service and the Civil Service were managed.

When John Major became Prime Minister in 1990, many administrative arrangements were already there for him to use in pursuit of his policies. He also found the public finances in a better state than they had been when Margaret Thatcher became Prime Minister, with no public sector borrowing requirement. He used the centralized controls to implement his version of conservatism, which was concerned to reduce the role of the state because he felt that state intervention, especially at local level, was the cause of lack of social cohesion, crime and other social problems. His, and his colleagues', solution was 'civic conservatism', which means voluntary action and voluntary associations, rather than the state, preventing and correcting social problems. In practice this meant stopping local authorities from doing things, especially building housing.

The politics of managing the state which the Major governments pursued were based on the idea that state employees are poorly motivated, unless they are on performance-related pay, that their activities need to be measured and controlled and that managers should be given the right to manage, that is to tell people what to do and expect them to do it. This approach was to be followed only if the function could not be privatized. There was a belief, which had been there during the Thatcher period, that the private sector was inherently better than the public. This was not a theoretical position about markets, rather a preference for business people over public servants.

Political alternatives to this approach come from two sources: the Left and the management theorists. For a period, Labour-controlled local authorities pursued management policies which flattened hierarchies, trusted workers, developed teams and promoted public service values. Meanwhile the 'new human resources management', as some people called it, recommended a similar set of features: it was argued and implemented in progressive companies that organizations are likely to be more able to change if the workers are committed to their employer, are willing to be flexible because their job is safe, and are likely to be more motivated if they can participate in decision making.

The Labour government showed some signs of being a more sympathetic employer, taking some categories of staff off short-term contracts and allowing pay rises, especially for occupations where there was a shortage of staff, such as nursing and teaching. On the other hand, it showed itself quite keen on performance pay and very critical of some public sector workers such as doctors and teachers, whom it saw as unwilling to change.

Foundations of the public sector 1945–79

The 'welfare state'

There was not a social revolution between 1939 and 1945, although the war did change the relationship between the state and civil society: industries were run by government during the war and the reconstruction after the war was led by government. During the immediate post-war period there was rationing of industrial and building materials and planning in the economy, in land use and in public services. Industries such as coal, steel and the railways were taken into state ownership to ensure their survival. It has sometimes been argued that the 'welfare state' was invented during the war and implemented after it in a spirit of consensus and social harmony. The National Assistance Act, the Education Act and the establishment of the NHS during and just after the war have been seen by some as the creation from nothing of a new type of state. While institutions were created and legislation passed, many of the elements of the welfare state were in place for working-class people before the war, including a state social security system, means-tested access to secondary education and a national health insurance scheme. What happened in the period from the mid-1940s was that these benefits and services became universal. This meant that contributions were no longer voluntary and that the middle classes gained access to services now provided by the state, which they had previously funded from savings or insurance. To ensure universality, services were largely controlled by the central government rather than left to local institutions and organizations.

There may have been general agreement that the welfare state was a good idea, especially from those who benefited from it, which included most of the population. There is no doubt that the returning soldiers and others who had lived through the war were keen for a form of state and welfare provision which would prevent a return to the deprivation of the Depression. However, the welfare state was not without its opponents. Glennerster[1] has shown that there has always been a right-wing group in the Conservative Party opposed to universal benefits and tax-funded services. This Right has had periods of influence ever since 1950 and did not emerge without precedent during the first Thatcher government of 1979. The Conservative administration elected in 1951 reduced income tax, introduced prescription charges, cut education spending and reduced NHS staffing levels. This difference of opinion about the right scale and scope of the state has persisted both between and within parties ever since.

One interpretation of the immediate post-war period is that there was a settlement between the trade unions, government and employers. Unions would moderate wage demands in exchange for job security and social benefits, employers would respond by offering stable employment and union recognition, while the government would be responsible for managing the services and benefits as well as steering the economy towards full employment. While the post-war government had full employment as an objective, it was achieved as much through foreign aid, reconstruction and the growth of world trade as it was by economic management. If there was an agreement, it was never as explicit as it was in, for example, Sweden, where there were talks between the three parties — employers, government and trade unions — and an explicit agreement was reached and signed at Saltsjøbaden in 1936.[2] An alternative explanation is that the employers found themselves in a very weak position at the end of the war: factories were destroyed or had been converted to arms production, the workers were returning from the armed forces with ideas about collective bargaining and rights, and materials were scarce. The Marshall Plan was making funds from the United States available for investment through the government, which was also organizing the reconstruction. In such a weak position, the employers had to agree to a process of national wage bargaining and a tax and national insurance regime to finance benefits and public services.

The Civil Service

The Civil Service has not been the subject of a consensus among politicians; rather it has had much scrutiny since the war. The Conservative manifesto for the 1951 election promised to cut waste and extravagance in the service[3] and the non-industrial Civil Service was cut from 425,000 to 386,000 by 1955, mainly as a result of the end of rationing and relaxation of controls. After then there were many efforts to increase efficiency and modernize the management of the service, culminating in the Fulton Report of 1968, which called for improved accountability, a unified system of grading and recruitment on merit. However, growth in numbers and spending soon restarted and the number of civil servants (including industrial civil servants) reached a peak of 747,000 in 1975. Prior to the Thatcher administration of 1979 there were efforts to improve accountability and efficiency but no government had much enthusiasm for the task until the Thatcher administrations and their attempts to introduce 'business' methods, or at least business language, initially through Michael Heseltine's attempt to find out who did what in the Department of the Environment (the Management Information System for Ministers), and later, from 1982, through the Financial Management Initiative.

At each change of party control there have been suspicions about the neutrality of the Civil Service, although few ministers, with exceptions such as Tony Benn, sustained their complaints. One aspect of this suspicion was that the Treasury ran economic policy and the Civil Service, if not the government. Two short-lived attempts were made to rectify this: the establishment of the Department of Economic Affairs in 1964, to manage economic policy, and the Civil Service Department in 1968 to manage the Civil Service.

Generally, the Civil Service, and especially the senior ranks, survived the first thirty years after the war well. Despite criticisms, reports and attempts to reorganize, the size, scope and influence of the service remained fairly stable.

The National Health Service

The NHS was established in 1946, based on the principles of universal access and freedom from charges which were established during the war. The institutional arrangements were a compromise designed to satisfy a variety of interests, especially the medical professions, and have been adjusted many times, starting in 1948. As Klein[4] points out, the dilemmas faced by the original scheme for the NHS have been the sources of political controversy ever since. These included the problem of national responsibility for the service and local management of the facilities, the need to integrate hospital and family health services while preserving the independence of family doctors, how to make comprehensive plans for a service which excluded independent (voluntary) hospitals, how to achieve public accountability while involving professionals in decision making, and how to keep general practitioners independent and promote best medical practice. A further dilemma was between creating and running a national service and having local democratic control and accountability: the debate between localism and nationalism. Klein argues (p.26) that: 'The history of the NHS since 1948 can largely be seen as the working out of these contradictions: a continuing and never-ending attempt to reconcile what may well turn out to be irreconcilable aims of policy'.

In 1974 the NHS was organized into a hierarchical arrangement of regional, area and district health authorities for budgeting, planning and control purposes, with community health councils to represent consumers. Each tier was served by full-time administrators and advised by an array of advisory boards representing the professions. As with the Civil Service, the idea of management as distinct from administration, using consultation and consensus, was not a feature of the NHS until the introduction of general management in 1983. This is the first example of the attempt to control the actions of medical professionals using management techniques.

Local government

Many services which are now directly controlled by central government — or indeed now privatized — were initially local authority services. Water, gas, electricity supply, public transport, health services, public health and 'poor relief' were all originally local government services. The process of transferring powers from local to central government began during the first Labour government after the war and has continued since. These transfers were not necessarily the result of central government hostility. In some cases it made economic sense to have a national level of provision. In others the nationalization was the result of a desire for equal and universal provision. When municipal services were originally developed, local business people were involved in their own municipality and its development of gas and electricity, water and sewerage. When the ownership of industry became national and then international, such a local focus was less relevant. While local businesses still have an influence on local authorities, there is no longer a strong connection between either the owners of local industry or their trade unions and the membership of local authorities.

Despite losing control of local hospitals in 1948, local authorities were the implementing institutions for two areas of social policy which were to grow in importance in the post-war years — housing and education — as well as having powerful planning and development functions allowing them to shape much of the post-war reconstruction of the cities. As with the NHS, local government was reorganized in 1974 (1975 in Scotland) into a hierarchical structure. In London the Greater London Council (from 1965) and in the metropolitan areas from 1974 the metropolitan county councils had 'strategic' functions such as planning and transport, while the main services were performed at London borough and metropolitan district level. In Scotland and in the shire areas of England and in Wales, the upper tier had the main functions of social services and education. They had relatively reliable sources of revenue, the domestic and commercial rates, and were seen as the natural providers of local services. The reorganization strengthened the position of local government as a whole, as it provided a reason for allocating extra resources. Indeed, local government spending increases were a large contributory factor to the fiscal problems of 1975/76.

The Labour government attempted in 1975 to introduce controls on local government spending, a process which was continued by successive governments. The attempt by central government to control local authority spending and local authorities' attempts to evade those controls have been continuous since that time and contributed to the distrust which the Thatcher governments had of local authorities, a distrust which eventually led to the abolition of the upper tier in London and the metropolitan areas of England in 1985, and in Scotland and Wales in 1995.

The Thatcher years 1979–90

When it was elected in 1979 the Conservative government found itself in charge of a large and relatively strong public sector. Public spending was 43% of gross domestic product (GDP); this, although lower than its peak of 49% in 1975, was 3 points higher than it had been when they had last come into office in 1970. The institutions were fairly robust: the Civil Service had mostly resisted attempts to modernize it and the Treasury was still the most powerful department within it. Local government still had a degree of independence, a tax base and a grant system which forced the government to pay a grant from taxation to contribute to any spending the local authorities decided to make. The NHS was still strong and the medical professions, especially doctors, well placed to influence it. Only 5% of the population was covered by private health insurance, indicating a high degree of satisfaction with the state service among the middle classes.

New or Old Right?

There was a view during the 1980s that Ronald Reagan and Margaret Thatcher especially, but also other Right parties in Europe and the Labour Party in New Zealand, represented a new sort of politics, sometimes called the 'New

Right'. The idea was that the mid-1970s recession which resulted from the oil price rise of 1973 produced a break with the previous consensus about the role of the state, welfare services and individual responsibilities, which had lasted since the Second World War. The new circumstances produced a new set of right-wing politicians who would reverse the previous policies towards the economy, the labour market and the welfare state. The emphasis of economic policy would no longer be on managing demand to maintain full employment but rather on stimulating profits by removing regulations and making the labour market more free. Protection of workers, either by law or trade unions, would be reduced to allow wages to find their market level and to allow managers to manage.

Part of the project was to restore to the private sector those industries which had been nationalized in the 1940s. The circumstances which made nationalization desirable were now gone and such businesses should no longer need state support.

While the inclination of this group of politicians may have been similarly to restore the institutions of the welfare state to the private sector, or abolish them, this would be more difficult than selling nationalized industries. In the early years, the policy was confined to trying to control spending, either directly or by finding more efficient ways of managing.

For the public sector, there is an important question about the Thatcher period. Did the Conservative governments of the 1980s and 1990s produce a radical break in the history of the welfare state and public services? We have seen that there was not a universal consensus on the role and size of the welfare state or on the level of public expenditure, but there had been a period of relative stability or growth for most of the post-war period. Government spending on goods and services had been a fairly constant proportion of GDP since the war, apart from the aberration of the mid-1970s, when it grew to more than 25% before settling down to the trend of around 20%. If there was not a consensus, in the sense that politicians of all persuasions agreed, there had been no radical changes in the form of the welfare state or the money spent on it.

Of course there were rhetorical speeches about individual responsibility and the dangers of reliance on the 'nanny state', of the tyranny of taxation and the debilitation of dependency. But can we see a step change in policy towards the 'welfare state' which happened at the beginning of the 1980s? There was not a step change in 1979 in the significant areas of policy which the Conservatives claimed they would change. The targets for growth of the money supply were never met and were eventually quietly abandoned. Monetarism as the basis for economic policy was thus forgotten. Public expenditure was not drastically cut, public borrowing was reduced and debts were repaid briefly in the late 1980s but then the economic cycle continued and borrowing increased again. Taxation has fluctuated as a proportion of GDP but this has been cyclical rather than a strong downward trend. The only area in which a truly Right agenda was achieved was the privatization of nationalized industries, public utilities and public housing. The government offered inducements for people to withdraw from the state earnings-related pension scheme and join company or individual pension schemes. At the same time the value of the state pension was reduced by indexing it to prices rather than earnings. Housing privatization was achieved by selling houses and flats to their tenants, at a discount from their market value, and by virtually preventing local authorities from building any new accommodation for renting. However, the state has not withdrawn from housing, still paying housing benefit to those unable to pay their own rent.

As we shall see in Chapter 3, the distribution of expenditure between departments and programmes has changed over time, but the radical changes have been in the methods used to manage the institutions. The Thatcher governments hired advisers from business, especially retailing companies, to help them to think about how public services should be managed. The solutions included internal markets, competition with the private sector, performance measurement and management, decentralized operational management and revised payment systems. They do represent a change in attitude and practice, although not of the type described in the New Right rhetoric: the institutions were reformed rather than abolished.

The Major years 1990–1997

During the Thatcher administrations the manner of government was forceful and based on some overwhelming convictions about what was right. Consultation was reduced, normal processes of decision making were not used and opposing views were ignored or punished. In part, it was the style of government which finally produced opposition within the party: if the Prime Minister had listened to advice she might have made fewer policy disasters such as the poll tax. John Major reversed some of these tendencies during his period of office, adopting a more open, consultative style and more collegial cabinet.[5]

However, did the content of policies towards public services change with the change of Prime Minister? In a speech made at the Carlton Club in 1993, John Major reasserted some Conservative beliefs, invoking Disraeli and Burke, which underlay his policies. One of these was the danger of over-government:

> We know the State can destroy, as surely as it can preserve — and more conclusively than it can create . . . we utterly reject the idea that the State can manage economic and personal relations between people better than businesses and better than families.[6]

While in the same speech he spoke of quality public services and the need for good management, there was one passage where he revealed a deep belief in the evils of state intervention and the creation of crime: the council estates of the inner cities are the cause of problems, not the solution:

Look at our suburbs and small towns and villages — where people, by and large, own their own homes. Here you will find networks of the voluntary associations which tie people into their neighbourhood, from Rotary Clubs to the active PTA to fund-raising and to Meals on Wheels. The big problem lies elsewhere. It is from the inner cities, where the State is dominant, that businesses have fled. It is in the inner cities that vandalism is rife and property uncared-for. It is there that fear of violent crime makes a misery of old people's lives. Now that comes as no surprise for Conservatives . . . it is where, over many years, the State has intervened most heavily, that local communities have been most effectively destroyed.[7]

David Willetts, Minister of State for Public Services, saw the state as destroying genuinely local and voluntary organizations. While the government was deciding to close St Bartholomew's Hospital, for example, he blamed the fact that it was a state institution for its closure: 'it is no exaggeration to say that Bart's fate was sealed when it was nationalised in 1948 and lost control of its destiny, becoming a tool of health planners'.[8] In this version of 'Civic Conservatism', any institution is preferable to one owned by the state, whether at local or national level. Willetts even argues that market reforms are designed to strengthen local institutions: 'The market — contracts, choice, competition — is being introduced within the public sector to achieve the authentically Tory objective of strengthening local institutions'. This belief in the benefits of competition survived the change of government in 1997, although the antagonism (or 'visceral antipathy' as Prime Minister Blair defined it)[9] abated.

One result of this deep-seated belief was that institutions of the state and especially local authorities could not be trusted with any major programmes. So, for example, the creation of grant-maintained schools (see Chapter 4, p.81) was seen as 'the emancipation of governing bodies and head teachers, taking the local authority straitjacket off their back'.[10] Another consequence of lack of confidence in the state was that even in those areas where the Prime Minister recognized need for state intervention, if that could be carried out by the private sector on behalf of the state, then such an approach would be preferred.

Other members of Mr Major's government expressed views about the state which illuminated their approach to the management of the institutions. Michael Portillo, when Chief Secretary to the Treasury, made a speech in which he echoed Mr Major's attitude to people who live in the inner city, when he asserted the difference between the deserving and the undeserving poor:

To talk today of the deserving and undeserving poor is guaranteed to make people wince: a mark of the triumph of political correctness . . . So our system tends to treat alike the unfortunate and the feckless, the thrifty and the profligate. Consequently it undermines the provident and demoralises the industrious.[11]

The solution was to shrink the scope of the state and make people take more responsibility for themselves:

> Citizens grow to respect themselves and so come to accept that there are clear limits to what the State should do for them. Then support increases for a smaller State and for the necessary measures to put and keep the public finances on a sound footing. As the State shrinks and the public finances are kept under control there is scope for permanent reduction in taxes, increasing international competitiveness and the rewards for individual effort. (*ibid.*, 13)

The implications of this for people working in public services are twofold. The principle of universality is challenged: service providers have to distinguish between the deserving and the undeserving, between scroungers and the unfortunate victims of circumstances. For those working in services which are accepted as universal, such as child benefit or state pension distribution, there is no question of selectivity or rationing. However, when people working in community care are allocating services and budgets, the rationing process is very explicit. Applying eligibility criteria and allocating help to those who need it most has always been a feature of the daily work of people in public services. Applying criteria of deserving and undeserving is a different matter and relies on a moral judgement, rather than an assessment of need. At the same time, people have been encouraged to make their own arrangements for insurance or care or help, without relying on the state.

The second implication was that management effort was dominated by the need to make cuts in spending. The overriding priority was to shrink the state and reduce taxes. We will see in the next chapter that the scale of state spending has remained fairly consistent, especially when expressed as a proportion of national product. But it also has cyclical variations, both with regard to the periods of growth and stagnation and decline in the economy and with regard to the electoral cycle, deficits increasing in the approach to elections. But there were enough supporters of the 'small state, low taxes good' position for there to be a consistent presumption against public expenditure as a solution to economic and social problems.

Michael Howard, who served in the Departments of Employment and Environment before becoming Home Secretary in 1993, extolled the virtues of voluntary collective action and decried the efforts of local authorities:

> 'Communities' built on collectivism are characterised by town hall socialism and housing and social security dependency. Their predominant features are alienation, atomism, lack of confidence and crime. The strongest communities exist where voluntary collective action is most apparent. These communities are characterised by neighbourliness and a strong sense of identity.[12]

He proposed that the government should, when confronted with a problem, think first about the voluntary sector and volunteers, before considering state intervention. When it had found ways of involving this sector, it should distribute funds in a such a way as to create 'leverage' from the private sector. This is a conception of the state as pump-primer and fund-raiser, rather than as a tax-raiser and service-provider. Not all members of the Major governments held these views but they had a sufficient majority to press for such policies.

The first Blair government

In 1998 Prime Minister Blair published a Fabian pamphlet called 'The Third Way: New Politics for the New Century'. Social Democrats in Europe and the then Democratic President of the USA proclaimed that they represented a new type of politics, leaving behind old definitions of left and right. This was not the old third way between capitalism and communism but a new Third Way. As Blair explained: 'The Third Way is not an attempt to split the difference between right and left. It is about traditional values in a changed world. And it draws vitality from uniting the two great streams of left-of-centre thought — democratic socialism and liberalism'.

What this meant in practice is that policies could be picked from a fairly narrow menu without the prejudice of principles. If a market solution looks acceptable, then it is based on the good parts of liberal individualism. If public spending is required, for example to reduce child poverty, then the decision is based on the socially responsible parts of social democracy. But if anyone from the old Left suggested, for example, keeping the London Underground in public ownership or renationalizing the company that owns the railway tracks, they could be condemned as old-fashioned and dogmatic. On the other hand selling London Underground is not the product of dogma, rather of pragmatism and the Third Way.

The attitude towards the relationship between public services, voluntary organizations and individual volunteering and charitable giving was a development of aspects of the Major government's themes. Compare the quotation from Michael Howard, above, with this one from Blair's 1998 pamphlet:

> My politics are rooted in a belief that we can only realise ourselves as individuals in a thriving civil society, comprising strong families and civic institutions buttressed by intelligent government ... In recent decades, responsibility and duty were the preserve of the right. They are no longer, and it was a mistake for them ever to become so.

The idea that public services and benefits, as supported by the old Left, were responsible for a decline in individual responsibility and duty is broadly similar to Howard's and Major's beliefs that council estates create unemployment and crime. It certainly has the same results in practice in the social security system and the attitude to the management and ownership of public housing.

To win power the Labour Party had 'modernized' itself and re-branded itself as New Labour. It had changed the party constitution to give less power to organized and especially trade union interests. Internal processes of discussion and decisions through branches to the annual conference were changed so that the leadership could more easily control the policies adopted by the Party. Symbolically Clause IV of the constitution, calling for public ownership, was scrapped. Elections were from now on to be fought in the media and campaigns to be managed by the Party's public relations machine. Policies presented at the election were more defined by what they were not: the Party did not stand for higher tax (or at least for a higher rate of income tax); it was not in favour of re-nationalizing the public utilities and the railway; it did not align itself with the unions. Five specific pledges were made in 1997 for its term of office: class sizes for 5–7-year-olds to be cut to 30; fast-track trial and punishment for young offenders; 100,000 fewer people on waiting lists; 250,000 young people to go from benefit to work; no rise in income tax rates; and a cut in VAT on heating to 5%. The first four required the government to be able to influence departments and local service delivery in the school system, the courts, the NHS, and Social Security and Education and Employment Departments.

'Modernization' meant many different things. Detailed diagnoses of problems varied in local government, the civil service and the NHS. The solutions, as we shall see in the rest of the book, followed a pattern of trying to assert control over organizations that were seen variously as too bureaucratic, too professionally dominated and in some cases self-interested and self-serving. The methods used were chosen eclectically. 'Modernization' of government was closely connected to the modernization of the Party and especially the abandonment of the commitment to public ownership. It was also about methods of service delivery and service design, especially getting access to services through the Internet and call centres. A quotation from the 'Vision' chapter of the White Paper gives an idea of the interpretations of modernization:

- We live in an age when most of the old dogmas that haunted governments in the past have been swept away. We know now that better government is about much more than whether public spending should go up or down, or whether organisations should be nationalised or privatised. Now that we are not hidebound by the old ways of government we can find new and better ones.
- Information technology is revolutionising our lives, including the way we work, the way we communicate and the way we learn. The information age offers huge scope for organising government activities in new,

innovative and better ways and for making life easier for the public by providing public services in integrated, imaginative and more convenient forms like single gateways, the Internet and digital TV.

- We must unleash the potential within the public service to drive our modernising agenda right across government. There is great enthusiasm and determination within the public service to tackle the problems which face society, to do the job better.
- Distinctions between services delivered by the public and the private sector are breaking down in many areas, opening the way to new ideas, partnerships and opportunities for devising and delivering what the public wants. (*Modernising Government* 1999, para 1.2)

We will see that while asserting that the new was now able to sweep away the old, many of the actions taken were a continuation of the old ideas of the preceding governments. Even so, the Prime Minister was often frustrated by the progress of the 'modernization' programme. He said in a speech to a group of venture capitalists:

> People in the public sector are more rooted in the concept that if it's always been done this way it must always be done this way than any group of people I've ever come across . . . It's not that there aren't wonderful people now with a tremendous commitment to public service, but you try getting change in the public sector and public services — I bear the scars on my back after two years of government. (Prime Minister Tony Blair, 7 July 1999)

Previous Conservative governments had felt the need to break down resistance to change, whether it came from professional groups, trade unions or departmental interests. They had used market mechanisms, managerial authority and the undermining of public support for particular groups. The incoming government in 1997 obviously felt that the struggle had to continue. Part Two is about the managerial and other devices used to try to exercise control of the organizations of the public sector. Perhaps there was less overt antagonism between politicians and these organizations than in previous governments that were openly hostile to the public sector, but the tension and frustration brought forward some strong measures to try to deliver the election pledges and more generally to make services more efficient, effective and popular.

We will also see in the next chapter that the overwhelming emphasis on cost reduction for public sector managers during the Conservative era was slowly relaxed towards the end of the first Blair government. It had become the only priority with successive rounds of either simple budget cuts or 'efficiency savings' included in budgets. While such savings were still called for, they were within an expanding overall total, with quite large increases in some sectors.

The politics of management

While the Major governments still did not achieve a big cut in the role of the state, ministers' attitudes such as those expressed above had an impact on the way services were managed and funded. The managerial agenda of the Thatcher period continued with even more vigour. It was rooted in a general set of ideas about how people behave.

The first element is that people always act rationally and in their own self-interest, whether they work in business or public services.[13] They respond to incentives, such as the incentive to expand their budget and the number of staff in their unit. They cannot therefore be trusted to act in any interests other than their own. Producers 'capture' services and the users of those services are disempowered. The consequence of this belief is that the power of producers has to be reduced and that incentives have to be found to make the producers act in the interests either of the government or of the consumers.

The second is that competition is the main incentive to improve perform-ance: the fear of going out of business, or losing a job, is the main motivator for individuals. Monopoly in any form is a bad thing and public monopolies allow costs to stay high and quality to stay low. Without competition, man-agers will have no incentive to make improvements either in cost or quality, and therefore will not do so.

The third is that managers should have the right to manage. Any force which reduces that right, such as trade union rights or professional organiza-tion, should be removed. Managers with incentives and authority are essential to good organizational performance. The right to manage is seen as the right to tell people what to do and expect them to do it. It is not about the right to develop staff, encourage commitment, form teams or instil loyalty. It is an instrumental view of management, implying hierarchy, authority and fear. The Labour government shared some of these attitudes with its predecessors, although from the beginning it emphasized the possibility that motivations other than selfishness can be present in people working in the public sector. It also played down the beneficial effects of competition and emphasized the need for co-operation in many areas of public sector work.

The belief, through both the Thatcher and Major periods, that the private sector is innately superior to the public sector was replaced by an agnostic stance, represented by the Deputy Prime Minister:

> Traditional values in a modern setting should be our guide, not an ideo-logical argument about public or private ownership (Deputy Prime Minister John Prescott, Local Government Association Conference, 8 July 1999)

In practice the policies implemented often pushed managers towards deals with the private sector or outsourcing, but this was presented as a pragmatic approach not an ideological one.

There have been other political approaches to management. Some Labour local authorities, especially in the 1970s and early 1980s, promoted an approach to management which reflected their political values. They encouraged collaboration rather than competition. Another belief was that everyone had the right to have good ideas, so that consultation and non-hierarchical relationships were encouraged. Some of these beliefs came from the feminist movement, which sought alternatives to hierarchical and authoritarian ways of working. People with such views lost influence during the 1990s, partly as a result of the politics of the Labour Party favouring more male-oriented and hierarchical ways of working. The other reason for the loss of popularity was the need to compete with private companies, whose attitudes to workers were more authoritarian and which concentrated on costs rather than quality or innovation.

Strangely, experience of 'human resources management' in successful private companies has shown that flexible and adaptable companies are those which adopt the less hierarchical, more consultative style and operate through developing commitment rather than fear. Companies such as Hewlett-Packard and Microsoft have developed such approaches to managing their workforces. There is little sign of these ideas in the Labour approach to management. In fact one of its innovations is the introduction of call centres, through NHS Direct and the Employment Service among others, a method of service delivery that is notorious for its regimentation and mechanistic managerial control over the workforce. There has been talk of greater 'partnership' between managers and trade unions but this has not extended to the agreements under the Private Finance Initiative whereby companies take over basic services along with building construction and financing. 'Modernization' has included implementing Investors in People, an accreditation scheme for how employees are involved in their organization and how staff development is managed, in all government departments but this may be more of a ritual than a genuinely participatory style of management.

A new consensus?

From the mid-1990s the Labour Party's themes about the public sector were similar to those of the Conservatives: the need to control expenditure in order to keep taxation levels down, the importance of a mixed economy of private, individual provision and state services and benefits, and the need for efficiency. A new consensus seems to have emerged, which is at least as strong as the supposed post-war one, if not stronger.

The size of the public sector is one element in the consensus. The Labour government's spending plans, as we shall see in the next chapter, were for an increase in public spending as a proportion of GDP. Previous governments had tried, mostly without success, to bring this figure down. In the campaign for the 2001 general election the Conservative Party mostly accepted the spending plans as necessary to improve public services, implying a more relaxed attitude to public spending and its impact on the economy than that of the Conservatives in power.

The Labour Party's rejection of its constitutional commitment to public ownership represented more than a change in attitude towards nationalized industries; it also represented a shift towards the idea of a mixed economy in general and a tolerance or encouragement of private pensions, schools, hospitals, home helps and refuse collection companies.

What may be emerging is a consensus on management. It was natural for the Conservatives to adopt the approaches which were common in certain businesses in the late 1980s and early 1990s: they had friends and allies in business, recruited business people as advisers and in some cases as civil servants, and were generally more impressed by the style and manner of business than they were by public service. The Labour government shares both the belief and the use of business people as advisers. On some of the fundamentals of management, such as the use of performance control and performance pay, outsourcing, benchmarking and competition, there is little difference between the main parties.

Conclusions

Politics has affected the public sector both in policy and in management. If ruling politicians are deeply opposed to the activities and institutions of the state, managers at senior levels may feel the need to protect services as well as manage them. At worst the tensions between managers and hostile politicians can produce stressful and unproductive relationships. If politicians have strongly held views about the motivation and performance of public sector workers which lead them to insist on authoritarian styles of management, managers have little discretion: they will be forced to behave or appear to behave in such a way. If not, they can be replaced by managers who will.

Management is not a neutral, technical activity. Management techniques and styles are themselves political and people with different political views will have different ideas about management. In the United Kingdom this does not mean that each party has an identifiable set of ideas about management: all parties have their share of authoritarians.

There has been a period of what was felt by many people working in the public sector as political attack which, to date, the institutions have been fairly well able to resist. However, the management style which managers are now encouraged to follow is the result of a political attitude of low trust. Some of the details of how this style or styles were encouraged in the different sectors are in Chapter 4.

In the next chapter we look at public spending and how it has been affected by changes in government.

Further reading

Deakin, N. (1994) *The Politics of Welfare: Continuities and Change*, 2nd edn. Hemel Hempstead: Harvester Wheatsheaf. A detailed account of the political debates and decisions about the main areas of welfare provision.

Newman, J. (2001) *Modernising Governance: New Labour, Policy and Society*, London: Sage.

Timmins, N. (1995) *The Five Giants: A Biography of the Welfare State*. London: HarperCollins. A very detailed account of the development of the welfare state.

Notes and references

[1] Glennerster, H. (1995) *British Social Policy Since 1945*. Oxford: Blackwell.

[2] Wilks, S. (1996) 'Class compromise in the international economy: the rise and fall of Swedish Social Democracy'. *Capital and Class*, 58.

[3] Theakston, K. (1995) *The Civil Service Since 1945*. Oxford: Blackwell.

[4] Klein, R. (2000) *The New Politics of the NHS*, 4th edn. London: Longman.

[5] Kavanagh, D. and Seldon, A. (eds) (1994) *The Major Effect*. Basingstoke: Macmillan, 154–66.

[6] Major, J. (1993) 'Conservatism in the 1990s: our common purpose', Fifth Carlton Lecture. London: Carlton Club Political Committee and Conservative Political Centre.

[7] *Ibid.*, 16–17.

[8] Willetts, D. (1994) *Civic Conservatism*. London: Social Market Foundation, 22.

[9] Blair, T. (1998) *The Third Way: New Politics for the New Century*. London: Fabian Society, Fabian Pamphlet 588.

[10] Willetts, D. (1994) *Civic Conservatism*. London: Social Market Foundation, 29.

[11] Portillo, M. (1993) 'The blue horizon', speech to Conservative Party Conference 1993. London: Centre for Policy Studies.

[12] Howard, M. (1994) 'Conservatives and the community', the 1994 Disraeli Lecture. London: Conservative Political Centre.

[13] The academic name for this is 'public choice theory'. For an explanation, see Dunleavy, P. (1991) *Democracy, Bureaucracy and Public Choice*, Hemel Hempstead: Harvester Wheatsheaf. There have also been critiques of this theory, for example Stretton, H. and Orchard, L. (1994) *Public Goods, Public Enterprise, Public Choice. Theoretical Foundations of the Contemporary Attack on Government*, Basingstoke: Palgrave; and Udehn, L. (1996) *The Limits of Public Choice: A Sociological Critique of the Economic Theory of Politics*, London: Routledge.

3

PUBLIC SPENDING

Introduction

This chapter looks first at trends in public spending over a forty-year period. It shows that aggregate expenditure as a proportion of GDP is relatively stable at around 40% except during recessions, when expenditure increases and GDP growth slows down. Within the total the distribution of spending has changed.

It then looks at the changes in fiscal policy brought in by the 1997 government. There was a break with previous policy to reduce spending as a proportion of GDP and a new set of rules about how much should be spent and how it should be financed. The chapter then asks where the revenue comes from and describes some trends in taxation.

Trends

Despite the variety of political opinions about public expenditure and the relative weight of the public sector in the economy, the trend in public spending has been fairly stable. Figure 3.1 shows the trend in total managed expenditure as a percentage of gross domestic product from 1963–4 to (projected) 2003–4. The variance over that period can partly be explained by politics. The growth in the first half of the 1970s was partly a response to demands for social spending, and its decline after the IMF visit was a response to creditors' pressure to cut spending. In 1975–6 public spending as a percentage of GDP almost reached 50% and by the time the Thatcher government was elected in 1979 the figure had been cut to under 45%.

Although the first Thatcher government may have been ideologically inclined to cut the public sector, there was a steady rise in the public sector proportion to 48.2% in the financial year of the general election in 1983. Then economic growth and spending restraint brought the proportion down

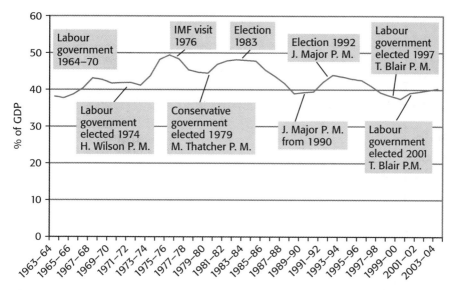

Figure 3.1   Total managed expenditure as a % of GDP 1963–2004
Source: Comprehensive Spending Review, HM Treasury, 2000

and it went below 40% in 1988–9. After John Major became Prime Minister in 1990 the proportion went up again prior to the 1992 general election and then fell again in the period up to the next election in 1997.

If we turn from spending as a proportion of GDP to the real terms[1] level of spending we can see a fairly small variation around a growth trend. Figure 3.2 shows both the real terms level of spending and the trend.[2] It shows that the acceleration of spending in the early 1970s was already slowing before it was corrected by the IMF visit in 1976. The first Thatcher government's spending was above the trend line and then the growth rate was reduced and reversed after the 1983 election. Growth got under way again after the selection of John Major as leader of the Conservative Party in 1990, and slowed again in 1995. Labour spending plans did not bring planned expenditure up to the trend line until 2001.

In the medium term of a couple of years, or half a parliament, spending levels are fairly committed: to reduce spending requires cancellation of employment or supply contracts, while to increase spending on, say, education or health requires training and recruitment of professional staff. This inertia in spending is played out through the expenditure planning process through which departments negotiate for their budgets with the Treasury. A Treasury determined to cut spending is likely to be offered the easy short-term option for cutting spending, which is to cancel or not start capital projects.

Figure 3.3 shows the trend in public sector net investment, or purchase of assets less disposals, as a percentage of GDP from 1963–4 to (projected)

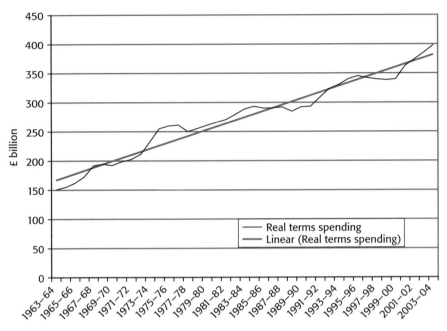

Figure 3.2   Total managed expenditure, real terms and trend 1963–2004
Source: Comprehensive Spending Review, HM Treasury, 2000

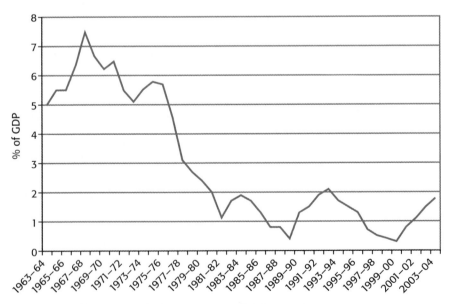

Figure 3.3   Public sector net investment as a % of GDP 1963–2004
Source: Comprehensive Spending Review, HM Treasury, 2000

Table 3.1 Spending as a % of GDP, United Kingdom 1981–2, 1995–6 and 1999–2000

	1981–2	1995–6	1999–2000
Social security	11.5	12.8	11.5
Health and personal social services	6.2	6.7	6.8
Education	5.4	4.9	4.6
Defence	5.0	3.0	2.6
Trade, industry, energy and employment	2.5	1.3	1.1
Transport	1.9	1.6	1.0
Law, order and protection	1.8	2.2	2.1
Housing	1.6	0.7	0.4
Other environmental services	1.5	1.2	1.0
Overseas, inc. aid	0.6	0.5	0.4
Agriculture and fisheries	0.6	0.6	0.6
Heritage (culture, media, sport)	0.5	0.5	0.6
Miscellaneous	1.3	1.4	1.1

Sources: *1981–2*, HM Treasury (1996) *Public Expenditure: Statistical Analyses 1996–7*, Cm 3201. London: HM Treasury; *1995–6 and 1999–2000*, HM Treasury (2000) *Public Expenditure: Statistical Analyses 2000–2001*, Cm 4601. London: HM Treasury

2003–4. It shows that the response to the IMF visit was to cut the building and investment programme from 1976 onwards. Investment was boosted prior to the 1983 and 1992 general elections and was then increased again in the spending plans of the Labour government but, as with current spending, not until three years into the administration. Capital investment never recovered to its mid-1970s level.

One consequence of the depression of capital spending was the accumulation of a backlog in building and repair programmes in all public services including the railways, hospitals, schools and public housing. The incoming Labour government of 1997 tried to correct this long-term deficit by changing the accounting arrangements for investment, making it a distinct category of central government spending for the first time. The idea was that people responsible for public services would think of capital spending as investment and that it would be more acceptable to borrow for investment than to cover current account deficits.

They also used alternative methods of financing an investment programme, the Private Finance Initiative and Public–Private Partnerships, that had been invented by the previous government. Spending plans announced in 1999 included an increase in capital spending to restore it eventually to its 1992 level.

Table 3.1 shows the main trends in spending by service as a percentage of GDP in 1981–2, 1995–6 and 1999–2000. It shows that while the total of spending has remained a fairly constant proportion of GDP, its distribution between services has changed somewhat over twenty years. Education spending has been squeezed by 15% as a proportion of GDP, defence by 48%, trade, industry etc. by 56%, transport by 47%, and overseas (especially aid) by 33%. The housing reduction represents a switch in housing subsidy from a building subsidy to a rent subsidy, counted under social security.

About one-fifth of social security spending goes to unemployed people and to those who are economically inactive who might otherwise be in work if jobs were available. The only ways in which governments could avoid this effect are either to reduce eligibility to benefits or to cut their level. Both are difficult in the short term.

Labour's fiscal policy

Gordon Brown, the Chancellor in the 1997 Labour government, made 'prudent' his favourite word, using it in the title of the 2000 Budget statement.[3] Prudence was represented by the 'golden rule' of fiscal policy, that the public sector current budget should be in balance or at least not in deficit on average over the economic cycle. Borrowings should be made only to finance capital spending, rather than to finance current account deficits.

The 'sustainable investment rule' was that investment as a proportion of GDP should be brought up and then maintained as a proportion over the economic cycle. A target proportion was not set. In any case the level of outstanding debt should be reduced to less than 40% of GDP. This fiscal stance produced by these two principles was presented and largely accepted by the media as being a necessary prelude to joining the euro.[4] In practice they were slightly more fiscally conservative than the required criteria: deficits of up to 3% of GDP were permitted and outstanding debt was required not to exceed 60% of GDP.

The buoyancy of the economy allowed the Chancellor to meet the prudent targets earlier than originally planned. By 2000 the budget surplus had grown to £17 billion, much higher than the 1999 estimate. This was mainly because the continuing growth in the economy brought extra tax revenues. In the March 2001 Budget the Chancellor announced that the surplus projected for the 2000–01 financial year was £23.1 billion. This allowed some repayment of debt and by the end of 2002 net debt was to be reduced to 30.3% of GDP and thereafter to be kept at around 30%. Reducing the outstanding debt allowed the government to reduce its debt-servicing payments and allowed for an expansion of spending in future years without having to proportionately increase revenue. The 2000 budget planned to increase public spending in line with economic growth, estimated to be 2.5% for the subsequent three years. In addition an extra £3 billion of current spending and £1 billion of capital was allocated to 2000–01. This reflected a view of the public finances that was in contrast with previous governments' positions, which had been

Table 3.2 Public expenditure 1995–96 to 2001–2, billions of pounds and % change

	Real terms departmental expenditure	Real terms Education	Real terms Health	Cash SS benefits	Aggregate as % of GDP
1995–96	167.8	37.6	34.8	86.1	42.7
% change	*−1.0*	*−0.8*	*−0.3*	*4.3*	*−3.7*
1996–97	166.2	37.3	34.7	89.8	41.1
% change	*−2.1*	*−2.9*	*1.7*	*1.4*	*−3.6*
1997–98	162.7	36.2	35.3	91.1	39.6
% change	*0.8*	*2.5*	*2.3*	*4.8*	*0.8*
1998–99	164.0	37.1	36.1	95.5	39.9
% change	*3.5*	*5.1*	*5.5*	*5.2*	*0.3*
1999–00	169.7	39.0	38.1	100.5	40.0
% change	*3.5*	*5.9*	*4.7*	*2.5*	*1.0*
2000–01	175.6	41.3	39.9	103.0	40.4
% change	*2.8*	*4.4*	*4.0*	*5.7*	*0.5*
2001–02	180.5	43.1	41.5	108.9	40.6

Source: Calculated from Comprehensive Spending Review 1999

based on a desire continuously to reduce spending as a proportion of GDP. While the golden rule put an upper limit on spending it also indicated that the consumption of public services and income transfers could grow at the same rate as the economy.

These increases had been foreshadowed in the 1999 Comprehensive Spending Review. Table 3.2 shows the aggregate expenditure plans announced in the 1999 Comprehensive Spending Review. It shows the cuts in spending that had been inherited, a 3.7% and 3.6% cut in spending as a percentage of GDP in 1996–7 and 1997–8 respectively. From 1998 onwards the plan was to build up the figure to around 40% again, much of the extra money going into social security benefits, health and education, all of which were given planned real terms increases.

Where does the money come from?

Table 3.3 shows general government receipts in 1996–7 and 2000–01. Figure 3.4 shows the 2001 receipts graphically. The incoming government of 1997 pledged not to increase spending in real terms in the first two years and not to increase the income tax rates for the whole of the parliament. Taxation was increased, partly to transform the overall budget balance from a deficit of £24 billion to a surplus of £17 billion or about 4% of spending. Within this adjustment there was also an increase in the proportion of tax gathered by the

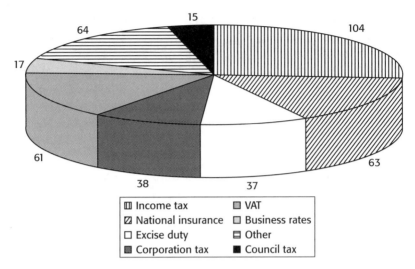

Figure 3.4   General government receipts 2001 £billion
Source: Budget March 2001, Chart 1.1, HM Treasury

Table 3.3   General government receipts 1996–7 and 2001–2

	1996–97 £ billion	%	2001–02 £ billion	%
Inland Revenue	**102.6**	**36**	**156.6**	**39**
Income tax	70.2	25	109.6	27
Corporation tax	26.6	9	38.7	10
Petroleum revenue tax, capital gains tax, inheritance tax, stamp duties	5.9	2	15.2	4
Tax credits			−7	−2
Customs and Excise	**84.1**	**30**	**107.4**	**27**
Value-added tax	47.9	17	61.5	15
Fuel duties	17.4	6	23.6	6
Tobacco duties	7.7	3	7.6	2
Others	11.4	4	14.7	4
Other taxes and social security contributions	**82**	**29**	**108.8**	**27**
Social security contributions	46.9	16	62.3	16
Business rates	14.7	5	17.7	4
Council tax	9.9	3	14.7	4
Oil royalties, vehicle excise duties, others	10.5	4	14.7	4
Interest, dividends, rents etc.	**16.1**	**6**	**31**	**8**
Current receipts	284.8	100	399.4	100

Sources: HM Treasury (1995) Financial Statement and Budget Report 1996–7 Table 4A.1; HM Treasury (2000) Pre-budget report, Table B11

Inland Revenue, generally progressive taxes, and a decrease in the proportion of the direct taxes collected by Customs and Excise. While there was never an explicit commitment to shift the burden of taxation from indirect to direct taxes, this was the effect of the budgets. One of the more striking changes is the increase in the category 'petroleum revenue tax, capital gains tax, inheritance tax and stamp duties', which increased by 250%.

A further innovation was the introduction of the Working Families Tax Credit, which appears in the public finances as a negative tax, rather than an item of expenditure. In 2000–01 this amounted to £4.3 billion.

Why is the level of public spending important?

Taxation is an important political issue. Voting behaviour is influenced by expectations about the level of tax a party will charge. While public opinion polls consistently report people's preferences for improved public services, even at the expense of higher taxes, politicians of all parties are nervous about testing that proposition in a general election. Some taxes are less visible to voters than others and it is easier to raise taxes on businesses than individuals without generating adverse reactions from voters.

Some taxes are redistributive. If parties gain their support from people who are mostly net losers from progressive taxation, they will either make sure that most taxes are regressive or neutral or will try to keep tax levels down, or both. The Conservative governments before 1997 gradually shifted the balance of taxation from income tax to other sources.

At local authority level, the link between politics and local taxation has been effectively broken. Council tax accounts for an average of only 20 per cent of local government spending; spending is actually or potentially 'capped' and the distribution of grant and the business rate is subject to manipulation. It is virtually impossible for politicians at local level to offer a programme of improved services, financed by a proportionate increase in local taxation. Bristol City Council held a referendum in 2001 offering a better education service in exchange for a higher council tax rate. The proposition was rejected. In any case, although the Labour government removed the cap on local spending the powers are still there and authorities know that they are subject to central government control as a last resort.

Before 1985, government policy was to reduce the volume of public expenditure. From 1985 to 1997 the policy was to reduce public expenditure as a proportion of GDP. Part of the 'New Right' philosophy was that public expenditure and investment 'crowd out' private sector investment. Government borrowing puts up interest rates and deters investors, hence reductions in borrowing (and, by implication, spending) will encourage investment and growth. The government was successful in pursuing spending and borrowing targets between 1985 and 1988, when there was a negative public sector borrowing requirement (PSBR) and spending was below 40 per cent of GDP. However, such targets are subject to cyclical pressures and borrowing was required again by 1992 and was necessary until 1998–9.

There have also been arguments about the public sector starving the private sector of physical resources, including people. Some have argued that the public sector used to expand in times of recession as governments spent money to encourage an up-swing and that such expenditure could never be reduced during periods of growth because of the vested interests of those benefiting from the expenditure, either as users of services or employees. Over time, therefore, there would be a cumulative growth of the public sector at the expense of the private.

A variant on the argument about the scale of the public sector has been that the 'social wage' is itself a determinant of economic success. This argument has two parts:

1. Inward investment to the United Kingdom (or anywhere else) is attracted not just by low wages and the fact of UK membership of the European Union but also by the low taxes and other social costs payable there. Low taxes are a national competitive advantage. As tariffs are reduced and capital becomes more mobile as part of the process of globalisation, such pressures on national competitiveness get stronger.
2. For those companies already operating in the United Kingdom, low taxes are themselves an important element in a competitive strategy based on achieving low unit costs.

The strength of these arguments depends on the actual impact of taxation levels on competitiveness with the other European economies. It is unlikely that unit costs would be made comparable with very low-wage economies, such as China, the Philippines or North Africa, where salaries are about £50 per month, just by reducing taxes. If production workers' wages are at a small fraction of European levels, tax reductions are unlikely to attract manufacturers back to Europe. The important issue is attracting investment from companies wanting to operate within the European Union. The policy has been successful to a certain extent, in that the United Kingdom spends slightly less than the EU average on social expenditure as a proportion of GDP. It spends somewhat less than Germany, Denmark and France and much more than Portugal, Ireland and Greece.

Other public expenditures, such as those on education, training and infrastructure, could be seen as contributing to competitiveness rather than detracting from it. A well-educated workforce, using modern transport and communications, is an important element of an economy which is competing on quality and value rather than low labour costs. The post-1997 government tried to distinguish between expenditures that contribute to growth and competitiveness and those which create a burden.

Conclusions

During the 1980s and early 1990s there was a presumption against public expenditure. Conservative philosophy was that tax rates should be lower and that people should make their own, individual, decisions about what to spend their money on. There was a belief in the Labour Party that it lost the 1992 general election partly because its policies implied higher taxes. In practice, although cuts were made it was difficult for a succession of governments to make big inroads into the proportion of national production that went into public spending. Government practice has normally been to increase spending before elections, not necessarily with a concomitant increase in taxation.

The 1997 government promised to keep for two years to the previous government's spending plans, and its fiscal stance was for a balanced budget over the economic cycle and for an increase in public sector investment. This implied that once spending was in balance with taxation, it would increase with growth in the national product. In 1999 it revealed its plans for the following three years and the growth was slightly ahead of growth in the national product. In the campaign for the 2001 election, the Conservative opposition did not promise to reverse the trend in spending, although it said that it could reduce taxation. The other parties, including the Liberal Democrats, Plaid Cymru and the Scottish Nationalists, accepted a relaxed attitude to public spending and rejected previous policies of trying to cut back the scale of state activity. While there was some dispute about the remaining proposed privatizations, especially of Air Traffic Control and London Underground Public–Private Partnership, there seemed to be a new consensus around public spending at about 40% of GDP.

For managers this may mean that the pressure on spending is slightly eased. Certainly the restoration of capital spending has led to an easier task in keeping the infrastructure going. We will see in more detail in Chapter 12 how public money is managed.

Notes and references

[1] 'real terms' is defined as cash increases deflated by the GDP deflator to remove the effects of inflation.

[2] Table 3.4 Public expenditure aggregates 1963–64 to 2003–04: total managed expenditure

Table 3.4 Public expenditure aggregates 1963–64 to 2003–04: total managed expenditure

	% of GDP	Real terms (£ billion)		% of GDP	Real terms (£ billion)
1963–64	38.4	150.2	1983–84	48.2	289.2
1964–65	37.8	154.7	1984–85	47.9	293.7
1965–66	38.9	162.7	1985–86	45.4	290.3
1966–67	40.7	173.2	1986–87	43.8	291.7
1967–68	43.3	192.3	1987–88	41.9	293.1
1968–69	42.8	193.5	1988–89	39.1	285.5
1969–70	41.8	192.9	1989–90	39.5	293.3
1970–71	42	199.1	1990–91	39.6	293.7
1971–72	42	203.1	1991–92	42.3	309.8
1972–73	41.3	210.9	1992–93	44.1	325.2
1973–74	43.9	232.9	1993–94	43.7	331.3
1974–75	48.4	255.7	1994–95	43.2	341.9
1575–76	49.6	260.1	1995–96	42.7	346.3
1976–77	48.4	261.5	1996–97	41.2	343
1977–78	45.4	250.8	1997–98	39.5	340.7
1978–79	44.8	255.5	1998–99	38.5	339.4
1979–80	44.6	261.6	1999–00	37.7	340.7
1980–81	47.1	266.6	2000–01	39.3	363.5
1981–82	47.9	271.3	2001–02	39.7	374.9
1982–83	48.3	279.9	2002–03	40.1	386.7
			2003–04	40.5	399.2

Source: HM Treasury (2000) Comprehensive Spending Review

[3] HM Treasury (2000) *Prudent for a Purpose: Working for a Stronger and Fairer Britain.*

[4] e.g. '. . . arguably the best kept secret in British politics: the extent to which our public spending is now dictated by our obligations under Article 104 (c) of the Maastricht Treaty to get the British economy into shape to join the single currency'. *Sunday Telegraph*, 14.05.2000, p.16.

4

SOCIAL POLICIES AND MANAGEMENT

Introduction

In this chapter we look at some of the main areas of social policy and the changes that governments have made in recent years. It is not intended that this should be a complete review of all aspects of social policy. There are several books that do this.[1] Rather, the intention is to examine the main changes that affect the way in which managers in the different sectors have to work. In some cases the trends we look at are directly about management itself, rather than what has traditionally been known as social policy. Management and social policy have become closer as governments have pursued different aims of policy through a series of managerial measures.

Six clear themes emerged during the period of Conservative rule, some of which applied to all the sectors we look at and some of which were apparent only in some. Since the election of the Labour government in 1997, there have been many changes in social policy and the way in which the services are managed. One way of making sense of these changes is first to look at the continuities with previous policies and then to ask whether there are different themes.

The first theme of Conservative policy was a move from equality of treatment to the promotion of different treatment for different people. The most obvious example of this was the change in the school system from a comprehensive system towards selection by schools, providing some degree of choice by parents and children and differences between types of school. Of course the education system never was completely comprehensive: the private schools survived and remained the preserve of people who could afford the fees and a few scholarship winners. Direct grant schools, such as the King Edward schools, retained selection even under Labour governments and Labour education authorities. But the changes brought about by the Thatcher and Major governments were designed to increase inequality (or 'diversity' as it was called). Another example was the move away from a universal entitlement to unemployment benefit for unemployed people. First, the increased use of means testing meant that people with savings were excluded. Second, the introduction of the Jobseekers' Allowance meant that entitlement was not universal but dependent on persuading a civil servant of the applicant's diligence in seeking work. This has continued through the New Deal, although this scheme offers more help with finding work or training. Another example is the change in policy towards older people and elderly people's homes. Until the NHS and Community Care Act people could refer themselves, if they chose, to a home and the state would pay the rent and care costs, subject to a means test. Now, they can only receive such care if they are judged to be in need by a social services department. In all these cases, the management of the services has changed from being focused on making sure that everyone receives the same service towards allocating different services to different people.

At the extreme, this change involves the second theme, which is the change from universal eligibility to rationing against strict eligibility criteria. For example, when housing subsidy was payable to all local authority housing construction, it was relatively easy for working-class people to obtain a council house. Points systems were in operation, according to size of family and current housing circumstances, but most people, especially if their parents lived in a council house, would eventually be housed. Now a majority of people housed in social housing are homeless and are not working. While the Housing White Paper[2] aims to improve access to housing it continues the policy of home ownership as the preferred tenure and says that local authorities should continue to divest themselves of housing management and, if possible, of ownership.

This is one example of a third theme that represented a strongly held belief of the Conservative governments, the presumption that public services should not be provided by public bodies but through private or mixed private and public provision. Public housing was privatized by selling houses and flats to tenants, by diverting money from local authorities to housing associations and by privatizing housing management. The prison service introduced private companies into the management of prisons. Elderly people's homes are predominantly privately owned. The incoming Labour government of 1997 claimed to be agnostic on the question of ownership. Ministers said that they wanted 'what works' and if the private sector is better then that is where services should be provided. An example is the abolition of compulsory competitive tendering for local authority services, under which most services had to be periodically tested against private competitors. However, under the Best Value[3] regime local authorities have to demonstrate that cost and quality are the best available, and that means competitive with the private sector. There is also a presumption that building projects should be financed using the Private Finance Initiative or Public–Private Partnerships through which private sector participation in service provision is required. So, although there is no longer an ideological presumption in favour of the private sector, in practice private or mixed public/private provision is the norm.

A fourth theme, which had more limited application, is the move from a position of no choice for the service user to some choice or the illusion of it. One example is the abolition of school catchment areas so that parents and pupils could choose their schools. There is some choice of service and service provider in the community care regime, once people have passed the need and eligibility tests. Choice is not available for patients needing hospital care, unlike in Sweden for example, where any citizen has a free choice of hospital; nor is completely free choice of social care available, unlike, for example, in the Netherlands, where people receive care vouchers.

The fifth theme is the move from local policy autonomy to central control, combined with a contrary tendency towards more local managerial and financial autonomy. An example is the Probation Service, for which the Home Office imposed a set of national standards for how probation work should be done, took more central control over the cash limits for the service but made probation committees more managerial. The Labour government went a stage further and established a single, national probation service accountable to the Home Office. Similarly in schools, budgets are now handled locally and governors and headteachers have more freedom in daily management, but there is a strengthened system of national curriculum, national testing and national inspection and publication of test and examination results. Labour's policies are mostly centralist. Institutions defined as 'failing', whether education authorities, schools or NHS Trusts, are subject to intervention from government. There has been no abatement of the instructions and directives from the centre; nor has there been a reduction in the flow of monitoring and control information.

A sixth theme involved changes in funding regimes. Increasingly, funding is based on some measure of performance or volume of work. Schools are funded according to pupil numbers, universities according to student numbers and a measure of teaching and research quality. Local authority capital budgets are allocated according to a competition, called 'Challenge Funding', in which money is dispensed according to official judgement of the proposals' merits. This idea was extended by the Labour government to include competition based on proposals for collaborative working. In various sectors cash for 'modernisation' was distributed after competition on the degree of (apparent) collaboration between public, voluntary and private organizations.

On balance, the preferences that were labelled a 'third way' seem to be mainly a continuation of the older, Conservative policies. Were there themes that distinguish the Labour governments from their Conservative predecessors? Michael Freeden[4] analysed the ideology underneath the government's first two years of policies and showed how its eclecticism allowed it to have a variety of practices from liberalism, conservatism and social democracy. In social policy the mix of policies contains elements from all three. From conservatism comes an emphasis on 'family values' and a desire to exercise strict control over individual institutions, from liberalism a belief in a mixed economy and a contractarian relationship between the state, civil society and the individual, and from social democracy a belief in progressive taxation and a concern for the very poor. In addition to these broad beliefs, Freeden identified the desire for 'modernization', which he sees as itself essentially conservative, quoting Prime Minister Blair: '"modernization" is in reality . . . an application of enduring, lasting principles to a new generation'.

Because of the mix of beliefs apparent in government policies it is more difficult to explain or predict policies than under previous free-market, anti-state governments. For example, the scrapping of the internal market in the NHS represents a break from previous governments' belief in the superiority of market forces, while the sale of organizations such as Air Traffic Control seems to endorse privatization. Ministers make speeches decrying Old Labour attitudes to public sector organizations and continue the process of, for example, transferring public housing from local authorities, and yet the government's spending programme increases the level of public spending as a proportion of GDP. The eclecticism allows a variety of approaches across policy areas, although within a relatively narrow range of options.

Income maintenance

Governments concerned to contain the total of public expenditure have sought to limit the growth of social security spending, by dissuading people from claiming benefits, changing eligibility criteria, changing the levels of benefits, preventing fraudulent claims and encouraging private insurance for some elements of social security. At the same time, the agencies responsible for distributing income maintenance payments have been trying to improve cus-tomer service by making benefits more accessible and understandable and by paying more promptly.

Table 4.1 shows the level of spending on the main social security benefits in 1991–92 and 2001–2. The main benefit is pensions. Of the total of benefits and tax credits, 45% are contributory and about 12% are 'cyclical', which means that they vary with the level of unemployment.

The number of people claiming income support, the main means-tested benefit, grew from 5 per cent of the population in 1980 to over 10 per cent in 1993.[5] While some of this growth was caused by unemployment, much of it was due to the growth of the number of economically inactive people, such as people who were made redundant in their fifties but did not sign on as unemployed because of the small prospect of finding another job. Another contribution was the erosion of the value of pensions, which made more pensioners entitled to income support, and the restriction of the eligibility for unemployment benefit, which had the same effect. One of the ways of trying to get social security spending under control was the attempt to 'target' the spending on those in most need, or to avoid paying benefits to those in least need.

Table 4.1   Expenditure by benefit, Great Britain, £ million, 1998/99 prices

	1991–92	% of total	2001–02	% of total
Retirement pension	30,753	38	37,434	36
Income support/supplementary benefit	13,981	17	12,376	12
Housing benefit	7819	10	11,852	12
Child benefit	6247	8	8239	8
Invalidity benefit	6604	8		
Incapacity benefit			6591	6
Unemployment benefit and JSA	1931	2	3384	3
Grand total benefit expenditure	**79,938**	100	**98,253**	96
Working Families Tax Credit			4421	4
Total benefit expenditure and tax credits	**79,938**	100	**102,792**	100

Source: Department of Social Security (2000) *The Changing Welfare State*. London: HMSO

The other aspect of policy was a result of the government's belief that the benefits system could produce disincentives to work, especially after it had deregulated wages so much that the bottom end of the labour market had reduced wages to levels very close to benefit levels. The solution to this was that the benefit system should 'work with the grain of policies to help unemployed people to compete effectively for jobs and find employment as quickly as possible, by creating and supporting incentives to work'.[6] This policy was continued by the Labour government, which tried to create a benefits system that contained incentives to work and penalties for staying on benefits without trying to find work or training. Another continuity was the continuation of the Child Support Agency, whose role is to ensure absent parents contribute to the maintenance of their children.

Unemployment benefit, income support, Jobseeker's Allowance and the New Deal

Up to October 1996 unemployed people were entitled to unemployment benefit (UB) for twelve months if they had paid the right amount of National Insurance contributions, or means-tested income support if they had not. The replacement benefit regime, Jobseeker's Allowance (JSA), has a non-means-tested element if National Insurance contributions have been paid and is a means-tested benefit for those who have not. The main difference between JSA and the previous system was that automatic entitlement was reduced from twelve to six months, people aged 18 to 24 have a lower rate of benefit than others, and the previous allowance for an adult dependant has been removed. The effect has been to reduce the amount of benefit paid to unemployed people. As well as this increased incentive to work, unemployed people had to sign and keep to a Jobseeker's Agreement, setting out what they would do to look for work. Failure to keep the agreement results in loss of benefit. The Labour government introduced what it called the New Deal, a continuation of the Jobseeker's Agreement, initially for young unemployed people and then extended from February 2001 to all unemployed people under 50 years old, except single parents and people with disabilities. Under the New Deal unemployed people have to pursue one option, whether employment, education or training, as a condition of receiving benefit. If no job is available the options are a subsidized job, work for the voluntary sector, or a job with the Environment Task Force. Refusal to follow an option results in the withdrawal of benefits for 26 weeks. Social Security Secretary Angela Eagle emphasized the responsibility of unemployed young people to find work: 'We promise the New Deal will provide every reasonable chance for young people. But in return we will not tolerate those few who shirk the system. Our plans draw the line in the right place'.[7] In January 2001 the government re-introduced home visits to claimants, a measure to reduce fraudulent claims that was cancelled in a previous round of cost savings.

Working Families Tax Credit and the Social Fund

One of the policy problems in social security is that people who can command only small incomes may have no incentive to get off benefits and take a job. The net change in income may be so small that it is not worth the individual's while to take a job, especially as this involves stopping being registered for benefits and having to re-register if the job does not last. Also, there are other benefits, such as free prescriptions for medicine and free dental treatment, which are available for people who are on benefit. If these benefits are also lost, the disincentive effects are even greater.

There are three potential solutions to this problem: reduce benefits so that staying on benefit becomes less attractive; introduce a minimum wage so that work becomes more attractive; or extend the chances of being able to work and claim benefit at the same time so that people have a reason to take a job. An early effort to tackle the problem of the benefits trap was the introduction of Family Credit, a benefit for families with children. To reduce the benefits trap, people were allowed to claim Family Credit if they worked part time (from 1992) and were allowed to offset childcare costs against earnings (up to £40 per week). Family Credit was part of the policy designed to remove the disincentives to work, especially in low-paid work, provided by the removal of benefits when people started earning.

The Labour government's main effort to eliminate the benefits trap was the introduction of the Working Families Tax Credit to provide a minimum income for families with children. This benefit is designed to maintain the incentive to work even at low levels of pay by topping up the earnings. It replaced the Family Credit system at the beginning of 1998 and is administered by the Inland Revenue department. Alongside this benefit is a new child care credit to pay for childcare and a national minimum wage to try to stop very low wages being paid.

The Social Fund is a cash-limited fund held at local level for loans to help people in emergencies, repayable from future benefits. It was an innovation in social security in that whether a person receives a loan or not now depends not only on whether they meet the eligibility criteria but also on whether the fund has any money left in it when they apply. This placed a burden of discretion and responsibility on Social Fund managers and workers which did not apply to other benefits: the rest of the system consists of applying a set of rules and criteria to applicants for benefit, whereas the Social Fund also implies rationing, in the same way that cash-limited funds for community care have to be allocated according to eligibility rules and available budget. However, the fund is a very small proportion of the social security budget and the principle of cash limiting has not been applied elsewhere.

Pensions

The Conservative governments claimed that publicly funded pensions, providing a reasonable standard of living for pensioners, are unsustainable in the long term. Other parties have also said that there must be alternative ways of funding pensions than the National Insurance scheme and taxation: personal and occupational pensions have to substitute for the state pension or at least enhance it up to a level which will provide a decent living standard. Pensioners' relative living standards have been cut by indexing them to inflation, rather than to the growth of earnings. In practice, those pensioners without personal or occupational pensions have had their earning enhanced by income support and in some cases by housing benefit. The other way in which the Conservative governments tried to contain spending on state pensions was to encourage people to withdraw from the state earnings-related pension scheme by offering them money to withdraw and start personal pension plans.

For the social security system, these changes have meant that the state pension is becoming a small residual amount, rather then the main source of income for people over retirement age. An increasing number of pensioners have been eligible for means-tested benefits, putting more demands on the means-tested parts of the social security system. The Labour government came under public pressure to improve the basic state pension, and its decision to increase the single pensioner's income by 75p per week, in line with inflation, was met with disapproval. While the government did not introduce earnings indexation for pensions it did put up the rates by more than price inflation. At the same time the government tried to make private pensions easier to arrange and more portable, with a new 'stakeholder pension' to be available along with personal and occupational schemes.

Housing benefit

Housing benefit, a rent subsidy, is financed by central government but administered by local authorities. It is the main means by which government subsidizes housing costs. About 3 million council tenants have their rent subsidized in this way in Great Britain, together with 1.5 million private tenants and 412,000 housing association tenants. Table 4.1 shows that housing benefit now costs about £12 billion per year, or 12% of all benefits and tax credits.

At the same time, the regime of spending controls and rent levels imposed on local authorities and housing associations means that most 'social housing' is allocated to people on benefits. This is for two reasons: the volume of housing is so limited that it is allocated only to those most in need; and rent levels which cover the cost of providing housing are comparable with the cost of renting in the private sector or buying accommodation with a mortgage. This has resulted in geographical polarization, with economically inactive and unemployed people concentrated in social housing while those in work live in private rented or owner-occupied property. As the Rowntree Inquiry into Income and Wealth said:

> The concentration of social housing resources on those in greatest need has led to concentration of disadvantaged households, leading to communities where there are few adults who have jobs. Nearly half of non-pensioner council tenant households have no earner.[8]

The policy of council house sales has also had a polarizing effect. The most attractive council houses were individual houses with gardens, and these were the ones which sold in greatest numbers. The stock available for rent as social housing is therefore limited to less attractive properties. Not only are social housing tenants most likely to be unemployed or economically inactive, they are also likely to be living in the least attractive housing.

Implications for managers

The social security system is both a safety net for people in temporary difficulties and a system devised to encourage or force people to go to work. For managers and workers in the system, this expresses itself as a dilemma: good customer service demands that people are helped to receive their entitlements while unemployed claimants are encouraged to look for work. When UB was paid through a separate system the distinction was easier to make, whereas the JSA is designed to encourage the search for work, whatever the probability of finding it.

There are conflicting expectations from the benefits system. Ministers expect certain things: an efficient delivery of service, especially to those people considered 'deserving', such as genuinely disabled people, widows and pensioners, while making benefits difficult to obtain by the 'undeserving' who might be differently defined by different ministers: single and never married parents, fit unemployed people, new age travellers. Service management is difficult if such distinctions have to be made at the point of service delivery. In practice, staff have commonly dealt differently with different classes of claimant, although managers have encouraged them to deal equally with everyone.

Senior management, especially in the Benefits Agency and the Employment Service, encouraged good customer service, through middle-management initiatives, the development of innovative solutions, the establishment of telephone help lines and better-designed forms. The Labour government decided that better service would be provided by a merged organization, called ONE, containing the benefit elements of the Benefits Agency and the Employment Service, reverting to an arrangement that had existed before the agencies were founded. For more complete integration, Housing benefit, which is currently administered by local authorities, often through contractors, could be treated in the same way.

Health services

Since it was founded in 1948 the National Health Service has been subject to many reviews and reorganizations. From the beginning, there have been debates about how local the management of the service should be, how politically accountable, whether it is a national service and how reasonably equitable national standards might be achieved. The role of doctors in the service has similarly always been controversial, as has the nature of the contractual relationship between the NHS and the various medical professions and factions. Structural changes have been frequent, including the creation and destruction of a wide variety of organizations at subnational levels, sometimes for small areas, sometimes for large areas, sometimes with two tiers of administration between the Department of Health and the service providers, sometimes with indirectly elected boards and sometimes with appointed boards. The only option which has not been tried is the transfer of health responsibilities to local authorities, which was rejected from the beginning.

The Conservative governments of the 1980s and 1990s made two main changes. They divided the service into a set of 'purchasers' and a set of 'providers' of health services and started a set of controls which give the Secretary of State for Health and the National Health Service Executive considerable control over what happens in most parts of the NHS. Previous reorganizations and interventions failed either to equalize access to health facilities or to bring doctors under political control. The second main change was to introduce explicit objectives about the incidence of ill health, rather than the volume of treatment to be provided for people who are ill.

Working for patients: markets and competition

The White Paper *Working for Patients*, 1989 (whose title implied that before then the NHS was working for someone else), established a different form of financial management in the service. The idea was that budgets would not be allocated to people providing services, rather to another set of people who would specify what they wanted the providers to do. These people would, initially, be the district health authorities and the larger GP practices. The new arrangement meant that service providers, such as hospitals, would not have a plan for the year and a budget, but rather a set of contracts for the year with agreed prices. Where there was only one large contract with the local health district, the arrangement was very much like a budget and a plan. Where there were a variety of purchasers and many providers in competition, the new arrangement had some characteristics of a market and a set of contracts.

In these latter cases managers and medical professionals were put into competition with each other. In the previous system the volume of work which a hospital did was determined by how much budget it received, how many patients were referred to it and how efficient it was. The budget was based mainly on historical patterns, with some adjustment from 'over-provided' areas. Referral patterns were mainly historical, based on where people lived and which general practitioners knew which hospital doctors. Efficiency was set by how well managers were managing, how good the facilities were and how hard the medical staff worked. In the new system, the idea was that hospitals would compete on price and/or the quality of work. Most contracts were large 'block' contracts which contained not only an allocation of funds but also a specification of what the providers were expected to do for the money. Efficiency was slightly more easy to measure, because procedures would have their unit costs defined. At the same time, purchasers would ask for an efficiency improvement each year, expressed as a reduction in the unit prices, achieved by individuals doing more work, by speeding up the through-put of patients (sending them home sooner) or by paying people less.

Another big change was to transfer a proportion of the health budget to GP fundholders, who could purchase services for their patients from hospitals or other providers of their choice. As the amount spent by GP fundholders grew, their influence on hospitals increased. While there is evidence that costs did not diminish as a result of this, the change did alter the relationship between general practitioners and their traditionally more senior hospital colleagues.

The Health of the Nation

In 1992, the government published a White Paper, *The Health of the Nation*, which set out targets for improvements in health in five 'key areas': coronary heart disease and stroke, cancers, mental illness, HIV/AIDS and sexual health, and accidents. Twenty-seven specific targets were also declared. Some referred to incidence of diseases such as the proportion of people with coronary heart disease or lung cancer. Some were causes (proportion of people smoking or obese) and some were outcomes (accidents and suicides). The paper recognized that the targets were achievable through a variety of preventive measures and that their achievement required the collaboration of a range of organizations.

The idea was that regional health authorities should adopt their own targets to contribute towards the achievement of the national ones. Each year, progress towards the targets is monitored[9] and published. While the achievement of the targets was not within the competence of any single body within the NHS, is did provide a focus for efforts to prevent the main avoidable causes of death and disease. It especially provided a way of making primary healthcare more important than hospitals in improving health standards as well as helping with collaborative efforts.

What is radical about these targets is that they are not concerned with the activities of any organization, but rather the effect of organizations working together to achieve a particular result. As we shall see in Chapter 10, it is only when results are measured or assessed that management can be fully turned towards achieving what people need.

The NHS Plan

The Labour government's policy towards the NHS contained some continuities with the past and some changes. What did not change was the struggle to maintain some central control through a system of target setting and managerial mechanisms and incentives. The old power battles between professionals, managers and politicians continued in an atmosphere of crisis and problems. Reducing the size of waiting lists and the time spent waiting for treatment were specific manifesto commitments by the Labour Party, and the government was not satisfied that the inherited arrangements were adequate to allow it to fulfil its promises. The internal market was dismantled and new institutional arrangements established. As the NHS Plan (2000) said:

> Competition between hospitals was a weak lever for improvement, because most areas were only served by one or two local general hospitals. Other methods of raising standards were ignored. The market ethos undermined teamwork between professionals and organisations vital to patient-centred care. And it hampered planning across the NHS as a whole, leading to cuts in nurse training and a stalled hospital building programme. (para 6.3)

The new arrangements replaced the market with an attempt at centralization in which the 'centre' would 'set standards, monitor performance, put in place a proper system of inspection, provide back up to assist the modernisation of the service and, where necessary, correct failure' (*ibid.*, para 6.6). Underneath the NHS Executive and its regional offices are the health authorities, which, together with the local authorities, are responsible for setting the health targets for their area. NHS Trusts, including primary care trusts, run services, whether in hospitals or in the community. Services are commissioned by primary care groups, which make 'commissioning plans' but do not organize competitions or market mechanisms as they commission care from the trusts and, in certain cases, from the private and voluntary sectors. This replaced the system of GP fundholding. The other organizational innovation was the establishment of the National Institute for Clinical Excellence, whose job is to set national guidelines for prescribing and treatment. Its principle is 'evidence-based treatment', which is interpreted as treatment based on nationally collected evidence about 'what works'. These changes were introduced early, following a White Paper called *The New NHS*. While the internal market and competition were abandoned, the changes did not reverse the decision to separate the functions of commissioning and providing services, with budgets allocated to the commissioners. This was one of the most significant of the previous changes as it aimed to change the balance of power away from the service providers. The power shift was not as great as it might seem, because the service commissioners are dependent on the providers for the services they fund.

The changes were not enough to solve the political problem that the NHS was causing the government, expressed in the size of and time spent on waiting lists and in a general feeling of crisis and under-investment. The main new solution was to commit more money and aim to increase the amount spent on healthcare to a proportion of GDP closer to the European average. The problem of the backlog of hospital and clinic building and maintenance was to be solved through extensive use of the Private Finance Initiative. Neither of these measures could produce immediate results. Healthcare professionals have long training periods, and instant staff increases can be achieved only by importing qualified staff, a solution that was tried. A lasting solution to a shortage of staff can come from expanding the medical schools and other training, and paying staff enough to keep them in the service and in the United Kingdom. The building programme got under way but not without controversy, as we shall see in Chapter 12, because of the additional costs involved in providing a profit for the PFI partners.

Apart from the financial solutions, the institutional arrangements replaced the market but continued with a series of targets, national standards, service frameworks and a system of inspection and monitoring with attached incentives. The Commission for Health Improvement was expanded and all parts of the NHS were classified as green, yellow, or red, with organizations that achieve green status having easier access to cash for investment and a light-touch inspection. While initially a very centralized system, the ambition was eventually to devolve performance management to health authorities, provided that they achieved 'green' status.

The new arrangements, as with so many other changes, were announced as 'modernization' and indeed one of the new bodies was called the Modernisation Agency, whose job is to help service providers to redesign their service access arrangements. The 2000 White Paper claimed that the organizational form and management methods were rooted in their 1948 origins, despite the extensive reorganizations and system changes that were put in place during the previous twenty years, with planning, targets, general management, the internal market and the switch of budgets from providers to commissioners.

It was as if 'modernization' was an absolute term in the sense that organizations and services are either modern or not. For practitioners, it was just another set of institutional arrangements in a long series of attempts at change.

Private healthcare

There are two sets of providers of private healthcare: private and charity hospitals and private wards and wings in the NHS hospitals. People pay for private care either through individual or employee insurance policies or with cash. In 1996, about 6 million people were covered by private health insurance, or 11% of the population. By 2000 the proportion had grown slightly to 12.3%. Of these, about one-third were individually insured and the rest were covered by company schemes. Not all those insured were covered for all possible health treatments, but 20% of elective surgery was done privately.

While the proportion of the population covered by private health insurance has grown slightly, the capacity of the private sector, as measured by available beds, is shrinking. Between 1995 and 1999 the number of beds was reduced by 13% to 10,144.[10] Of those, about one-third were in the not-for-profit and charitable sector. The other private provision is in NHS hospitals, where the number of dedicated private beds is 1400.[11] Spending on private healthcare is just under £3 billion, compared with NHS spending of around £45 billion.

The doctors who work in the private sector mainly also have jobs in the NHS. They are paid by the operation in their private capacity and may earn two or three times their NHS salaries by doing so. For managers, this sort of competition produces different problems from simply managing the service: they have to attract insurers by offering high quality at a competitive price; they have to attract insured patients by a level of 'hotel' facilities and speed which matches those of the private hospitals. They also have to offer consultants and other specialists enough money to persuade them to do the extra, private work.

One of the ways in which the Labour government tried to control the consultants who work in the private sector as well as the NHS was to specify the number of hours that NHS consultants must work for the NHS before going off to their private practices. New arrangements for clinical governance were designed to hold managers responsible for the doctors they hire, rather than being protected by doctors' clinical independence. Together these are the main means to solve the problem that has indeed been apparent since the establishment of the NHS, that of how to control the clinicians, especially the doctors.

The Labour government have been willing to use the private sector, either contracting out items such as psychiatric services and termination of pregnancy or using private provision for waiting list initiatives. The government seems to have come to the view that the mixed economy is appropriate in healthcare.

Implications for managers

There are three main implications for managers of these changes. Competitive behaviour is dealt with as a special topic in Chapter 7, but clearly managers have to analyse the nature of their competitive environment, assess how the competition is being organized and behave accordingly. While the internal market has been officially abolished, some providers face more competition than others.

One result is that the relationship between managers and professionals changes. All previous attempts at imposing management on the NHS since 1983 were weakened by the power of doctors, especially their power to commit beds and therefore other resources. The contractual regime meant that their interest was in performing the sort of work and in the volumes that would generate revenue for their hospital. Doctors became more involved in managing this process, through mechanisms such as clinical directorates and in co-operating with general managers and finance directors, for whom the business side of the NHS is important and who previously had been considered inferior and irrelevant to the real task of treating individual patients.

A third result of the allocation of budgets to commissioners is the concentration on volume and unit costs. Information systems have been improved to comply with the need to count activity to claim payment, and have allowed managers and medical professionals to be clearer about how much work they do and what it costs. This process itself was not cheap, doubling the number of administrative and clerical staff. The abandonment of the internal market removes some of the need for clerical effort in writing contracts, administering transactions and measuring all the services being bought and sold. The inspection and monitoring system put in its place, however, also requires a good deal of administrative and clerical effort.

Relationships between central and local government

John Major expressed a view that local authorities and especially Labour local authorities were the cause of alienation, crime, poor environments and most other social ills through their policies of collectivism. The previous Prime Minister had had a similar attitude to local authorities. But the relationship between central and local government has always been tense, as governments of all parties have sought to implement national policies at local level. The Labour Party collectively remembers the humiliation of the 1976 IMF intervention, caused in part by the spending growth of local government. The 1997 government, while apparently loosening controls over local authorities, retained reserve powers to prevent too fast a rise in spending.

There has always been tension between local and national governments, especially when the central and local government have been controlled by different parties, as they frequently have been. Throughout the period of

Conservative rule, local authorities spent as much energy trying to evade central government control as central government spent trying to subjugate them. Despite these efforts, local authorities retained a surprising degree of autonomy and difference.[12]

Funding

Local authority spending is almost all directly controlled by central government. There is a formula by which the Department of the Environment, Transport and the Regions (DETR) calculates a spending level for each service for each local authority, the amount which the government says would provide a standard level of service (the Standard Spending Assessment or SSA). This level is then used to distribute the business rate, which is aggregated nationally and redistributed, the revenue support grant, and the amount of council tax which authorities are expected to raise. Council tax accounts on average for about 20% of local authority spending. Business rates are collected locally but pooled and redistributed according to population size. Revenue Support Grant is allocated on a formula and there are various grants dedicated to particular services, such as the Standards Fund for education and money for such things as services for asylum seekers. Less than 10% of the total central government support is earmarked in this way. Capital expenditure is subject to direct control, through a process of application, approval and now competition. Sources of revenue are shown in Figure 4.1.

The Labour government tried to lift the amount of central government support for local government spending. Support had been declining in real terms in the last three years of the previous government and the incoming government announced plans to make it grow by 4% per year. Some of the money came with strings attached. As we saw in the plans for rewarding the

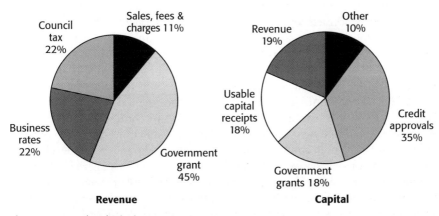

Figure 4.1 Local authority income sources
Source: Department of the Environment Transport and the Regions (September 2000)
Modernising Local Government Finance: A Green Paper, p.10

'green' organizations in the NHS, local authorities that achieve their Best Value targets are allowed extra central government support of up to 2.5% of their budget. The revised financial regime also includes a three-year planning period and a formula to limit annual changes in the formula-allocated grant in an attempt to produce more predictability and stability.

Direct controls

As well as control over spending there are many aspects of policy and management through which central government controls local authorities. The compulsory competitive tendering legislation, in place until 1998, determined the answer to one of the questions which any organization has to ask: how much of what we do should we consider contracting out? Changes in education legislation determined the proportion of the budget that education authorities can spend on activities other than that which goes on inside schools. Planning controls have been weakened by a process of upholding a greater proportion of appeals against local authority planning decisions. House building by local authorities has virtually stopped, and housing management is subject to outsourcing.

These direct controls have affected the way in which local authorities are managed. As individual departments and services are to a large extent controlled by regulations, managers have reduced discretion and are increasingly concerned with implementing national policies rather than managing the interface between local politicians and their organizations. In turn this leads to fragmentation of decision making within the authorities.

Overall allocation of resources among the services is still largely a local matter. While SSAs are published for each service, these figures are only indicative. Within services decisions are circumscribed and this means that there is a reduced possibility for overall planning and management of the organization as a corporate whole. In any case it is fragmented as a result of outsourcing. Contracts operate for a variety of services, whether they are carried out by the private sector or an in-house team. The contracting process makes the contracted parts relatively independent and subject to specific constraints. For example, if there is a five-year contract which specifies how a service is to be delivered, it is difficult to make any fundamental decisions about that service until the contract is up for renewal. The competition process also sets constraints. If the price for the contract is set through competition, management must ensure that costs are at or below the contract price. This has implications for staffing levels, wage and salary levels and, often, conditions of service: some of the major areas of managerial discretion are therefore dictated by the market, itself created by legislation and regulations.

As well as these financial, policy and managerial controls, central government ultimately has the power to create and abolish local authorities. The Local Government Review, completed in 1995, caused great uncertainty in those areas where the authorities' boundaries and functions were subject to change. Management and political effort was diverted away from service delivery towards campaigning and lobbying for survival. Local government is subjected to such fundamental change approximately once a decade. London government was reorganized in 1965, the rest of England, Scotland and Wales in 1974/5; the metropolitan areas and London had their upper level of authority abolished in 1985. The 1995 review completely reorganized Scottish and Welsh local authorities, while leaving London and the metropolitan areas of England unchanged.

Modernizing local government in England and Wales

Local government was to be 'modernized'. A White Paper[13] was followed by a Bill in July 1998. This time the intervention was not to be concerned with boundaries and functions but with internal political and management arrangements. The White Paper had a long list of diagnoses of local governments ailments:

- it was inefficient and inward-looking;
- there were variations in service quality;
- some councils had failed badly in particular services;
- some members and officers put self-interest before the public interest;
- there were corruption and wrong-doing because of a lack of scrutiny and openness;
- voters could not be bothered to vote in local elections; councillors were unrepresentative of the people in their area;
- previous initiatives had caused demoralization;
- committee structures were opaque and inefficient;
- voting methods (ballot boxes) were old-fashioned;
- local accountability for local taxation was weak;
- personal conduct and ethics had reduced public confidence;
- there was insufficient partnership with and influence by local businesses.

The proposed changes started at the top: new political management arrangements were demanded, with a choice of three options: directly elected mayor with a cabinet; cabinet and leader; or directly elected mayor and appointed council manager. Whichever option was chosen by authorities the change implied that fewer people would be involved in decision making and the rest of the councillors would be relegated to a back-bench role, much like the relationship between central government and Parliament.

The lack of interest by voters was to be cured by making voting easier. This was probably a forlorn proposal, since voting arrangements for general elections are identical to those for council elections and people manage to find the polling station on the relevant day. Freeing local government from central control to make the elections meaningful was not an option considered in the White Paper. While capping of local spending was stopped, reserve powers were retained to make sure local spending decisions were taken within nationally set constraints.

There was also to be a new ethical framework policed by standards committees and Standards Board, designed to raise standards and improve public confidence.

Partnerships were to be encouraged, rather than direct service delivery, now considered to be 'old-fashioned'. John Prescott's introduction to the White Paper was blunt:

> . . . councils need to break free from old fashioned practices and attitudes. There is a long and proud tradition of councils serving their communities. But the world and how we live today is very different from when our current systems of local government were established. There is no future in the old model of councils trying to plan and run most services. It does not provide the services which people want, and cannot do so in today's world. (p.6)

A significant proposal was the establishment of a 'Best Value' regime. The old rules about compulsory competitive tendering were scrapped and a new set of rules installed. These were very similar to a previous set of rules in central government, known as the 'prior options'. Councils were to ask fundamental questions about whether their services were necessary and then whether the ways in which they were delivered were the best option. Competition was no longer to be compulsory for any service but fair competition had to be considered as an option for all of them. The whole process was to be documented in annual performance plans and reviews, and policed through a new Best Value inspectorate.

Implications for managers

The increasingly centralized local government system has two main implications for managers in local government. The first is that the task of making strategy or a considered allocation of resources at local level is constrained. Individual departments have their policies and increasingly their funding dictated by someone outside the local authority. These outside referents in turn cause fragmentation within the authorities. The group of services which any local authority provides is the result of a series of historical accidents, withdrawal of functions and reorganizations, but the fact that individual committees and chief officers can refer to directives, guidelines or recommendations from inspectors rather than take notice of corporate policies reduces the coherence of the organization. This reduces not only corporate managerial influence but also the power and influence of the local elected representatives. It remains to be seen whether the new arrangements for political management will improve this situation.

Attempts by the DETR to set out in detail how services should be run, whether through CCT or Best Value, generates mixed responses among local authorities. Enthusiasts for the imposed methods follow the spirit, while opponents will find ways of conforming with the details without necessarily following the spirit.

Community care

Older people

Before April 1993, elderly people who wanted to live in an elderly persons' home could do so and have their rent and other costs funded by the Department of Social Security. This right had been established in 1980 in the supplementary benefit regulations and was exercised by a large number of people. Private residential homes expanded to accommodate the demand. This policy was an expensive, open-ended commitment: once someone decided to enter an elderly persons' home, the state was committed to pay for them for the whole of their stay there. The NHS and Community Care Act of 1990, among other things, closed the commitment and made access to services by older people subject to an assessment of need and a means test. From April 1993, the budget for old people's care was transferred from the Department of Social Security to local authority social services departments, which were then responsible for deciding whether individuals were entitled to help as a result of some dependency. If they were entitled, an individual care plan was drawn up, which might enable the person to stay at home or might allocate them to a residential or nursing home. Figure 4.2 shows the impact of this policy on the number of local authority beds in homes for elderly people and

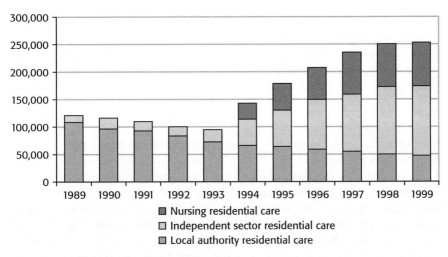

Figure 4.2   Adults in local authority care
Source: Social Services Inspectorate (2000) *Modern Social Services*, 9th Annual Report. London: HMSO

Table 4.2 Adults receiving personal social services, England

	1993–94	1994–95	1995–96	1996–97	1997–98	1998–99
Households receiving home care	514,600	538,900	512,400	491,100	479,100	447,200
Of whom, % receiving intensive home care	12%	15%	21%	25%	28%	31%
People aged 65 or over in residential care	89,827	103,120	116,117	129,358	135,271	137,779
People aged 65 or over in nursing care	23,113	39,874	52,845	60,787	67,451	67,548

Source: Social Services Inspectorate (2000) *Modern Social Services*, 9th Annual Report. Appendix A, p.101

the slowing of the growth of private residential beds. Figure 4.2 also shows the impact of the change in 1993. Since April of that year, local authorities have been able to support people in nursing home care and by 1999 they were caring for 73,500 people in nursing homes.

The funds for these services were integrated into local authority social services budgets, where they had to compete with other demands. The Audit Commission[14] (1994) reported that while some authorities faced budget problems, most were managing to stay within their budget. Those authorities which later faced difficulties suffered from an accumulation of commitments: as people were allocated places in residential care or care at home, the authority was committed to that expenditure for as long as that person remained in need:

> Authorities face hard choices. It is also particularly worrying that some authorities audited were unable to assemble the sort of information needed to check the financial implications of placements already made . . . rates are actually rising through a combination of rising demand from within the community and increasing pressure from hospitals. (p.19)

The combination of accumulated commitments and increased expectations from older people themselves, and from hospitals wishing to reduce their long-term care liabilities, put serious pressure on community care budgets. Authorities had to adjust their eligibility criteria, offering help only to those in greatest need.

The purpose of the rationing process was to target the care available on those in greatest need and to try to help people to stay in their own homes as long as possible. Table 4.2 shows a reduction in the numbers of people receiving home care since 1993, but an increase in the proportion of people getting 'intensive' home care, the people in greatest need of help. This indicates that the home care service is being targeted at the most needy group. However, Table 4.2 also shows a growth in the numbers of people supported in residential and nursing homes.

The White Paper *Modernising Social Services* drew attention to these trends, criticized the way in which care services are allocated and recognized that many people are excluded from services:

> Eligibility criteria are getting ever tighter and are excluding more and more people who would benefit from help but who do not come into the most dependent categories. (para 2.3)

Of course, that is what targeting intended, to allocate services to those in greatest need. The White Paper re-stated what councillors had been saying since 1993, that it is unpopular to withdraw services from a large number of people to make more intensive services available to a smaller number.

The solutions proposed in the White Paper were better reviews of individual cases, more joint working between health and social services, and greater use of direct payments to help people to look after themselves.

Mental health

Since the late 1950s mental health policy has been designed to transfer mentally ill people from large mental institutions into 'the community', which may include supervised accommodation in staffed community houses, or residential care staffed during the day, or may involve occasional visits from mental health professionals.

It has been argued by some that the policy has not been supported by sufficient resources for the care required in the community. The Health Select Committee (1994) expressed concern about the uneven success of the policy, especially the fact that minimum levels of provision had not been established, and the low priority given to mental health services by health purchasers. One source of concern was the publicized growth of attacks, murders and suicides by people with mental illness who were not in secure accommodation, either prison or a special hospital.[15] In September 1994 the Royal College of Psychiatrists reported that inner London mental units were operating over their capacity and turning patients away.

It became clear that the policy of transferring people from mental hospitals to the community was not without problems, of resources and co-ordination between agencies. Part of the problem was caused by a large increase of people suffering from mental illness transferred from prison to hospital, from 227 in 1984 to 1018 in 1994.[16] One solution was to introduce supervised discharge of certain categories of people with mental illness, whereby a worker would be assigned to each patient discharged. Even so, many such 'key workers' claimed to have too many people to oversee properly.

There was some good collaborative work between the various agencies involved in the process of discharging people with mental health problems from hospital to the community, but there remains a problem of resources and a clear idea about which agency is responsible for the people discharged and the services they need to survive.

A series of scandals occurred involving people with mental illness, whose supervision was inadequate, committing violent crimes. The various reports repeated the analysis of poor co-ordination and lack of accountability. During 1999 the government proposed a change in the 1983 Mental Health Act, especially the introduction of compulsory treatment. The changes involve small changes in the process of compelling people with mental disorders to accept a compulsory assessment, in exchange for an undertaking that appropriate treatment will be made available whether in hospital or at home. The changes included a new definition of a mentally ill person, 'dangerous person with severe personality disorder'. Once defined as such, people with this 'condition' could be detained before committing any offence.

Implications for managers

There were two main implications for managers in community care. Those running statutory services increasingly had to compete with the private and voluntary sectors, as purchasers looked for value for money for their budget allocations. Purchasers of services had to learn how to contract with other agencies and companies and to stimulate the provision of services, while working within a strict rationing regime. For some the new activities contradicted their professional values, which made them feel uneasy about having to be gatekeepers for services. These values, combined sometimes with poor management information systems, allowed many local authority community care budgets to be overspent.

The new arrangements caused many social services departments to reorganize. Because services had to be commissioned partly from the independent sector and because in-house services were in effect in competition with the independent sector, many social services departments divided themselves into two parts. One part was responsible for assessing needs and commissioning services. The other was responsible for running services, such as a dwindling number of residential homes, homecare services and day centres. The rationale behind this was that the former group would 'purchase' services from the latter, thus establishing an internal market. While we will see the implications of this sort of arrangement in more detail in Chapter 5, this change was similar to those in other parts of the public sector: central government direction combined with devolved accountability for services and the establishment of market-type relationships. However, underlying the community care changes was a desire to cash-limit an apparently open-ended commitment to spending on older people and to reduce the number of people in mental institutions.

Children

One side-effect of the community care changes was the reversal of the trend towards 'generic' social work through which integrated teams carried out social work functions for all the people in an area. Specialization returned, along with the separation of assessment of people's needs and rationing the resources from the provision of care services. One specialism that re-emerged was children's services, on which many social services departments had originally been founded.

Improving the quality of life for children was part of the Labour government's policy on social exclusion. Over one-fifth of children live in poverty, according to the government's definition, and 333,000 are in care[17] under the Children Act; a further 1.5 million get some social care services each year. Some of the income support measures we saw above were designed specifically to help poor children, as was a programme for pre-school children called 'Sure Start'.

Children's services were subject to periodic scandals and evidence of poor services, resulting in efforts to improve the quality of services culminating, in England, in a programme of efforts under the heading 'Quality Protects' from 1998. The programme aimed to improve the procedures by which children's services were delivered. An easier and clearer choice was to be offered between fostering, adoption and residential services. Processes of assessment, care planning and record keeping were to be improved, not only to improve service standards but also to avoid the mistakes reported in repeated childcare disasters. Management information systems and quality assurance procedures were also to be improved or put in place. Special attention was to be paid to listening to the children being looked after and to providing support to children after they left care. Authorities were also asked to improve the education and health provision to children in care. To help all this, a special grant was established, of £885 million over five years.

A programme of inspections by the Social Services Inspectorate was set up to monitor progress on Quality Protects. After two years, progress on process improvements was said to be encouraging but it was not yet possible to demonstrate that the outcomes for children were any better: 'many of the achievements this year are still concerned with *process*, and are hard to translate directly into better lives for children. Few councils have yet reached the point of *both* being able to identify, implement and monitor a strategy for change, *and* then demonstrate the effect of that change in terms of outcomes'.[18] For managers, Quality Protects brought a tightening of procedures and an increase in record keeping.

Education

Education was subject to all the sorts of reform which the Conservative governments promoted: competition between schools and colleges; centralization of control by ministers and ministries; decentralization of financial management; publication of performance standards and results; bringing professionals under control by national curriculum and national tests and through an inspection process; and the introduction of appointed people to sit not just on boards of governors of schools and colleges but also on a set of central institutions created by the Secretary of State for Education.

Although Margaret Thatcher had been Secretary of State for Education, education was apparently not a high priority of the early Thatcher governments. The main changes did not occur until 1988, nine years into the Thatcher period. The pace of change increased during the Major administrations, completing a transformation of the governance and management of education.

Labour made an election issue of educational standards. Its Secretary of State for Education and Employment, David Blunkett, had been the leader of Sheffield City Council and therefore had direct experience of local education authorities. With few exceptions they followed the lead of the Conservatives in their mistrust of local authorities to run an effective education service and their belief that teachers needed to be subjected to more control, inspection and incentives if they were to teach well.

Schools

School education in Britain is a centralized affair. Over 90% of pupils attend a state-run school and follow a national curriculum. Standards are set and monitored nationally and there are national standard attainment tests and public examinations. All teachers in state schools have to have qualified teacher status. There are some schools that vary from the standard comprehensive school system. Some secondary schools are allowed to select their pupils on educational merit and an interview with their parents, despite being state-funded. There are over 500 'specialist' schools, comprehensives that follow the national curriculum while offering extra teaching in technology, languages, sports or arts. In addition, at the end of 2000, city academies were announced, replacements for mainly inner city schools whose buildings and equipment are funded partly through sponsorship by companies and voluntary organizations such as the Church of England. Specialist schools and city academies are all in inner city areas. The types of school that pupils attend in the United Kingdom are shown in Table 4.3.

Secondary schools all have boards of governors made up of elected parents, teachers and members of the local community. The governors are supposed to set the direction for the school, select the headteacher and make decisions on staffing and the use of the school's budget. Local education authorities have education departments that are responsible for a limited range of support functions, many of which are provided to schools in competition with other service providers. The LEAs are in principle responsible for the educational standards in their area and for the provision of school places but their powers and budgets were curtailed during the Conservative governments.

The 1980 Education Act stopped education authorities restricting pupils to the secondary schools in their area. While apparently minor, in practice this change started the process of allowing parents and pupils to choose their

Table 4.3   School pupils by type of school, United Kingdom, thousands

	1990–91	1994–95	1999–00
Public sector schools			
Nursery	105	111	144
Primary	4955	5230	5338
Secondary			
Comprehensive	2,843	3093	3277
Grammar	156	184	204
Modern	94	90	94
Other	300	289	283
All public sector schools	**8453**	**8996**	**9339**
Non-maintained schools	613	600	618
Special schools	114	117	114
Pupil referral units			9
All schools	**9180**	**9714**	**10081**

Source: Office for National Statistics (2001) *Social Trends* 31, Table 3.1. London: HMSO

school and, perhaps more significantly, of allowing schools to choose their pupils. Comprehensive education was not favoured by a government which believed in individualism and the attainment of privilege through ability. The establishment of compulsory boards of governors for schools was a prelude to the process of handing control over state institutions to appointed bodies and taking them away from both the professionals and the elected local authorities. This process was completed by the Education Reform Act 1988, which made the management of schools more independent of the local authorities, both by transferring financial management to schools and by allowing them to opt out completely from local authority control. Both these measures appeared to give the schools more autonomy, at least from their local authority.

While the introduction of this legislation was accompanied by rhetoric about autonomy and self-management, the Act increased central government control. A national curriculum was introduced, to be overseen by a new body, the National Curriculum Council (NCC). National testing was also introduced, again overseen by a national body, the Schools Examination and Assessment Council (SEAC).

Some of these measures were further strengthened in the 1993 Education Act, which took more steps to encourage schools to opt out of their education authorities. Of course, those schools which decided to leave the control of their education authorities had to have their budgets allocated centrally so a national funding body, the Funding Agency for Schools, was established. At the same time in England the NCC and the SEAC were combined into a new central body, the School Curriculum and Assessment Authority (SCAA), later replaced by the Qualifications and Curriculum Authority.

These changes had a big impact on the management of the education system. The local education authorities previously had a great deal of influence and direct control over what happened in schools. They planned the distribution of schools in their areas, appointed headteachers and had a large say in curriculum and teaching methods. After the 1992 changes their powers were greatly reduced. Governing bodies appointed heads, schools ran their own budgets, and those schools which opted for grant-maintained status were completely independent. Those functions through which the education authorities exercised influence, such as in-service training for teachers, inspection and curriculum development, were subject to the market. Local authorities had to allocate a small fixed proportion of their budgets for education authority functions, the rest being allocated to the schools. If the authorities wanted to provide services for schools whose costs exceeded the fixed proportion of the budget, they had to be paid for out of school budgets. Schools were free to choose from whom to buy support services, including inspection, and the educational professionals changed from being powerful superiors to competitive service providers.

In many cases the education authorities had to reduce their staffing levels to match the amount of budget they were allowed to retain and their success in competing to supply services to schools. It also increased the power and responsibility of headteachers. While governing bodies were nominally more powerful, in practice the headteachers gained power through their expertise and knowledge and the fact that they were full-time.

Heads had to use their new authority, in part, to ensure the survival of their schools. Competition for resources meant competition for pupils. In areas where there is spare capacity in the number of places, there is competition for numbers. In areas in which schools are close to each other, there is competition to attract those pupils who will achieve the best examination results. The publication of the proportion of pupils who achieve five GCSE grades C and above makes some schools look better than others. Competition is based on a variety of factors: school discipline, uniforms and the fact that a school is single-sex as well as its examination result scores.

As in all markets, the market for pupils produces winners and losers. Schools with good results are able to attract pupils who will achieve good results. The reverse is true for the rest: bad results deter parents. In practice, much of the differentiation between schools is based on the class background of their pupils. There is a high correlation between examination results and social class. Attracting successful pupils means, in effect, attracting middle-class parents. Although schools are allowed to select only 10 per cent of their pupils, priority can be given to siblings of existing pupils. In any case, although catchment areas are no longer in force, there are practical limits to the distances pupils can travel. While comprehensive schools were segregated according to geography, the current system exaggerates the differences.

The 1992 White Paper *Choice and Diversity: A New Framework for Schools* promoted such diversity. It advocated the creation of different schools for different sorts of pupils: academic schools for those of more academic ability and practical schools for the rest. There was an experiment with a new sort of school, the city technology college, which would be technically well equipped and sponsored by industry. While a few of these were established, industry was, in general, reluctant to fund education.

There was not a complete victory for the government in these changes. While mechanisms were established to run the whole of the secondary school system from the Department for Education and the quangos it established, the people who staff the educational system were not prepared simply to submit to central government changes. Despite the financial inducements for schools to opt out of local authority control and become grant-maintained, fewer than 1000 schools voted to do so, about a quarter of the secondary schools in England and Wales. The rest decided to maintain their links with their education authority, albeit within a new regime which gave them more financial and managerial autonomy. One reason for this is that many head-teachers see themselves as part of a local education system, rather than a small enterprise in the education business. They respect the support they receive from the education authority and the stability provided by a system which manages through planning, to the limited extent that the education author-ities can in the current system. Another reason may be the difficulty which schools found in finding members of governing bodies who were willing to volunteer enough time to run their schools. Just as business largely refused to fund schools through the city technology college initiative, individual people showed unwillingness to manage their local schools.

The innovations introduced by the Labour government from 1997 were based on many of the same principles as the previous government's: selectiv-ity rather than universality and uniformity; a belief in the mixed economy; a mixture of central control and individual accountability; and an element of competition for funds. They also included the newer principles identified at the beginning of this chapter: a desire to exercise central control over indi-vidual organizations, in this case schools; an eclectic attitude to ownership; and a belief in 'modernization'.

The system established by Conservative governments was largely preserved by the Labour administration. Selection was upheld, although selective schools could hold a ballot among the parents of children currently attending feeder primary schools of the selective school in question about whether to continue selection. A variety of schools was maintained, whether specialist schools or the old state-funded grammar schools, and more schools were encouraged to become specialized. Grant-maintained schools lost their privileges in 1999 on the grounds that their status gave an unfair advantage to their pupils.

As well as continuing the main elements of the Conservative approach, the new government introduced some innovations. Some were concerned with the general level of standards, and others with what to do about schools that were doing very badly. On general standards the national scheme of testing pupils and publishing the results school by school was extended down the age range. A new pay and performance regime was introduced from September 2000, after much opposition from the teachers' unions, under which teachers assessed as reaching a threshold of competence would get extra pay and the chance to get on a pay scale with a higher top end.

By January 2001 650 schools had been declared as 'failing' by the Office for Standards in Education. Failing is defined as 'failing to give its pupils an acceptable standard of education'. The 'special measures' that result include an action plan to be approved and monitored by the Secretary of State for Education, through the inspectorate. Of failing schools, 546 were declared successfully saved from failure within two years by a variety of management interventions and staff changes; 84 were closed. Twenty were given a 'fresh start' under new leadership and a lot of publicity for the newly appointed 'superheads', but without much success.

A similar scheme applied to LEAs. If they were declared as 'failing' they could be prescribed a rescue package or could be handed over to private managers to run. Some authorities decided to contract out the management of their LEA services before being forced to by the government.

As well as these measures for individual schools and LEAs, groups of schools in deprived areas could be declared an Education Action Zone, 73 of which were established from September 1998 to September 2000. A further 26 smaller ones were established in 2000 and 2001. Schools in the zones would get extra funding and special help, and were supposed to attract sponsorship from the private sector, amounting to about 10% of the government funding.

Funding for all schools was also increased, as we saw in Chapter 3. Some of the capital funding was given a special label, such as the New Deal for Schools in 1997, but the funding was a necessary response to the long backlog of repairs and renewals and to the need for the provision of new school places.

As with other parts of the public sector, Prime Minister Blair called for changes in the education system. A typical remark came in a speech at Cranfield School of Management in September 2000:

> We want first-rate secondary education for all, with the excellence and flexibility within every school to make the most of every pupil. Let's be clear what this means. It means big change from the old comprehensive model. Modern comprehensives should be as dedicated as any private school or old grammar school to high achievement for the most able.

After over two years in government, after an election in which 'education, education, education' had been declared as the three main priorities, this showed a degree of frustration with the public education system and the changes the government had so far made.

Post-school education

Administrative changes were made to all those parts of education in the post-school years. In part these changes were a response, common in most European

Table 4.4 Enrolments in further and higher education, United Kingdom, thousands

	1990/91	1993/94	1998/99
Further education			
Full-time	480	738	1065
Part-time	1759	1756	2978
Higher education			
Undergraduate			
Full-time	665	948	1127
Part-time	342	471	535
Postgraduate			
Full-time	84	116	117
Part-time	86	129	254

Sources: Office for National Statistics (1996) *Social Trends* 26, Table 3.21; and (2001) *Social Trends* 31, Table 3.15. London: HMSO

countries, to changes in the labour market. While employers were demanding better-qualified workers, unemployment rates among school leavers increased from the early 1980s and accelerated during recessions. Increased participation rates in higher education were one answer to both of these problems. At the same time, the UK government was unwilling to continue to pay the same unit cost for the extra students as they were paying for the existing ones. The expansion was to take place without a proportionate increase in funding, resulting in a sharp drop in the amount of funding per student in further and higher education.

As well as these underlying considerations, the changes followed the familiar pattern. Local authority control, first of polytechnics and then of further education and teacher training colleges, was to be replaced by rule by board. Both sets of institutions became corporate bodies (in 1989 and 1992 respectively). Funding arrangements were adjusted to make student numbers a more important determinant of income, and the institutions then competed for students. The number of full-time students in further and higher education grew by 47 per cent between 1990/91 and 1993/94 and a further 44 per cent by 1998/99, and the number of part-time students by 8 per cent and then by 70 per cent by 1998/99. The figures are shown in Table 4.4.

The competition process in the higher education sector increased when the polytechnics were allowed to become universities with degree-awarding status from 1992. The creation of corporate status took some institutions from the status of technical college to university in three years. Sometimes the development of the facilities did not match the change in status and activity but that was not the purpose of the exercise: the changes successfully increased the proportion of the post-school population at university, a growth that continued until the end of the decade.

As well as the competitive environment, changes in the post-school sector included the establishment of instruments of control: the funding arrangements imposed a planned system of student numbers and subjects, while inspection mechanisms for teaching and research gave central leverage through direct intervention and financial inducements.

Outside the educational institutions, other changes have taken place. Training and enterprise councils (TECs), another set of quangos, were funded by government (through the departments of Education and Employment, Environment and Trade and Industry) to commission a variety of training, work experience and other activities aimed at creating an employable workforce and, to some extent, jobs for that workforce. They operated through an operating agreement and a funding agreement with the government, which set out in detail what they would do during the year. In turn the TECs entered contracts with service providers, including the state further education sector. This mode of control, from ministry to TEC (itself a quango) to private and incorporated providers was an ideal type of how the Conservative governments preferred to operate: appoint people you can trust (preferably from business) who are accountable to you and establish funding and control mechanisms which enable you to determine what they do. Eventually the Labour government replaced the training functions of the TECs with a new arrangement, the learning skills councils that were set up under the Learning and Skills Act 2000. From April 2001 these new bodies also took over the functions of the Further Education Funding Council in allocating money to sixth forms and further education colleges. In its first year the LSCs' budgets were £6 billion.

Early in its period of office, the Labour government commissioned Sir Ron Dearing to look into funding and other issues for higher education. It accepted his recommendation that fees be charged for all higher education and that the systems of quality and other controls be further strengthened. The Scottish Parliament did not accept that fees should be charged for higher education and abolished fees in Scotland.

Implications for managers

Managers of educational institutions are in an increasingly competitive environment, for students and pupils and for resources. More financial independence means that managers have the responsibility for keeping costs down, by whatever means are available. Local discretion leads to local bargaining and decisions about staff recruitment and retention. For example, half of further education colleges now negotiate their staff terms and conditions of employment.

Competition reduces collaboration. In the secondary education sector, for example, headteachers are unwilling to share good practice developments and to share in-service training for fear of giving their neighbouring schools a competitive advantage over theirs. In higher education, the competition for research funding led to a 'market' for researchers. Each institution is graded according to the quantity and quality of its research output. A transfer market for researchers developed so that research output looked better on the day on which the research assessment exercise was carried out. As well as the impact of competition and relative independence, there was a simultaneous decrease in local discretion, as more influence was wielded by the new bodies attached to the Department for Education and Employment, including resource allocation, curriculum content and inspection of standards. The Office for Standards in Education has claimed that the inspection regime has improved standards in schools. This has been at the cost of some stress to teachers in schools, called by one group of researchers 'pre-inspection panic and post-inspection blues'.[19]

The main result for managers of the expansion in further and higher education is that they have to achieve two things: to attract enough students to generate revenue, and to increase productivity (measured in cost per student) of the staff in order to cope with the reduction in unit funding. Few people living in the United Kingdom can have missed the efforts made to achieve the first of these: universities even advertise with posters on buses and on television. The second objective has been achieved less visibly, with larger classes, more use of part-time and casual staff, and an increased workload for existing teachers. Local bargaining in further education has created a new set of negotiations on pay and hours of work. Fortunately for the managers, the over-supply of graduates has contained the pressure for pay rises from teachers and lecturers, although the National Association of Teachers in Further and Higher Education has retained a national agreement in many colleges. (There is more on the industrial relations implications of these and other changes in Chapter 11.)

Housing

One of the main objectives of Conservative housing policy was to promote home ownership by allowing council and housing association tenants the right to buy their house or flat, at a subsidized price: 1.5 million units were bought in this way, bringing owner occupation up to 69 per cent of the housing stock in 1999. The other tenures were social housing, including housing associations and local authority and other public sector 22 per cent, and private rented 9 per cent. The sale to tenants of municipal housing was the biggest of the privatizations and one which had a direct impact on the policy towards publicly owned housing. Whereas local authority housing was a normal tenure for working people in the post-war period, the policy of privatization and reduction of the volume of construction made council and housing association housing into 'social housing' available only for those with no alternative: new lettings by the 1990s were predominantly for poor people,

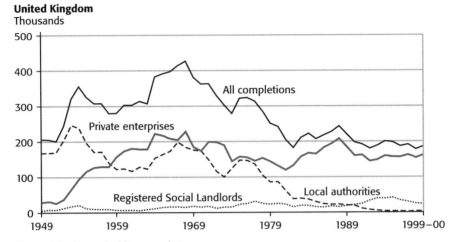

Figure 4.3 House building completions
Source: Office for National Statistics (2001) *Social Trends* 31, Figure 10.3

either economically inactive or unemployed. In some areas, especially in the north of England, there are surpluses of social housing and estates have become 'difficult to let'.

Local authorities and housing associations

The policies have virtually stopped the construction of local authority homes for general use, almost all 'social housing' now being provided by the Registered Social Landlord (RSL) sector, as is shown in Figure 4.3, which also illustrates the dominance of private sector housebuilding in the last two decades.

Other forms of privatization

Another objective of government policy has been to transfer the management of the residual housing stock which local authorities own. Various schemes have been tried. Housing management is included in the compulsory competitive tendering regime. Local authority housing managers have to compete for the management contract of the authorities' houses if companies are prepared to bid for the work. As an alternative, the 'large-scale voluntary transfer' was a way for councils to transfer the management to private companies or housing associations, sometimes formed by existing managers. In many authorities, tenants now control the management of their estates, including maintenance and security.

Meanwhile, housing associations have become more reliant on private finance. The Housing Corporation, which provides funds to housing associations, used to provide 100 per cent funding through the Housing Association Grant, but it now provides funding of 58 per cent, the rest being made up by private borrowing, in line with other initiatives to introduce private finance into public spending. The flow of funds in these schemes is interesting: lettings are mainly to people in receipt of housing benefit, so the private investor or lender's risk is underwritten by the Department of Social Security's rent guarantee. The scheme does not transfer much risk to the private sector, but it does reduce the figure for public sector capital spending. The main foreseeable problem (apart from the difference in rates of interest) is that the right to buy for housing association tenants potentially removes a revenue stream to the private investor, as homes are removed from the rental stock. This is an example of the contradiction between individual choice and offering the private sector guaranteed return on its investment. In practice the private sector does not want to take the risk of investing in property which the tenants have the right to buy at a discount.

The Labour government maintained the overall policy of encouraging home ownership and trying to divest local authorities of their direct housing provision function. As in other sectors the government recognized the huge backlog of housing repairs and maintenance in the residual public sector housing stock, which it put in the Green Paper at £19 billion. This was to be remedied, eventually, by an injection of cash and permissions to enter PFI schemes. It also increased the allocation of funds to the Housing Corporation to increase the scale of RSL building.

As far as the management of public sector housing was concerned, the main policy was either to transfer management to RSLs or to persuade local authorities to set up 'arm's-length' companies through which to manage the housing stock. The White Paper said that the government would support the transfer of up to 200,000 homes each year from local authorities to RSLs.

Housing was one of the policy areas that was devolved to the new administrations in Scotland and Wales and had always had different arrangements in Northern Ireland through the Housing Executive.

Housing benefit and subsidy

The other main policy has been to stop subsidizing house building and subsidize people's housing costs. Local authorities and housing associations have to charge rents which cover the full cost of building and managing housing. Those tenants who cannot afford the rents receive housing benefit to cover the difference.

The switch in subsidy was from 'bricks and mortar' to housing benefit. In Great Britain, about 1.8 million local authority tenants and 1 million privately rented tenants receive housing benefit. The switch in housing subsidy by the Conservative governments is shown in Table 4.5. The Labour government phased out the tax relief on mortgage interest.

Table 4.5 Housing subsidy 1979/80 and 1994/95 (England and Wales, £ billion)

	1979/80	1994/5
Mortgage tax relief	4	4.4
Housing benefit	1.84	8.9
Subsidy for building	12.5	4.9
Total	**18.4**	**18.2**

Source: Department of the Environment and Welsh Office (1995) *Our Future Homes, Opportunity, Choice, Responsibility*, Cm 2901. London: HMSO

Remaining housing problems

Replacement rates

Housing policy is not producing a balance between supply and demand, especially for social housing. In 1994 Ford and Wilcox[20] estimated that England required 120,000 new social rented houses per year. The 1995 White Paper showed that the government planned 70,000 new lettings in the social housing sector for England and Wales together, including letting made available by inducing people to move to the owner-occupied sector. The 2000 White Paper[21] announced a doubling of the funds available to the Housing Corporation.

'Ghettos'

The cumulative effect of the two policies, of increasing rents to cover costs and the housing benefit regime being the main source of subsidy, results in fewer tenancies in the local authority and housing association sector being for working people. Social housing is increasingly available only to those for whom the state pays the rent. Prescott-Clarke *et al.* estimated[22] that there are 240,000 new local authority lettings per year, or about 11 per cent of the stock. They found that 66 per cent of new tenants were not in work, including 64 per cent of the under 35s and 51 per cent of those aged 35–54. Half of new tenants had incomes of £75 per week or less and 60 per cent of new tenants were in receipt of housing benefit.

Owner occupation is not a universal solution

Owner occupation makes owner occupiers vulnerable to changes in interest rates and entrants to the housing market vulnerable to the level of house prices. House price booms in the mid-1980s and again in the mid-1990s led to big temporary increases in the proportion of incomes devoted to mortgage repayments. Recessions have led to repossessions of homes by lenders as people made unemployed are unable to meet their repayments. In areas of housing surpluses because of scarce job opportunities, previous council houses bought under the right to buy remain unsaleable.

One of the problems caused by the dependence on owner occupation as the main form of tenure and the overwhelming tenure of newly built housing is that there is a class of workers who cannot find anywhere affordable to live in prosperous areas. Many of these are public sector workers such as nurses, teachers, ambulance drivers and other essential staff. The problem was made worse by policies of selling off nurses' housing and replacing police housing with housing allowances. In recognition of this problem the government introduced a starter home initiative for 'key workers' in 2001.

Implications for managers

Some estates have become more difficult to manage. The implications for people working in housing is that the tenants are increasingly concentrated among poor people. Housing estates which are populated by people with low incomes have the problems associated with poverty, such as families breaking up and poor health. Once public housing becomes a residual function for people with nowhere else to go, its management becomes less of a housing management job and more of a social welfare and crisis intervention one.

Criminal justice

The Conservative governments frequently claimed that 'law and order' were a major priority. However, the volume of recorded crime increased during the period of Conservative rule. Figure 4.4 shows the increase in the number of offences recorded by the Crime Survey in England and Wales between 1981 and 1993 and its decline after 1995. Table 4.6 shows the trends in activity in the criminal justice system in England and Wales and the people employed to carry them out.

There have been many attempts to reform the main institutions of the criminal justice system: the police, courts, prisons and probation services. In each case there have been similar themes: a desire to increase central control and direction, especially by the Home Office; and a desire to improve performance and increase efficiency. The approach has been similar to that used in other parts of the public sector. Management methods have included the establishment of performance targets and indicators, attempts to link pay to performance, standardization of work processes, removal of both local and professional autonomy, and the introduction of competition. Although the organizations of the criminal justice system were relatively late in receiving the attention of the reformers, when it happened they were by no means

Table 4.6 Criminal justice, England and Wales 000s

	1981	1991	1999
Probation orders	36	45	56
Community service	28	42	51
Combination orders			21
Probation service employees	13	18	15
Prison service employees	24	33	43
Prison population	44	46	65
Police	120	127	124
Civilian staff in police service	28	46	53
Recorded crimes	2964	5276	5301

Source: Office for National Statistics (2001) *Social Trends* 31, Tables 9.3, 9.19 and 9.23.
London: HMSO

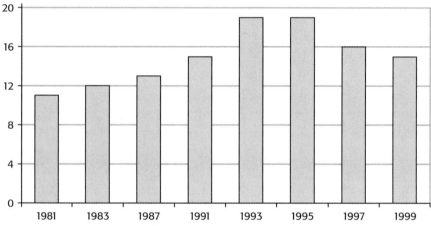

*All incidents measured by the survey, whether or not they were recorded by the police.
Surveys were not carried out in 1985 or 1989.*

Figure 4.4 Crimes identified in the British Crime Survey, England and Wales 1981 to 1999
Source: Office for National Statistics (2001) *Social Trends* 31, Figure 9.2

immune from it. However, the target in this case was rather stronger and
more able to resist change than some other groups. When magistrates and
chief constables are asked to change, they can call on their connections with
powerful interests.

There was one specific manifesto commitment about criminal justice, to
reduce the time taken to bring prosecutions against young people. This involved speeding up court and reporting processes, rather than any change in
policy about prosecutions.

Prison population[1]

Great Britain
Thousands

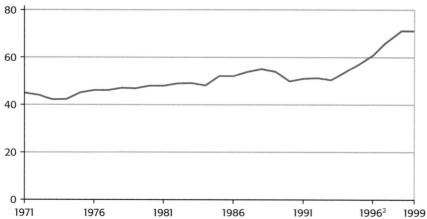

[1] Includes those held in police cells up to June 1995. Includes non-criminal prisoners.
[2] From 1996 onwards the Scottish prison population is for financial years.

Figure 4.5   Prison population, Great Britain, thousands
Source: Office for National Statistics (2001) *Social Trends* 31, Figure 9.17

Prisons

The prison population has grown rapidly over the past two decades and especially the last ten years. Figure 4.5 shows the total numbers of prisoners in Great Britain from 1971 to 1999. Table 4.7 shows that the growth in prison population was in both local prisons and closed training prisons. The prison population slightly exceeds the official capacity. The Home Office *Prison Population Brief* in June 2000 said that the England and Wales prison population exceeded the certified normal accommodation level by 2%. This figure disguises the overcrowding that occurs in some prisons.

A report[23] published in 2000 on the management of prisons found much to be improved: standards needed to be established, accountabilities clarified, the volume of instructions from headquarters to prison governors reduced, financial management improved and personnel policies brought up to date. In fact there was hardly any area of prison management for which improvement was not recommended. This was despite at least ten years of efforts to reorganize and improve the management of prisons. The two mechanisms used were market testing, an attempt to test the Prison Service against the cost and quality of private organizations, and the establishment of the Prison Service as an 'executive agency', the managerial solution of preference for the Conservative governments.

'Market testing' of prisons was introduced to promote changes in management. The first to be market tested was Manchester Prison.[24] In 1990 there

Table 4.7   Prison population by type of establishment 1980–1999, thousands

	1980	1990	1999[1]
Local prisons	17.3	15.5	25.1
Closed training prisons	13.0	17.1	24.3
Young offender institutions[2]	–	5.3	5.2
Remand centres	2.4	2.3	4.5
Open prisons	3.7	3.7	3.9
Juvenile institutions	–	0.3	1.6
Closed borstal institutions	3.9	–	–
Open borstal institutions	1.6	–	–
Senior detention centres	1.3	–	–
Junior detention centres	0.7	–	–
Short sentence institutions	–	0.3	–
Police cells	–	0.9	–
All prisons	**43.9**	**45.5**	**64.5**

[1] *Based on population at 30 June.*
Source: Office for National Statistics (2001) *Social Trends* 31, Table 9.18

had been a riot in this prison, the consequence of which was a repair bill of £70 million and a damaged reputation for the establishment and the Prison Service in general. In 1992, following a report by the Inspector of Prisons identifying the causes of the riot, the management of the prison was put out to tender. The causes identified were many and complicated and included a problem of inadequate staffing. However, many of the problems were due to poor management, especially by middle managers.

Putting the prison out to tender produced quick changes in management and in the regime in the prison. The managers realized that it was not going to be credible to promise an improved regime in the bid document if such a regime could not be demonstrated in practice. The governor of Manchester Prison has argued that the process of redesigning the regime and the management arrangements was evolutionary rather than revolutionary.[25] He may have displayed undue modesty, because the change in the relationship with the Prison Officers Association was significant. The threat of losing the prison to the private sector provided an incentive to produce a better service. The success of the process led some to believe that market testing was just a mechanism to reduce the power of the Prison Officers Association to resist operational changes. This was not to be the case and the programme of competition continued. Private companies were invited to run new prisons without a counter-bid from existing employees of the Prison Service. The first contract to manage a prison was awarded to Group 4 Remand Services Ltd for the management of the newly built Wolds Remand Prison, which opened in April 1992 for 320 adult prisoners. The stated aim of this process was not to save money, rather to improve the regime. In the event the winning tender was not the lowest bid and the actual running costs exceeded the accepted tender because of mistakes and omissions in the tendering process.[26]

By 1996 there were six private and 140 public prisons in Great Britain. The plan was clearly to have a parallel private system alongside the public one. The private operators could be used as a standard for the public prisons and a useful item to employ in negotiation with prison officers and managers. However, a proposal to subject twelve public sector prisons to competition from private companies was delayed by the Home Secretary in May 1995 until after the general election.[27] Since the 1997 election the Prison Service has had some success in tendering, for example retaining Manchester Prison and winning Blakenhurst, a prison that had been an exemplar of the successful private sector.

In addition to the privatization programme for the management of prisons, other elements of the service, such as the prison education service, drug and alcohol services, and transport from court to prison, were subjected to competition from private companies and voluntary organizations.

HM Prison Service and the Scottish Prison Service were launched as executive agencies in April 1993. The new agencies were given the task of improving the way prisons were run. They produced corporate plans setting out their targets and proposals for meeting them, including ideas about devolving operational responsibilities to individual establishments, changing the pay and grading system and introducing competition for certain services.

As well as the structural changes and the introduction of companies into the management of prisons, the 1995 Budget brought a budget cut to the Prison Service, at a time of increased prisoner numbers. Ironically, the private prisons were protected against both these changes, as their legally binding contracts guaranteed their income and prisoner numbers. Such pressures have shaken up the management of the Prison Service but have not solved its problems. Recent inspectors' reports have indicated that some of the problems identified by Woolf[28] persist, such as long hours in-cell, and insufficient rehabilitation, work, counselling and education. The main response by the Labour government was to announce the biggest ever building programme, £660 million for sixteen new prisons over three years, through the Private Finance Initiative method.

Police

The Major government introduced fundamental changes to the management of the police service. There was frustration with the increasing level of crime, which increased spending on the police forces failed to stop. A review of the way in which police officers are managed and paid was called for in May 1992. The report[29] made many recommendations, including the abolition of certain management grades and the introduction of short-term contracts, reduction in salaries for new recruits and performance-related pay. The various organizations representing police personnel and police authorities organized protests and lobbies and managed to make the reforms less radical than proposed by Sheehy.[30]

However, changes were introduced, including changes in pay and grading. A pay system was introduced which linked pay to the appraisal scheme. Short-term contracts were introduced for chief constables. The idea was to avoid the 'job for life' attitude which was believed to detach police officers from any need to do well. Meanwhile the structure was flattened, with greater account-ability for operational units, which became known as basic command units.[31]

The Police and Magistrates' Courts Act 1994 changed the relationship between the Home Office and the police authorities and made the police authorities more independent of local authorities from April 1995. Announc-ing the proposed changes, the Home Secretary, Kenneth Clarke, said:

> Given that I provide 90 per cent of the money on behalf of central govern-ment and that nine out of 10 people think that I run their local service, it is time that I held police authorities to account for performance and was then held to account by this House.[32]

The funding of the new authorities was subject to central cash limits, unlike the previous arrangement in which the government paid its share of the locally determined budget. While the original proposals were to fill the police authorities with nominees of the government, amendments to the legislation ensured the presence of local authority elected members on the authorities. The composition of the authorities is nine local councillors, three magistrates and five appointed members.

However, the new arrangements allowed the Home Secretary to set targets, implemented through a local policing plan. As with other public sector changes, these contained a combination of increased local accountability, through plans, performance measures and reporting arrangements, and increased central control through target and priority setting and direct control over finance. The targets related to the Home Secretary's priorities were set out in the form of key objectives and performance indicators. They included detection rates for violent crime and domestic burglaries; prevention of crimes which were a special local problem (performance indicators for this proved too difficult); visibility of the force to the public; and response times to emerg-ency calls.

The government pursued a model that was similar to its plans for the NHS. There would be national targets and indicators set centrally and moni-tored on behalf of the Home Secretary. Police authorities were to act as if they were purchasers of police services, specifying what should be achieved, rather than managing the operations. Basic command units would be the equivalent of trusts, operating within guidelines but with some managerial freedom. The main difference was the retention of local authority representa-tion on the police authorities, but this was forced on the government as the Bill progressed.

Probation

The Probation Service has also been subject to policy and managerial changes. Since the Probation Rules of 1907 the ethos of the service was that it was to 'advise, assist and befriend' offenders. Probation work was based on social work ideas about intervening in the lives of offenders to help them to avoid crime. The qualification for those working in the service was a social work one and officers worked in a relatively autonomous way, with a professional relationship with the courts. While there was 'supervision' by senior officers, this was conducted as a conversation between professionals rather than between a boss and a subordinate. Practice was based on legislation and learned practice rather than predefined routines of behaviour.

The Home Office made various attempts to assert control over the service. In 1984 it published a statement of objectives specifying that the purposes of the service were to prevent re-offending, reintegrate offenders and divert them from custody. While these were uncontroversial they were a prelude to a series of attempts to bring the service under national control. This became a more important matter when the government decided to change the role of the Probation Service. Probation was to become 'punishment in the community', rather than a social work-based process applied to offenders. The Green Paper *Punishment, Custody and the Community* 1988 and the Criminal Justice Act 1991 made it clear that the government wanted non-custodial sentences to be punitive and to be a sentence and punishment in their own right, rather than an inferior alternative to custody. This was part of a wider concern that the Conservative government had to be 'tough' on crime. This was essentially a political stance, that harsh sentences on those who were convicted of crime were likely either to prevent crime, to satisfy a need for retribution or at least to assure the electorate that the government was concerned about the rapidly increasing level of crime. This approach was strengthened after the 1992 election. As Faulkner said:

> the Government . . . approach . . . relied on law enforcement, and especially the disabling effect of imprisonment and the supposed deterrent effect of conviction and punishment more generally, as the principal means of tackling crime. This approach paid little attention to prevention, to the social and economic circumstances in which crime becomes prevalent, or to the influences which affect a person's behaviour or pattern of life.[33]

In 1992, the Home Office issued a set of national standards for the Probation Service. These were partly a description of the activities carried out by the Probation Service and partly an attempt to enforce routines of behaviour.[34] Many probation officers were concerned that such precise prescriptions changed the nature of the activity from that of an autonomous professional making judgements within a legal framework to a service which consisted of following routine. In practice the framework still allows professional judgement within a framework of timetables and reporting regimes.

The national standards were a prelude to an attempt to detach the Probation Service from its social work origins. The Dews Report[35] questioned the relevance of a social work qualification as a prerequisite to becoming a probation officer. In particular, it questioned the relevance of social work values: 'We . . . heard much of the importance of "social work values" but nothing to suggest these were different from the values of many professions and we noted that this was not a concept embraced by the Home Office' (p.26).

The solution to social work values was to change the qualification of probation officers. Dews recommended a diploma in probation studies, which would be 'skills-based and the assessment would focus entirely on whether the trainee was competent to begin practising core probation work' (p.35). The Home Secretary was keen to replace social work attitudes with attitudes more appropriate to punishment in the community, by recruiting and qualifying a different sort of probation officer, including people with police or military experience. The Dews Report was met with hostility by the Association of Chief Probation Officers and the National Association of Probation Officers. The hostility was partly motivated by protection and partly by the challenge to the underlying values of the service. There were those who argued that the social work qualification was not adequately geared towards probation practice, but there were few within the profession who agreed with the proposal for a competencies-based qualification without educational content.

The Labour government completed the process of transforming the Probation Service into a national service for punishment in the community. From April 2001 the Probation Service in England and Wales was reorganized as the National Probation Service[36] with a national director accountable to the Home Secretary in charge of 42 areas, coterminous with police authority boundaries. A review[37] of the prison and probation services published in 1998 said:

> Successive Governments have neglected the organisational framework which supports the work of probation officers. A series of Acts of Parliament have merely served to consolidate an outdated reflection of a service that has been engaged in change and modernisation for many years. Legislation still directs probation officers to 'advise, assist and befriend' offenders. This is completely out of line not just with the expectations of the courts but also with the reality of the work which probation staff undertake day in and day out.

The optimism with which the Home Office pursued the centralization of the service does not reflect the concerns of the report on the Prison Service quoted above, in which poor centralized management and unclear accountabilities for performance were seen as the major items creating bad prisons.

One problem for managers in the probation system is the workload created by the increase in prison numbers and in the number of people under probation orders. Figure 4.6 shows a crude measure of probation workload, the number of probation orders (ignoring community service and combined orders) and the numbers employed in the Probation Service. It shows a decline in staff

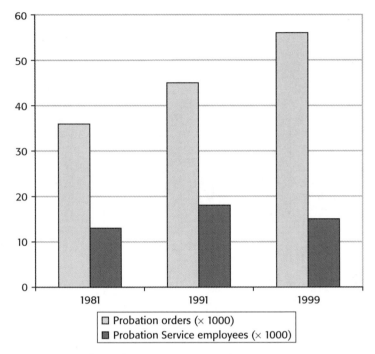

Figure 4.6   Probation orders and Probation Service employees
Source: Office for National Statistics (2001) *Social Trends* 31, Figures 9.23 and 9.19

since 1991, despite the obvious increase in workload. The Labour govern-ment responded to this trend by announcing an expansion of the probation training and recruitment programmes in February 2001.

The numbers employed in the Prison Service have increased roughly in line with the prison population, as shown in Figure 4.7.

Implications for managers

Raine and Willson (1993) interpreted the changes in the criminal justice system as a shift of power from professionals to the Home Office and called for a restoration of discretion:

> The Home Secretary and the Lord Chancellor should now recognise that the period of detention is up. Reformed and rehabilitated, the professionals must now be resettled and supported so that we can benefit from their capacity to exercise discretion in the complex and uncertain circumstances which characterise criminal justice.[38]

Such a conclusion probably applies more to the courts and probation than to the Prison Service. The management of professionals, who have their own ways of working derived from training and professional ethics, is appropriate

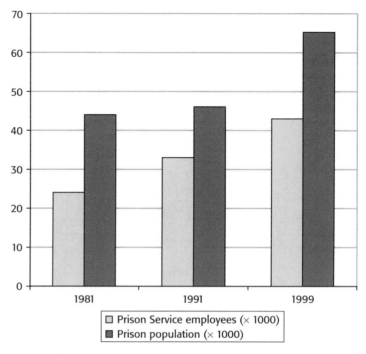

Figure 4.7   Prison Service employees and prison population
Source: Office for National Statistics (2001) *Social Trends* 31, Figure 9.23

only where such conditions apply. Prison officers receive training in the routines of the prisons and in counselling and talking to prisoners but never established a profession in this sense. The Police Service is in an ambiguous position: individual police officers, including constables, have always had a great deal of discretion about how they behave when they are in contact with the public and with criminals, because direct supervision is not possible.

What managers have had to do has been to reduce the autonomy and independence of action of the practitioners and make them conform more to a set of expectations and rules of behaviour. In the cases of the Police Service, the managers have always themselves had experience as workers in the service and have learned directly how practice operates. In the Prison Service, the head of the service has normally been a career civil servant and in one case someone with no public service experience. Very senior probation officers were traditionally selected from career probation people but there have recently been appointments from other backgrounds.

This distinction is important: the application of a set of rules and procedures is possible only when individual discretion is reduced to a set of decision rules. When the top managers are former practitioners, it is harder for them to argue for a reduction of discretion: outsiders are better placed to tell workers and middle managers to follow rules rather than use their experience to inform their discretion.

Relationships between policy areas

One of the problems for managers operating in these policy areas was that the policy process itself was fragmented from the highest level. Ministries and policy divisions within them are concerned with small areas of policy. For example, policy on housing and housing subsidy was set in the (then) Department of the Environment, while income support was a matter for the Department of Social Security. Mental health was the concern of part of the Department of Health, while prison policy and practice is thought about in the Home Office.

These divisions produced both inconsistencies and contradictions. For example, managers concerned with the welfare of people with mental health problems have to cope with a range of policies. The policy to close the mental hospitals and let people who previously lived there live in 'the community' was mainly developed by the Department of Health. Local authorities were involved in the process of finding accommodation and support for the people who moved. Housing, when it was provided, was the concern of housing associations and the local authority. The police became involved when people committed offences. Such fragmentation inevitably led to failures to provide adequate services for people at whom the policy was aimed. A series of reports on the disasters which occurred (many resulting in murders) emphasized the fragmentation of policy and service delivery.

Another example was the treatment of children with behavioural and emotional difficulties. The Children Act says that such children's interests should be central to what happens to them and that they are entitled to help. The Education Reform Act set schools in competition with each other and allowed schools to exclude and eventually to expel children with behavioural problems. Schools excluded the children because they disrupt the activities of the school and threaten its results in the competitive examination result league tables. Such children were therefore excluded from the help, socialization and integration which they would receive in schools. Meanwhile, the special schools to which they could have gone were being closed because they are too expensive to run within the constraints of overall budgets.

The Labour government saw fragmentation of policy making and service delivery as one of the main problems facing it. It had two solutions: organisational changes, such as giving magistrates' courts, police and probation services the same boundaries; and co-ordination and collaboration mechanisms to help policy makers and service deliverers work better together. At the heart of government it set up a large range of new task forces, committees and units to pursue its declared aim of 'joined-up government'. The most publicized was the Social Exclusion Unit and its eighteen policy action teams, attached to the Cabinet Office. Task forces brought outsiders (mainly business people) into government to give advice on issues that mainly crossed over departmental boundaries. A review by Cranfield School of Management carried out nine months after the 1997 election found more than 75 task forces and 200 policy reviews and counted 350 business people involved in the process. The reviews covered a very wide range of issues, including 'Music Industry and New Creative Industries', 'Better Regulation', education, youth justice, tax and benefits, drugs, banking, construction, contraception, rebranding Britain (appropriately called 'Panel 2000'), human rights, cleaner vehicles, literacy and coalfields. After 100 days of the new government, Sir Robin Butler, head of the home Civil Service, called a moratorium on policy reviews.

Actions to encourage organizations to work together included area initiatives for health, education, urban renewal, crime prevention and mental health. Often funding was linked to resource allocation. The implications of collaborative working are explored in Chapter 7.

Conclusions

In the introduction to this chapter we saw that there were six themes which we could identify in the Conservative government's intentions for these policy and managerial changes. We have seen that most of these intentions have been successful and were pursued further by the Labour government. The move from equal treatment of everyone to difference has been reasonably successful in some sectors. Universal access to state services has been reduced; even state pensioners only receive an income on which they can live reasonably if they apply for means-tested benefits. Child benefit and retirement pension are the only remaining universal state benefits. The changes should not be overemphasized. There is still universal access to education and healthcare.

The private and voluntary sectors are involved in public services in a way which seemed unlikely when the welfare state was established. The involvement of the private sector in the Prison Service was a great surprise to people in the Prison Service, as well as to many outside it.

Central policy control has been a very clear success. The autonomy of local authorities and the professions has been greatly curtailed. Social workers are engaged in rationing services, probation officers are offering punishment in the community, teachers have been controlled and even doctors are acting under instruction from managers. The success of output-based funding of capital schemes has yet to be seen. If the intention was mainly one of limiting the amount of money spent, however, it has been a success.

As well as reasonably successful implementation of the government's intentions, other changes have taken place in the management of public services as a result of these policy and management changes. The first is that managers and professionals have become more competitive and less collaborative. We look in more detail at the impact of the competitive regimes in Chapter 5. The reduction in collaboration had negative effects. The first was the reluctance to share skills, knowledge, information and good practice. In the case of schools and surgery, institutions which compete with each other do not like to share their successes. The same is true in the case of the competing and privatized government scientific laboratories. The second effect is that organizations in the private and voluntary sectors which may in the past have been collaborators are now seen as competitors. Professionals whose previous way of working involved caring for the service users and sharing good ideas have become focused on revenues and the competition for them. The 'modernization' may well have the impact of making professionals spend more time listening to service users.

The second effect is that professional discretion is reduced and managerial power increased. The centralization of policies and procedures reduces the autonomy of the professionals but at the same time increases the influence of managers. If central direction in the form of procedures is to be followed, it is the managers who transmit and interpret the procedures from the centre (whether the ministry, NHS Executive, Home Office, inspectorate or whatever) to the local organization. Whether the managers were previously professionals or not, the power they acquire derives from their relationship with the centre rather than their professional expertise or knowledge. Centralization shifts the balance from the professions to the managers.

The Labour government tried to correct some of these negative effects by taking the edge off some of the market solutions and encouraging collaboration. The success of these efforts is covered in Chapter 7.

A third effect was the residualization of many state services. The state pension is now a residual benefit for pensioners. Community care is increasingly a last resort. The least well-resourced schools have an atmosphere of simply surviving, rather than generating confidence and pride in their pupils. The effect of this on people working in the state sector is that they know that they are no longer doing the best possible, rather the best possible in the circumstances. Social workers, for example, spend a great deal of their time either telling clients that they cannot have the services which they need and thought they were entitled to or arguing to get access to those services. These results were accepted by the Labour government and some efforts were made to correct them, adjusting pensions, recognizing the over-targeting of social services and trying to turn around the worst schools.

A fourth effect is a greater concentration on measurable results. The emphasis on output-based funding means that managers and workers have to concentrate on the relevant numbers. We will see that this process has been strengthened by the Labour government through an even greater emphasis on measurable results and strengthened inspection systems.

Stakeholder expectations

Managers are expected to do different things by different people. Many are committed to providing sensitive and responsive services, which correspond with the expectations of the people who use the services. At the same time, most managers are expected to save money, either through increasing productivity or paying people less. They know that these two objectives are in contradiction with each other. When the workers are themselves professionals, managers have another set of conflicts. The language and behaviour of professionals are different from the language and behaviour of managers. Management language, with its emphasis on performance, measurement, budgets and rationing, is different from a professional language of individual clients, care, understanding what is likely to work well in individual cases and reference to professional ethics. When the professionals are important stakeholders, without whom the service cannot survive, managers may be forced to accept professionals' judgement, language and power.

Values

Managers in the public sector often have values which exist independently from those of the organizations in which they work. They may bring values with them from their training, especially when values are made explicit there, as they are in medical, social work, legal and education training programmes. If the managers have previously been members of these occupations, they may find it hard to adopt managerial values. If they are not from a profession and are managing people who still have such a value attachment, they may come into conflict with the people whom they are supposed to manage. This is especially the case when the managerial action changes. Generally, managers are expected to implement government policy. If that policy changes to include, say, competitive behaviour, managers have to carry out such a policy and may even hold values which are implied in such a policy: their values may be altered by the policy of the government in power. There is no doubt that in many areas, managers believe in the values of competition, of 'tough' management, of the 'right to manage' and other approaches which increase the power of managers and decrease that of the professions. This may be an irreversible change: once the power in the institutions of the state is held by people with a particular set of values, which is reinforced by the management schools and associations of managers, it would be difficult to produce a change in behaviour.

Further reading

Nicholas Deakin (2000) *The Treasury and Social Policy: The Contest for Control of Welfare Strategy (Transforming Government)*. Basingstoke: Palgrave.

Howard Glennerster (1995) *British Social Policy Since 1945*. Oxford: Blackwell. An overview of the development of the welfare state since the Second World War.

Howard Glennerster and John Hills (eds) (1998) *The State of Welfare*, 2nd edn. Oxford: Oxford University Press.

Rudolf Klein (2000) *The New Politics of the NHS*, 4th edn. London: Longman.
Eric Midwinter (1994) *The Development of Social Welfare in Britain*. Buckingham: Open University Press.

Notes and references

[1] See e.g. Glennerster, H. (1995) *British Social Policy Since 1945*, Oxford: Blackwell; Timmins, N. (1995) *The Five Giants: A Biography of the Welfare State*, London: HarperCollins; Deakin, N. D. (1994) *The Politics of Welfare: Continuities and Change*, 2nd edn, Hemel Hempstead: Harvester Wheatsheaf; Klein, R. (2000) *The New Politics of the NHS*, 4th edn, London: Longman; Glennerster, H. and Hills, J. (eds) (1998) *The State of Welfare*, Oxford: Oxford University Press.

[2] DETR (2000) *Quality and Choice: A Decent Home for All*. London: HMSO.

[3] Set out in DETR (1999) *Modernising Local Government*. London: HMSO.

[4] Freeden, M. (1999) The ideology of New Labour, *Political Quarterly*, 70, 1, Jan–March.

[5] Hills, J. (1993) *The Future of Welfare: A Guide to the Debate*. York: Joseph Rowntree Foundation.

[6] HMSO (1994a) *Jobseeker's Allowance*, Cm 2687. London: HMSO.

[7] News release 10.2.2000.

[8] Joseph Rowntree Foundation (1996) *The Future of Work: A Contribution to the Debate*, *Policy Summary* 7. York: Rowntree.

[9] Department of Health (1995) *Fit for the Future: Second Progress Report on the Health of the Nation*. London: HMSO.

[10] *Market and Business Development* 11.2000.

[11] *British Medical Journal* 2.9.2000, 563.

[12] See Atkinson, H. and Wilks-Heeg, S. (2000) *Local Government from Thatcher to Blair: The Politics of Creative Autonomy*, Cambridge: Polity Press, for a discussion of the degree to which local authorities retained their autonomy.

[13] DETR (1999) *Modern Local Government: In Touch With The People*. London: HMSO.

[14] Audit Commission (1994) Taking Stock: Progress with Community Care. *Community Care Bulletin* No. 2, December. London: HMSO.

[15] Wright, K. (1995) *The Mental Health (Patients in the Community) Bill*, Research Paper 95/71. London: House of Commons Library.

[16] Home Office (1995) *Statistical Bulletin 20/95. Statistics of Mentally Disordered Offenders England and Wales 1994*. London: Government Statistical Service.

[17] Figures from Department of Health (2000) *Tracking Progress in Children's Services: An Evaluation of Local Responses to the Quality Protects Programme, Year 2*.

[18] *Ibid.*, para 32.

[19] Ferguson, N., Earley, P., Ouston, J. and Fidler, B. (2000) *Improving Schools and Inspection: The Self-Inspecting School*. London: Paul Chapman/Sage.

[20] Ford, J. and Wilcox, S. (1994) *Affordable Housing, Low Incomes and the Flexible Labour Market*, National Federation of Housing Associations Research Report 22.

[21] *Op cit.*

[22] Prescott-Clarke, P., Clemens, S. and Park, A. (1994) *Routes into Local Authority Housing: A Study of Local Authority Waiting Lists and New Tenancies*. London: HMSO.

[23] Home Office (2000) *Modernising the Management of the Prison Service: An Independent Report by the Targeted Performance Initiative Working Group*. London: HMSO.

[24] Known colloquially as 'Strangeways'.

[25] Halward, W. (1994) Manchester Prison: mounting a successful in-house bid. In Prison Reform Trust *Privatisation and Market Testing in the Prison Service*. London: Prison Reform Trust.

[26] *Howard Journal of Criminal Justice*, 33, 3, 1994, 354.

[27] *Ibid.*, 365.

[28] Lord Woolf, now Lord Chief Justice, chaired a committee on the causes of the 1990 riot in Manchester Prison ('Strangeways') and identified poor management, long times in-cell and unhelpful routines as major causes of the troubles.

[29] Home Office, Northern Ireland Office and Scottish Office (1993) *Inquiry into Police Responsibilities and Rewards*, Cm 2280. London: HMSO (the 'Sheehy Report').

[30] Leishman, F., Cope, S. and Starie, P. (1995) Reforming the police in Britain. *International Journal of Public Sector Management* 8 (4).

[31] Lewis, M., Long, S. and Williams, A. (1995) What to do with what you've got. *Policing* 11 (4), 261–71.

[32] Loveday, B. (1994) The Police and Magistrates' Court Act. *Policing* 10 (4).

[33] Faulkner, D. (1995) The Criminal Justice Act 1991: policy, legislation and practice. In Ward, D. and Lacey, M. (eds) *Probation: Working for Justice*. London: Whiting & Birch, 63.

[34] Home Office, Department of Health, Welsh Office (1992 and 1995) *National Standards for the Supervision of Offenders in the Community*. London: Home Office Public Relations Branch.

[35] Dews, V. and Watts, J. (1994) *Review of Probation Officer Recruitment and Qualifying Training*. London: Home Office.

[36] Under the Crime and Probation Act 2000.

[37] Home Office (1998) *Prisons Probation: Joining Forces to Protect the Public*. London: HMSO.

[38] Raine, J. and Willson, M. J. (1993) Restoring a sense of law and order. *Justice of the Peace and Local Government Law*, 18 December, 808.

Part

2

Introduction to Part Two

The evolution of modes of control

Governments have introduced a variety of means to strengthen control over the public sector since the beginning of the 1980s. Sometimes the problem was defined in financial terms: spending has been seen at various times as excessive and commitments to increase spending interpreted as irreversible. Control over finance, whether through cash limits or budget cuts, was simple to design but often difficult to implement because of the non-discretionary nature of those expenditures that result from rights to social security, pensions and so on. However, systems of financial limits have been developed that now seem to work.

Apart from finances, governments have tried to exercise control over the institutions and the way they are managed. To make sense of the efforts it is useful to understand what governments did *not* want from the institutions of the public sector. There are two stereotypes of problematic organizations. One is the bureaucracy, managed in the interests of its senior staff, operating rigidly and inefficiently and more importantly not changing according to the political will of the government. Bureaucracy has been blamed at various times for rising costs and poor service and for the perceived failures to generate public support for public services. The merits of management, including the focus on results, better use of resources and customer orientation, were contrasted with rule-bound, inward-looking, hierarchical organizations run by bureaucrats.

The institutions were caricatured. Had they been as bad as they were drawn, the NHS would never have been created, and the housing programme, universal secondary education and all the other visible results of the 'welfare state' could surely not have been achieved. Looking further back, such rigid organizations could never have created the advances in public health, slum clearance and public utilities that countered the worst excesses of the industrial revolution.

In any case the bureaucratic principles upon which the Civil Service and local authorities were based were established as a counter to corruption, exploitation and arbitrary behaviour. The impartiality of treatment of civil servants and people wanting services could only be achieved by rule by rules. Discretion without rules can only generate inequalities. Of course rules were not universally followed and discrimination and nepotism were possible in the pre-managerial era, but they were not the principles upon which the systems were built.

The other problems to be addressed were those caused by rule by professionals. Self-serving and self-regulating doctors, teachers, nurses, road engineers, lawyers and so on do not operate in the interests of their 'customers' and their self-interest can only be contained by imposing some form of external controls. The professions could not be trusted to manage themselves. The positive aspects of professionalism, such as the fact that they take care of their own training and that they have ethical standards that may produce unrewarded efforts, were seen as less significant.

The twin problems, bureaucracy and self-governing professions, were apparent from the early days of the welfare state. The compromise with the doctors whereby they remained as independent practitioners rather than employees with employment contracts was a necessary condition for gaining their support for the establishment of the National Health Service. Where professionals have been employees the problem has been seen as less acute but the protection offered by membership of a profession or a trade union with restricted membership has been interpreted as a brake on progress.

What may be surprising after eighteen years of the Conservatives' enthusiastic pursuit of reforms and management changes is that the Labour government from 1997 still diagnosed the same problem. Prime Minister Blair's emotional condemnation of the 'forces of conservatism' in the public sector[1] included criticism of both professionalism and conservative bureaucracy: '. . . the British Medical Association and other professional organisations . . . are there to represent and promote the interests of its members . . . the Government is there to govern for all the people'.

Previous governments had relied on two main alternatives to professionalism and bureaucracy: the introduction of 'management' and the imposition of markets. 'Management' meant giving managers formal status and the ability to influence or control professionals and the introduction of targets, mainly concerned with the volume of outputs and unit costs. These and other managerial instruments were designed to bring professionals under control and make them susceptible ultimately to political control. They were also designed to solve bureaucracies' problems of rigidity, inflexibility and introversion. If managers could be given targets and a degree of control over their budgets and over their staff they could behave like managers rather than functionaries, and could be held to account for their results rather than their stewardship.

The other mechanism, the imposition of competitive markets, was designed to make managers aware of costs and alternative ways of organizing services, and make them and their workforces cut costs as a way of competing with alternative suppliers. If they lost in competition, the functions would be transferred to the winning bidders from the private sector, thus solving the twin problems at a stroke: the private sector would not tolerate professional self-interest and would automatically have good management. Of course this stereotype of the lean, focused, efficient private company had its limitations, as soon became apparent in some of the disastrous information and communication technology contracts.

For many years the twin solutions to the twin problems were pursued vigorously. From the early days of the Financial Management Initiative through the creation of the executive agencies to the revision of pay scales and introduction of performance-related pay and national performance targets, management methods have been introduced. Simultaneously governments have used competition and the market, first in local government and the NHS from the early 1980s and then in the Civil Service. Compulsory competitive tendering and market testing were eventually replaced by the Comprehensive Spending Review process in central government and Best Value in local government, but the underlying belief was similar: test costs and quality against what is available in the market and if the public sector organizations cannot match the competition then the service should be outsourced.

Both solutions had big impacts on the public sector. By the time the Labour government was elected these two approaches had achieved cost awareness and some cost reductions and had certainly made performance management more open to scrutiny. The extent of cost reductions has never been satisfactorily measured. Since costing systems were generally introduced at the same time as competitive tendering, actual costs[2] before the tendering process were often not known. Among others Walsh and Davies[3] argued that savings that were possible by speeding up manual work such as refuse collection were not replicable in white-collar jobs. Companies that are making profits from contracts to perform clerical and professional work have clearly devised ways to find a gap between the tender price and the cost of delivering services.

Certainly the processes of defining services for the tendering process and calculating their costs focused managers' and workers' minds on issues of cost and quality, in services ranging from refuse collection through prisons to accountancy and legal services. The growing unwillingness of companies to tender for local government contracts may be a testimony to public sector managers' success in improving management.

But there were also negative effects of the two approaches. The emphasis on outputs, accountable units and unit costs had made managers and their systems introspective and the internal and external incentives were such that they were concerned only with their own, narrow performance rather than the impact of their and other services on the service users. One example is the mix of agencies dealing with people who abuse or misuse chemical substances. Prisons, courts, doctors, charities, the police and probation services, housing and social services each have to deal with their own aspects of the

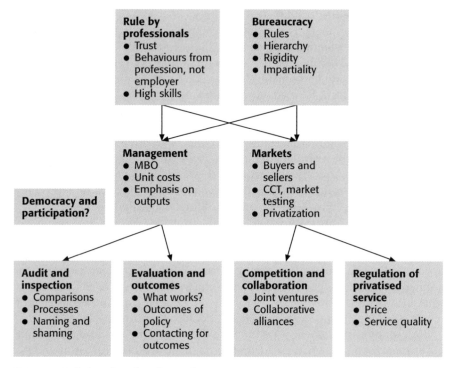

Figure 1   Evolution of modes of control

individual's behaviour and its consequences but no one takes a holistic view with the authority to take actions that might help resolve the problems. Each agency might do a good job and even meet its targets, while the problem remains unsolved.

The use of markets also had negative effects. While single-step reductions in costs were probably achieved by the process of competition, continuous exposure to market testing and retendering had a deleterious effect on morale and commitment, not just in the public sector but also among the companies involved in service provision. The evolution of the different modes of control is illustrated in Figure 1.

The Labour government did not abandon markets and management as solutions to the problems of bureaucracy and professionalism; rather it emphasized additional modes of governance.

The government inherited an enlarged and strengthened set of audit and inspection bodies. Hood *et al.*[4] have shown that in the twenty years to 1995 real spending on internal inspection and regulation had increased by over 100% and staff engaged in such activities had increased by 60% to about 20,000 people. The government has made use of these bodies to strengthen the power of central government over local authorities and individual institutions such as schools and prisons.

The Labour government also had ambitions to solve the problems of fragmentation caused by the overemphasis on individual organizations' output and cost targets. One solution is the concentration on 'outcomes' or the results of government actions, rather than outputs. The ambition expressed among other places in the White Paper *Modernising Government* included 'Ensuring that policy-making is more joined-up and strategic'. Partly this was to be achieved through new institutional arrangements, such as units in the Cabinet Office and a long list of task forces. It was also to be achieved by including policy outcomes in the process of deciding how public expenditure is allocated. The third element is a pragmatic commitment to 'what works', implying that policy changes are subject to an evaluation of their effectiveness.

'Joined-upness' also requires more collaboration among public sector organizations and between the public, private and voluntary sectors. Management by objectives and contracting out both produced fragmentation. Collaboration between agencies to deliver policies and programmes is an attempt to solve that problem. Often collaboration is mandated in a specified area or zone, such as Health Action Zones or Education Action Zones, which are designed and funded to force agencies to collaborate, at least at the stage of bidding for money.

'Partnership' became an important keyword and was applied to a variety of collaborative arrangements, some of which had already been put in place by previous governments but could be renamed and some of which were new. The renaming included changing the name of the Private Finance Initiative to Public–Private Partnership. This solved one of the problems identified in the competitive tendering process: the costs involved in frequent retendering. Under PFI/PPP, contracts are let for up to 60 years to one company, thus removing the worry of retendering.[5]

Meanwhile the privatized utilities and transport companies continue to be regulated by industry-specific regulators for water, gas, electricity and telecoms. Regulation of the privatized sector is an alternative mode of control for public services.

Modes of control and management arrangements

In the following chapters we look at the implications for managers of this variety of modes of governance and control. While Figure 1 shows the changes as a progression from rule by professionals and by bureaucracy to the other modes, in practice the different modes are used simultaneously and managers have to cope with them all. Figure 2 gives an indication of the implications for the main activities of management of different emphases in the modes of control.

Figure 2 gives shorthand descriptors of the main emphasis of the modes of control for strategy formulation, organizational form, performance

	Strategy	Organizational form	Performance management	Personnel policy	Financial management
Bureaucracy	Compliance with law and instructions	Hierarchy and stability	Conformance to procedures	Recruit at entry level. Promotion through seniority, up scales	Line budgets, input-based
Professional	Compliance with standards	Flat. Distinction between professionals and others	Peer review	Recruit qualified staff. Promotion through seniority	Budgets for programme areas
Management	Rational, hierarchical planning	Accountable, relatively autonomous units	Management by objectives	Open recruitment, promotion on merit and performance	Output-based budgets, unit costs
Markets	Market positioning, based on cost and quality	Profit centres, flexible structures	Profit and loss accounts and to contribution performance	Flexible practices and recruitment, PRP	Revenue depends on success. Tight cost control
Audit and inspection	Compliance with current targets	Clear accountability	Conformance with procedures and comparative performance data	Transparent rules	Line budgets, clear procedures
Outcomes and evaluation	Search for policy solutions	Flat, flexible, open	Outcome measurement-based	Flexible job descriptions	Outcome-based budgets
Collaboration	Search for strategic alliances and policy solutions	Boundary-less, links most important	Based on shared assessment of outcomes	Flexibility	Combined, outcome-based budgets

Figure 2 Modes of control and management arrangements

management, personnel and financial management. Bureaucratic control in a stable environment does not require much imagination in any area of managerial effort: strategy is given from outside, the organizational structure is by definition hierarchical, performance requires only that the organization conforms to required procedures, staff are managed by moving up pay scales, and budgets are for inputs only. Of course, such organizations hardly exist, if they ever have in recent times, but at least some elements of their management approach persist in various corners of the public sector.

Professional control requires a different set of management attributes: standards rather than instructions determine what and how services are delivered. In the areas where professionals work there are hierarchies according to rank and experience but usually in a narrow band, and there is a distinction between professionals and 'the rest', who are all considered inferior by the professionals, whatever their formal status might be. Performance is managed horizontally by some form of peer review or professional to professional assessment: outsiders are not welcome in the performance management process. Recruitment is controlled by qualification and promotion, partly on merit but mainly on seniority. Budgets may be bureaucratically determined or may be based on a programme area.

While these two ideal types, the bureaucracy and rule by professionals, may be scarce in their pure forms, they illustrate the difficulties involved in controlling by other methods. Even a simple form of management, based on unit accountability and agreement to some periodic objectives, can be a shock to either system. The idea of a planning process based on objectives to be achieved is not easily adopted by people used to working according to a set of rules or a set of professional standards. Accountability of individuals for their unit's performance is hard to accept by people used to being accountable only to their peers or only for their conformance to the rules. Recruitment and promotion on merit and performance rather than on seniority can be a shock in a cosy environment. Budgets based on outputs and the costing of outputs implied by them are often interpreted as 'bean counters' interfering with professional discretion.

The move to control through markets involves a different set of management arrangements: some are a step beyond those required for control through management. Units or sections that only survive by winning in competition cannot plan their future other than in the light of which contracts they are likely to get. They have to establish a position in relation to their competitors, somewhat akin to a company's strategy but in a much more limited market. To survive, people responsible for contracts have to make sure they make money or at least break even. Performance is measured by profitability, people are hired and promoted according to their contribution, and financial management is concerned with keeping cost below prices.

These adjustments have been made in large parts of the public sector. They were hard to achieve because while they appear to be technical questions they have had serious implications for security, for the locus of power, for individual and group self-esteem and for the degree of trust between individuals.

The growth of control by audit and inspection calls for further changes in managers' behaviour. First, targets are set from outside the organization and may change from year to year. Secondary schools have been set the test of three grades A–C at GCSE level, primary schools attainment levels in SAT tests. These are not necessarily the targets that headteachers and governors would have set for their schools, nor are they likely to remain the main targets for ever. In the NHS, waiting lists and waiting times targets are set as well as health status targets for the populations of their areas. Similarly these are imposed from above and are monitored by inspection. Police targets set by the Home Office do not necessarily reflect local priorities or local managers' judgements about most effective policing.

While managers are able to adjust to changing goals, increasingly the audit process imposes ways of managing, not just targets to be achieved. The Best Value process in government has an explicit set of procedures that has to be followed and a separate division of the Audit Commission to prescribe and monitor those procedures. While performance against externally set performance indicators is still important, managers now also have to comply with the procedural rules laid down.

Once the emphasis shifts to rule by outcome and an expectation that outcomes will only be achieved by collaboration between agencies and between the public and private sectors, the game changes again. Output targets are not enough: policy outcomes are required along with innovative solutions to policy problems. Eventually the Chancellor has even promised outcome-based budgeting, although this has not been achieved at the time of writing. Collaboration requires managers to seek out strategic partners, to make their organizations more open, to measure outcomes not only for their own work but also for the results of their collaboration with others. It also requires skills in evaluation so that the achievement of outcomes can be demonstrated.

The attempt to substitute management and markets for bureaucracy and professionalism has been widely discussed for decades. The difficulties of making the transitions are still problems for organizations involved in these changes. Professionals resist the power shift implied by the imposition of management systems. Managers have problems coping with the entrenched values and interests of professionals. Bureaucracies find it hard to make the cultural and attitude changes required by the introduction of markets.

As new layers of control are laid over management and markets, the cultural and technical problems for managers become more complex. For example, complying with audit requirements on output and unit cost targets or guidelines makes managers concentrate on individual or sectional performance and accountabilities for specific targets. Meanwhile the encouragement of collaboration (including making funding dependent on demonstrating collaboration) blurs accountabilities and shares responsibilities for achieving policy outcomes. Another example concerns financial accountabilities: while probity audit requires compliance with line-by-line subjective headings, an emphasis on managing for outcomes requires both combined budgets and accountability for results.

The tendencies identified in Figure 2, in other words, are neither simple nor sequential. As successive efforts are made to solve the problems caused by previous attempts, layers of practice are laid over previous ones. Control by outputs and unit costs does not replace an interest in the details of input controls. Competition does not remove the requirement to operate according to rules of behaviour designed to control arbitrariness and corruption. The requirement to collaborate to achieve results does not remove the imperative to account for individual actions. The demonstration of effectiveness does not remove the need constantly to reduce the costs of a unit of output.

In some ways the Conservative agenda was easier for managers to follow than that of the Labour government. An emphasis on cutting costs, backed by well-established methods of management accounting and work intensification, was hard work but the models and methods were reasonably well known and available, backed by changes in industrial relations legislation and powerful political backing for unpopular ways of making people work harder for less money. More recent agendas have fewer available methods. Evaluation has been relatively underdeveloped in the United Kingdom, especially compared with the industry that developed in the United States of America in response to the federal government's desire to see its money well spent by the states and cities. Competition based on cost and quality is an easier path to follow than collaboration based on synergies and complementary competencies.

The fact that new requirements are demanded while the old ones are not removed produces contradictions for managers. Being flexible while following detailed set procedures, looking for policy solutions that will produce results while competing with alternative service providers, collaborating with colleagues in other organizations while competing for funds, are among the many contradictions that managers have to live with. To be successful, managers have to assess which mode of control is dominant at the present time. If it is impossible to conform to all expectations, which ones are unavoidable, and which ones can be harnessed to produce the best services?

Notes and references

[1] Speech in February 1999.

[2] A true and fair measure of savings would compare the avoidable cost of contracting out with the contract price. This involves splitting off those costs of supervision that remain with the public body after the contract is let from the cost of delivering the service. Such calculations were rarely made, and cost savings often compared the previous total cost with the contract price.

[3] Walsh, K. and Davies, H. (1993) *Competition and Service: The Impact of the Local Government Act 1988*. London: HMSO.

[4] Hood, C., Scott, C., James, O., Jones, G. and Travers, T. (2000) *Regulation Inside Government*. Oxford: Oxford University Press.

[5] See pp.256–7 for details of the PFI/PPP arrangements.

5

MANAGING THROUGH MARKETS

Introduction

A central tenet of Conservative belief was that markets are an efficient way of allocating resources and reducing costs and improving efficiency. Think tanks were set up to promote the superiority of markets, were influential on Conservative opinion and were part of the ideological effort to counter the postwar development of planning and public services. 'Third Way' thinking was less enthusiastic about markets but promoted their use as a way of allocating resources.

In practice the markets which were constructed rarely conformed to the features of the economists' 'perfect competition', with freedom of choice as to what to purchase and from whom, free entry for new competitors and perfect information for consumers. In fact they were mostly very limited in comparison to this ideal. One reason for this difference is that the motives for establishing markets, whatever the rhetoric, were not to improve the allocation of resources or efficiency. One motive was to distance politicians from decisions which would be unpopular with the electorate: having a market to blame is convenient, whether for the closure of a popular facility, or a reduction in workers' incomes or the number of jobs.

The markets which were created mainly excluded the element of free choice of service or supplier for the service user. The market within the NHS was an internal market, transactions being made between NHS employees without involving patients. In local authority compulsory competitive tendering, the authority rather than the citizen had the choice of service provider. Market testing in central government is an internal matter designed to reduce cost and increase private sector participation in public services. In the community care markets, consumers do have a choice of services subject to their assessment as being in need.

As well as these internal markets, market mechanisms have also been introduced by getting the private sector involved in financing capital projects and in the market for labour.

The Labour government claimed to be less dogmatic about the advantages of markets and competition: it did not believe in them in principle but rather only if they worked. Very early the new government changed the internal market in the NHS, the competitive tendering regime in local government and the market testing arrangements in the Civil Service. While there was talk about partnerships and trust, the new arrangements subjected at least as many services to market pressures as the old ones and were designed as much to encourage private firms to provide services as to limit the destructive effects of competition.

Why rule by markets?

Ideology

Markets are one alternative to bureaucratic control of resources and to hier-archical management. They may also offer a solution to the problem of professional control of resources, organizations and services. For the Conservative Party, markets, competition and private sector participation were the preferred solution. To 'modernizers' the bureaucratic and professional organizations that were built as part of the welfare state, the NHS, local authorities, nationalized industries and powerful government departments, are part of the pre-modernized way of managing the state and delivering public services. The 'Third Way' rhetoric could not simply propose the same market-type solutions but had to find an alternative, apparently softer and more collaborative version.

Proponents of markets as a solution to economic and social problems organized a propaganda campaign. The Institute of Economic Affairs, for example, was set up in 1955 explicitly to promote market ideas in opposition to those of social democratic groups, such as the Fabian Society, which proposed planned state intervention into social and economic life. Another body, the Adam Smith Institute, was established with similar aims in 1977. The Conservative Party was keen to adopt a market-based philosophy as an alternative to the interventionist philosophy of the first three post-war decades.

The main argument was that markets allocate resources more efficiently than bureaucratic rules. Efficiency is defined in two ways. First, goods and services will be produced at the lowest cost. Any high-cost producers will be replaced by lower-cost producers as new entrants seize the opportunity to make profits. Second, only those goods and services are produced which people demand. Producers' response to individuals' demands are more likely to produce what people want than some bureaucratic mechanism deciding what people might want or need. The first type of efficiency is known as 'productive efficiency' and the second as 'allocative efficiency'. To enable these two aspects of efficiency to prevail, there are certain prerequisites: consumers must know what is available in the market and at what price, and be able to gain access to alternative suppliers; producers must be able freely to enter any particular market; existing producers should not have insurmountable advantages because of their existing operations; and capital markets must operate in such a way as to allow investment in profitable opportunities.

Proponents of markets argue that even if these conditions do not prevail, partial market solutions are better than none. If there can be a competition between a small group of producers, this is likely to produce efficiency gains even if there is no free choice for the ultimate consumer. Alternatively, if there can be a small element of consumer choice this will make producers more responsive to consumers than if there is no choice. In other words, even if there is not an optimal solution, the less than optimal solutions will be better than having no markets at all.

Anonymous decision making and arm's-length accountability

There is also a political advantage in market solutions. Just as it has always been one of the perks of a politician's life to open a building and have a name on the plaque, so closing a building has never won any friends. With the exception of the explosive demolition of unpopular tower blocks, the closure of facilities such as an under-resourced branch library, ill-equipped cottage hospital or unsanitary elderly persons' home always generates a high degree of popular support for those establishments. If the institution to be closed is the oldest hospital in London it can be assured of support not just from the local population but also a host of influential friends from both the medical establishment and members of the political elite. Any way of removing the decision from political accountability will therefore find favour. 'Market forces' or Adam Smith's 'invisible hand' are to blame, if indeed blame is due, or the responsibility lies with management, which has failed to behave in a sufficiently competitive manner.

The same applies to competitive tendering exercises, in which it is not politicians who reduce the number of jobs and reduce the job security of those remaining, but the 'market' which chooses the winning bid. During the Conservative governments even the Labour Party found this proposition convenient at local government level. Leaders of Labour-controlled local authorities have admitted that efforts to improve customer service and reduce costs in services such as housing maintenance and refuse collection were helped by exposure to competition from outside. Local politicians could not be blamed for asking their workers to produce more output for the same or less pay: a combination of government rules and market forces made them do it. The Best Value regime introduced by the Labour government puts extra pressure on managers to improve costs, quality and competitiveness as well as carry out consultation on the processes.

The market also allows operations to be divorced from policy. Whether a private contractor or an in-house organization wins a bid, there is a fairly clear distinction between the responsibility for setting policy and standards of service and organizing to deliver services. The managers of the service delivery units are clearly accountable for the management of their units and not for the amount of budget allocated to the service which they deliver.

Limits to market reforms

In practice, the markets which have been introduced into the public sector have been a very artificial creation, the product of rule books rather than anything which might be identified as 'market forces', and the conditions necessary for efficiency have not been established. The particular difference between the ideal type of free market and the artificial creations is the role of the consumer, with free choice and very good knowledge of the options and the ability to switch between suppliers. The reason for this difference is clear: the reason that services such as health, social security and the other major public services are in the public sector is that the market would not work. People who are regularly unemployed could not buy unemployment insurance. Children of poor parents would not be able to afford healthcare. The rationing system which has to be put in place for public provision immediately restricts the freedom of the 'customer': someone else is always involved in the rationing decision and is therefore likely to be involved in the choices made as part of the rationing process.

Therefore, in the health service, there was a possibility of choosing a general practitioner, but referrals to secondary healthcare have to go through the primary practitioner. In community care, access to services is through the assessment process in which a social worker or other official makes an assessment of need and an allocation of resources. Parents and children can choose schools but only if they can easily travel to them and in some cases, only if the school chooses them.

Whatever the nature of the market, the market mechanisms are combined with government control. The NHS Trusts are subject to Treasury control on capital spending and to a variety of interventions and instructions from the Department of Health. Schools may be more free from local authority control but are subject to the Department for Education and Skills and its inspection arrangements.

The political limits

In practice, the public are not stupid. If the process of market operation means that a hospital is about to close, nobody really believes that 'market forces' rather than political decisions are to blame. In the case of the London hospitals, the market had to be replaced by a plan before decisions were made to merge hospitals and close some down.

Markets for services

NHS

The White Paper *Working for Patients*, which was published in 1989, introduced market mechanisms to the NHS in two ways. Health authorities were to become purchasers of health services on behalf of the populations of their areas; and people providing services, whether in the community or in hospitals, were to become relatively independent trusts which would sell their services under contract to the purchasers. At the same time, general practitioners were to be given the option of having their own budgets with which to purchase medical services on behalf of their patients.

The structure of this administratively invented market varied. In the cities there was the possibility of competition between general hospitals and between teaching hospitals. Any individual hospital could therefore be faced with a range of potential purchasers, and purchasers had some choice of providers. In less densely populated areas, a single purchaser would be facing a single general hospital and competition would involve patients making long journeys to an alternative service provider.

The market was operated through a series of contracts which specified the services, the volume required and the price. The process of writing and monitoring the contracts was expensive, raising the costs of running services in exchange for the benefits of competition and the separation of the decisions about which services should be provided from the management of hospitals and community health services. The consumers of health services would see no immediate increase in their control over services. Indeed, their choice could be reduced: if their district had no contract with the preferred provider, it would have to be persuaded to make an 'extra-contractual referral' and pay for the service. As Klein said:

> there was nothing that the consumer could do directly: there were no decisions, informed or otherwise, to take — except, possibly, to opt out of the NHS and go private . . . the consumerism of the internal market was of a very peculiar kind: it was a top-down consumerism.[1]

However, the market did create reasons for managers and clinicians to change their behaviour in response to the purchasers' requirements, especially with regard to the volume of work done for a given amount of cash.

Simultaneously, the reform gave the NHS Executive more ways of controlling and directing the activities of both purchasers and providers, promoting the establishment of trusts, influencing the appointment of trust boards and chief executives, and promoting ministerial initiatives. In this sense, the changes were both decentralizing and centralizing: managers had to make changes in response to the market as well as in response to the NHS Executive and its regional offices.

The differences between the new arrangements and the free market were that the contracts were not legally binding (there being only one corporate entity); prices had to be based on average cost; there is in practice a geographical restriction on competition; and contracts were limited to one year. The regional office was felt to be exerting influence through help and guidance and through control of the capital expenditure programme.

The NHS market, therefore, was a mixture of market and central control and direction, both designed to reduce the influence of the medical professions in the hospitals. The abolition of the internal market in the NHS and the introduction of long-term contracts between health commissioners and health service providers was not as radical a break as it was presented. The Department of Health had already lengthened contract periods, and competition was really confined to areas where there were a large number of suppliers. The fundamental reform by which budgets were allocated to people commissioning services, rather than directly to those providing them, remained intact.

Compulsory competitive tendering and Best Value

Local authorities were subject to a regime of compulsory competitive tendering (CCT) based on the Local Government Planning and Land Act 1980 and the Local Government Act 1988 until the Local Government Act of 1999 established 'Best Value'. The CCT rules made authorities organize a competition with private contractors for any work which it undertook, initially in the areas of building and highways work and then in other 'blue-collar' areas such as refuse collection and parks maintenance, followed by 'white-collar' and professional services, including engineering design and legal, personnel, computing and financial services. A market developed as companies formed to undertake local authority work or expanded to enter this new field of work. In some cases, companies which had previously operated in other countries went to the United Kingdom to tender for the new contracts which were offered.

While the 1999 Act abolished compulsory tendering, it introduced rules and an inspection process that made some form of competition inevitable. As the White Paper preceding the Act said: '. . . retaining work in-house without subjecting it to real competitive pressure can rarely be justified' (para 7.28). The real competitive pressure did not need to take the old form of CCT, which had been unpopular with many firms because of its long and tedious procedures, but could include partial outsourcing to provide comparative information, outsourcing without an internal bid, forming a joint venture with a private provider, or disposal of a service and its assets to another provider. By using these alternative methods, the government thought that 'there is likely to be greater interest from the private and voluntary sectors in working wth local government to deliver quality services at a competitive price' (para 7.30).

Market testing and Better Quality Services

The government introduced a programme of market testing in the Civil Service in 1992. While some services were contracted out to the private sector without an in-house bid, which was called 'strategic contracting out', an expression that survived into the 1997 government proposals, others were to be subjected to competition in a process similar to CCT in local government. Departments and agencies were given targets for the volume of services which would be subject to tendering. In the first year, 389 activities had been subject to testing, costing £1.1 billion. The private sector was awarded £885 million-worth of work, £768 million of which was awarded without an in-house bid. Of this £525 million was accounted for by the Inland Revenue computer service and the Atomic Weapons Establishment.[2] The government claims that costs were reduced by an average of about 25% as a result of the competitive process, whether bids were won internally or by contractors. However, we may have a slight doubt about the scale of savings. As John Oughton, head of the Efficiency Unit, said: 'we need to be clear about what the data can, and cannot, tell us. For example, calculating savings is fine so long as there is a clear idea of how much an activity costs pre-test. This is not always the case'.[3]

The market testing initiative was short-lived. The targets for volume of work to be tested were dropped and other initiatives, such as the Private Finance Initiative, were given more prominence. However, departments were still encouraged to consider market testing as part of their search for cost savings. One of the reasons for the falling enthusiasm was the complaint by companies that they had to spend money on making bids, while 70% of work was won by the in-house teams.

The Conservative governments made various attempts to involve companies in the provision of public services in ways which have not involved a competition with the existing public employees. At the same time as the market testing initiative there were contracts with companies which were awarded without the existing employees being allowed to bid. A phrase was invented to cover this behaviour: 'strategic partnerships'. While it was never clear why this was done, there was always a suspicion that it was simply a manifestation of the 'private good, public bad' belief.

The Labour government continued with much the same approach. In 1997 it introduced 'Better Quality Services', which was a combination of performance review, target setting and competition. The guidance for senior managers[4] set out a list of options for the decision about how services were to be provided that was unchanged from the previous government's. The options were:

- abolish, if the service is no longer required;
- restructure internally, after 'benchmarking';
- strategically contract out — that is, outsource without an internal bid;
- market test — outsource but only if an external supplier bids successfully against the in-house team;
- privatize.

The market for care (community care)

The NHS and Community Care Act introduced market mechanisms to part of the work of social services departments. The rule that 85 per cent of the special transitional grant (STG) should be spent on services other than those provided directly by the local authority meant that authorities had to trade with the private and voluntary sectors. There were two sorts of transaction: a series of 'block' contracts through which services were purchased in advance and 'spot' purchasing of services as required by individuals. The Audit Commission estimated that 89% of STG and 21% of total budgets were available for 'spot' purchasing in 1994/95.[5]

This arrangement encouraged some authorities to allocate social services budgets to staff designated as 'purchasers', who could commission care from other staff designated as 'providers'. According to the Audit Commission progress report, this arrangement did not generally apply to the authorities' residential accommodation, which continued to be funded directly. Other authorities decided that it was not desirable to establish such market-type arrangements because the STG was such a small proportion of the total social services budget. The Audit Commission expressed the view that a market-type arrangement 'does not guarantee either greater flexibility or more responsive services. If handled clumsily it can introduce barriers and rigidity'.[6] In cases in which the authorities made a strict division between purchasers and providers, the providers became resentful if their services were not used. In some cases, purchasers found that external providers were both cheaper and more flexible. In the case of homecare in some authorities, for example, agencies could provide staff cheaply at unsocial hours in comparison with direct employees.

The market with the private and voluntary sectors is managed to a large extent by the local authorities. While in the case of residential care individuals have a choice of where to live, within a budget constraint, authorities use their market intelligence to recommend providers of whom they approve. In addition, authorities have been promoting the development of other services by offering contracts to provide homecare and other aspects of non-residential care.

Where budgets are delegated to 'purchasers' rather than allocated to the provision of local authority services, a competition is entered into between the direct providers and their independent sector competitors. However, this competition is normally managed differently from the competitive tendering regime for other services: authorities did not, generally, put their own services at risk by allowing spot purchases of their own services. They were committed to keeping the premises and staff, in the short term at least, and would have incurred the expenses whether or not the purchasers in the internal market bought them.

The community care market differed from the NHS market in these respects: in the NHS there was no presumption that a proportion of the budget be spent in the independent sector; in social services there was no compulsion to organize an internal market for all services.

Markets for labour

Conservative governments tried to deregulate labour markets, by a series of legislation to reduce the power of the trades unions and the removal of restrictive practices such as minimum wages supported by wages councils. In the public sector, they tried to allow the market for labour to operate more freely, by devolving bargaining to local areas. The idea is that in areas of high unemployment and low pay, public servants can be hired for lower pay than in areas where the local labour market is more competitive. Similar arguments apply to particular occupations. In some parts of the country there are shortages of people with certain skills and premium pay has to be offered to attract people to work. The move towards local bargaining reflects developments in the private sector, where plant-level bargaining or company bargaining has largely replaced whole industry deals, if indeed collective bargaining still takes place.

Markets for capital

Despite the increase in capital spending there is a very regulated market for capital. Local authorities have to obtain permission to make capital expenditures, however they are financed (whether through borrowing or the use of accumulated reserves), capital spending by NHS Trusts is tightly controlled, and in the Civil Service strict control is exercised.

It is inconsistent that markets are established for services, the market for labour has been deregulated, but the market for capital is still very controlled. While the introduction of accruals accounting apparently makes it possible to make more rational choices of investment, in practice the Treasury is always interested in one year's cash flow. There are chances to 'spend to save' or invest to improve productivity but these decisions are generally vetted by the

Treasury. Labour continued with these procedures, although some of the names of the funds changed slightly. In addition to the Invest to Save Fund there was, inevitably, a 'Capital Modernisation Fund' for approved investments.

The capital funds arrangements for local authorities were thought to be too restrictive, and proposals were made to change them.[7] Some of the proposals give more freedom, such as the overall control on borrowing being changed from an approval system to a rule about the rate of growth of debt. However, there are strong views about how capital spending should be done, and that it favours 'strategic partnerships'. The proposals recognize that it will not be able to ensure the growth of such partnerships 'merely by restricting the funding available to authorities and thereby forcing them to seek partners' (para 4.15). However, 'until private finance achieves more general acceptance, there is a case for continuing to provide ring-fenced grants to remunerate private finance deals' (para 4.16). The government was clearly frustrated by some authorities' reluctance to enter PFI-type arrangements because of what it described as their 'proprietorial attitudes to services'.

Markets and managerial behaviour

How have managers responded to the establishment of markets? First we suggest that the amount of change depends on how much competition is introduced, ranging from that which occurs in simple internal market arrangements which involve no competition, through degrees of competitiveness to a market in which buyers have free choice of supplier. In the least competitive position, managers have to define their services and calculate what their unit costs are. More competition, through price testing, makes managers ask questions about cost, while if this is accompanied by real testing against competitors, people start to try to reduce their costs. More change is required if there is an organized tendering process. The most change is required if there is a market in which all purchasers are free to choose their supplier, whether internal or external. In these circumstances, the organization becomes fragmented, jobs are insecure and managers and workers would probably benefit from leaving and setting up their own company. Managers have developed competitive strategies, competing either on price or uniqueness. In general, the argument about quality justifying higher price is difficult to sustain unless quality can be demonstrated.

Sometimes, competition has been a prelude to privatization. There are many examples of organizations developing a successful competitive strategy and then being sold to the private sector. This may be seen by some as positive and by others who believe in publicly provided services as a bad thing.

The chapter then looks at the evaluation of these changes. It concludes that there are probably single reductions in cost as competition is introduced,

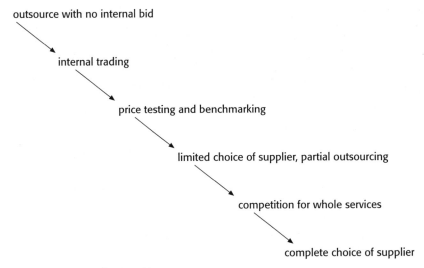

Figure 5.1   Degrees of competition

through cuts in either wage rates or numbers of jobs. However, it is difficult to justify such assessments without an adequate assessment of cost, volume and quality of services before and after the introduction of competition. If the tendering process causes managers to define, measure and cost services for the first time, it is unlikely that true comparisons can be made. However, there have been other results: flexible response to customers may be reduced, the nature of public accountability changes, and there has been a growth of public service companies.

A competitive spectrum

As we saw in the previous chapter, markets have been introduced in different forms in different parts of the public sector. It is useful to think of the markets as having degrees of competitiveness which in turn require different responses from managers. This is illustrated by Figure 5.1. At one end of the spectrum the service is outsourced, after competition between potential suppliers, but there is no internal bid. The second degree of impact on the competitive behaviour of the internal managers is simply an internal transaction in which each side plays at buying and selling services. At the other end there is a market in which purchasers have a free choice of provider and service providers have to compete. The requirement from managers changes according to how far along the spectrum the markets lie.

Outsourcing with no internal bid

In certain, mainly internal, services a decision was made to outsource to a company without a bid from the internal team previously supplying the service. This applied particularly to central government and some of the information technology contracts between the government and software and facilities management companies. Internal teams were transferred, at least partly, to the new employers and often had the same middle management. The impact was to remove some of the rigidities imposed by internal systems and to make staff make themselves attractive to their new employers, if they wanted to be transferred.

Internal trading

A minimal approach to the development of markets is to establish a supplier–customer relationship within an organization. This idea became fashionable in parts of the private sector during the 1980s as a way of helping people who are not in direct contact with customers to define what it is they do and for whom. In manufacturing and service industries, the development of internal relationships in this way became part of the quality improvement effort as value chains were defined, each part of the production process being identified as adding value to the product or service and each link in the chain being described as a market relationship. Only the relationship between a 'supplier' and a 'customer' was felt adequately to result in good service or value for money. The idea was applied in the public sector through contracts on the volume and quality of service to be offered. In local government these were called 'service level agreements'.

The first impact of internal trading is that managers have to define their position in the value chain, and decide who is the customer and who is the supplier in each relationship. Sometimes this is very complicated. For example, an accountant working in a local authority may have a large number of customers: line managers for whom he/she provides management information, the chief finance officer who receives finance data, members who receive advice. He/she might also be a customer of the personnel department, the legal department and the car park. Or the chain may be long. A software maintenance person may be a supplier to a school but the school has a contract with a purchasing division of the local authority, which commissions work from internal and external suppliers. If in turn the software maintenance section has subcontractors, the supply chain may be longer still. In other cases the process is more simple. Grounds maintenance is clearly a service to a school, personnel advice on disciplinary matters clearly a service to line managers. In these cases the definition of who is working for whom is useful: the school gets its cricket pitch rolled before the match, not after. The process can make the relationships more appropriate for good service delivery: rather than the personnel department dictating what managers can do, they are there to support management. One example is recruitment advertising, which can be a source of long delays for managers trying to replace staff. A customer–supplier relationship can help to ensure that managers are supported.

Once the supply chain has been established, the next task is to define what is being bought and sold. Taken to the extreme, the definition of the service provided by professionals can be an elaborate and lengthy business. However, the process can be useful, especially if it makes more obvious what professionals do. A negative aspect of professionalism is that individuals can create a mystery. A definition of the service provided both makes the activity explicit and allows others to judge the value of the service. Such definitions also expose the power relationships in the organizations. Traditionally, people in charge of money have been powerful, whether directors of finance or principal finance officers. They have controlled the flow of financial information and in many cases the flow of funds used by people providing services. They have also created the impression of crisis, only to solve the problem by mysteriously finding an extra packet of money at the last minute. Defining their job as a service to other people in the organization addresses this power and provides a starting point for discussions about who is in control.

The third requirement for an internal market is the need to estimate costs. It sometimes appears odd to outsiders, but it has often been the case that managers have no clear idea about how much services cost: they may know how much cash a department or unit consumes but have little idea of how much a particular service costs. Internal trading forces people to make these calculations. In some cases, the allocation of costs is necessarily arbitrary but even estimates are valuable. The calculation of costs itself puts managers under scrutiny. Even if there is no competition, the fact that costs are known makes people question the value of what is provided for those costs and whether that value could be obtained more cheaply. In some cases, questions are asked about whether the service is required at all.

Once the suppliers and customers have been identified, the services defined and the costs calculated, internal markets can then be accounted for in a series of trading accounts. In traditional public sector accounts, departments or units are allocated funds, usually at the beginning of the year, and the accounts are prepared to show how those funds are spent. Trading accounts are different: they have an income side as well as an expenses side. Credits are made to the account as work is performed according to the contract. In practice, most purely internal trading accounts are fictitious in that income is entered in regular monthly sums whatever work is done. Even in the NHS, purchasers hand over budgets to block contract providers. But, where the income side of the account represents real transactions, trading accounts become an important means for managers to see whether their trading activity is successful. It is surprising how much difference this change makes: managers no longer see themselves accountable only for money spent but also for work done and therefore income received. This change in attitude occurs even when there is no competition, although competition brings with it other changes as well.

Internal trading with price testing and benchmarking

A variation on this approach is to make an internal contract and then check the costs of providing that service against what might be offered by an alternative supplier. While there may not be a formal competition, the fact that alternative prices are estimated sets a 'benchmark' figure for the service. For example, it is possible to estimate how much a bank would charge for running a payroll system which could be compared with the internal charges. It is also possible to define the quality standards that an outside supplier would conform to.

Price testing with outside suppliers generates more change. The costing exercise has to be more precise: if prices are to be compared, the units in which trading occurs have to be defined. For example, if the recruitment part of the personnel function is to be compared with the cost of hiring a recruitment agency, the relevant comparison is between the cost of hiring one member of staff internally and the charge which the agency would make for this. Then, the costs of the department which is hiring need to be included in the total cost of the exercise and the difference in that cost between using the inside personnel department and an agency.

The next step is to compare the internal costs with the external prices. This always starts an argument about the allocation of costs and managers' discretion to affect their own costs. For example, one central government training department had its costs compared with the cost of outsourcing the training function. One of its major costs was the rent it notionally paid on a very expensive central London office which had a lease signed during the property boom. Unable to vacate the premises or negotiate the rent level, it was placed at a competitive disadvantage. Similarly, people always argue about the level of recharging for central departments. As more and more services are subjected to internal market regimes, these costs become more visible and what is provided for the money becomes more clear. There is a sequential process of questioning costs: those first exposed to comparison question the cost and value of the services which they receive from others, who in turn begin to ask the same questions of their internal suppliers.

Comparing quality with outside suppliers can also have an impact. In some cases, the internal customers for a service are convinced that the quality of outside suppliers would be higher and it is worth testing that proposition. Conversely it is often the case that existing services are of too high a quality and have too many refinements that internal customers rarely need and do not want to pay for.

Limited freedom to choose suppliers

A further step is when the customer end of the supplier–customer relationship is allowed, within defined limits, to choose an alternative supplier. An organization may have a printing unit, for example, but people who need printing may be allowed to shop around with a proportion of their printing budget. In community care, people making assessments and allocating care may have a proportion of their budget to spend on the open market. Once those exposed to price comparisons are exposed to actual competition, the pressure is even greater. Faced with the threat of losing their job, managers have to look seriously at their costs compared with the prices of the competition.

Both sides of the internal trade also look at the relevance of the services being provided and their quality. Some internal services are of a quality which is not required by the customer: for example, some payroll systems have a level of potential sophistication in reporting which is never used. Line managers question whether they need some services at all. When legal costs are attributed through a service-level agreement to a unit which never receives legal advice, they wonder why. If they face competition and those legal costs are a contributory element to their uncompetitive price, they protest. Such activity has its advantages: people are forced to think whether they are doing a useful job. It also has its disadvantages, in that it splits the organization into divisively competitive elements.

The transfer of budgets to the customer side of the transaction changes the power relationships. Take the accounting function — if there is an allocation of funds to the accountants, with no accountability to line managers, they are in a strong position. Such a position is difficult to imagine in the private sector, in which an accountant arrives at a firm, announces that he/she has been appointed as accountant, then defines what he/she is going to do and how much the customer is to be charged. Once the customer–supplier relationship is established and the customer has a budget for accountancy, the relationship changes. It can even change to the extent that the provider side starts to sell itself to the customers. This certainly happened in the education service. Education Department employees produced glossy brochures and made sales visits to schools when the budgets for support services were devolved. Some schools were surprised when previously haughty managers transformed themselves into humble salespeople.

There are also changes in the way in which services are provided, in line with customer requirements. For example, support staff are more likely to be physically sited where the customers want them, rather than in a head office building.

Competition for whole services

A more radical step is to put a whole service out to tender. Once the customer–supplier relationship has been defined, the customer side then seeks bids from people to become the supplier. They may do this because they have been told to (in the case of local government by legislation and regulations, in central government by ministerial edict) or because they see it as a way of reducing costs. The franchise approach is a variant on this. In London, bus routes were offered to bus operators by tender, as were individual train routes in the privatization of British Rail.

When a whole service is put out to tender, there is a sudden-death competition in which the in-house team is given a single chance to keep their jobs. If they have already been through the processes we have just seen, the next step is to see whether they can reduce their cost to the likely price of the competitive bid. Since most services are labour-intensive this often means reducing staff costs. While the European Union regulations that protect workers' conditions when their work is transferred to a new employer limit the extent to which companies can reduce staff terms and conditions after winning a bid, there is still competitive pressure on prices. While the competitors' likely prices are not known, at least the first time, they do have access to published accounts from the organizations whose work they are bidding for, and are likely to reduce costs.

The search for cost reduction may involve finding different ways of providing the service. For example, Capita provides council tax collection services on a series of centralized computers, rather than each council having its own. In-house teams have to try to find their own ways of matching such changes in service design if they can.

Sometimes, the in-house team decides that the constraints on its operations and its costs are such that it is unlikely to compete successfully. The only way to win is to make a management buy-out and put in a bid for the work as a new entity. An early example of this was a company called MRS, which was established by managers at Westminster City Council to win the bid for refuse collection. An alternative is to find a 'host company', already established in the field, to employ the in-house team. This happened in local government, especially, as a way of avoiding going through the competitive tendering process. Tendering was compulsory only if the council wanted to do the work using its own workforce. Once the work had been privatized, the rules no longer applied. Similarly there were examples of local education authorities contracting out the management of their departments in advance of being ordered to do so by the Department for Education and Employment.

Complete choice of suppliers for individual purchasers

At the extreme, all budgets are moved to the customer side of the relationship and there is neither a commitment to the internal supplier nor a periodic tendering process. Budget holders simply choose where to spend their money on each occasion on which they need services. The devolution of budgets from education authorities to schools, under the Local Management of Schools process, has this effect. Once the purchasers have complete freedom they may choose to exercise it by entering long-term contracts, but how to purchase is their decision.

Fragmentation of services

One impact of the competition process is that the organization is divided into discrete parts, each operating to its own contract. This has two effects. First, it is difficult to operate any corporate policies on matters such as redundancy policy or pay policy: each case is determined by the price and conditions in the contract. The second is that the contracting process reduces flexibility and responsiveness. For example, in emergencies such as floods, a workforce used to be able to be found from a variety of sources to deal with damage: road workers, refuse collectors and so on. Under a contracting regime such flexibility is much more difficult.

Conversely, dividing organizations into accountable units with very specific tasks can make the managerial task easier. Before privatization, London Buses was divided up into accountable units. Individual garages were managed by individual managers and functions such as maintenance engineering were managed separately and accountably. Much of the performance improvement in London Buses can be attributed to this change, rather than the subsequent privatization. There was a plan to split up the management of the London Underground into separate contracts in a similar way but this was opposed by the mayor of London.

In other words, dividing activities into parts which are easily seen and for which people can be held accountable is a positive result of the process of defining work for competition. When this is taken to excess, fragmentation occurs and flexibility is lost.

Competitive strategy

Managers have had to decide how to compete. Porter[8] has shown that there are three generic strategies in competitive markets. Companies have to compete on price if there are no special features of their product or service which would persuade customers to pay a higher price. The second strategy is the process of making one product or service appear more valuable to the customers, and is called 'differentiation'. This strategy could be adopted for part of the product range, while competing on price in the rest of the range. The third strategy is described as 'focus'.

Managers have had to decide whether to compete on price or differentiation and whether there are some areas where only price competition is appropriate. The rules about competition usually allow decisions to be taken on the value for money offered by the different bidders, but the differentiation has to be demonstrable. If there is a detailed specification against which the bid has to be made, it is difficult to show in advance how one organization might perform better than another. The more mechanical the work, the harder it is to make the case for higher quality. In services which have a high level of personal contact, such as leisure services or homecare, it is easier to argue the case for high-quality service justifying a higher price. However, there were cases where working practices did not make the service quality as high as it could be. The times at which services were available were often restricted by the working hours of the staff, for example. Such practices had to be changed if quality was to be used as a criterion for selecting the winning tender.

When local authorities wanted to retain their existing workforce, there were ways of organizing the tendering process which would make the in-house teams more likely to win. Some private sector competitors believe that local authorities favour their own workforces in the bidding process. One-third of those firms that had grounds for complaint said that the local authorities favoured their own workforce.[9] The strategy of protecting jobs for local people on reasonable pay and conditions is attractive to local author-ities, especially in areas of high unemployment, such as north-east England or east London. Transferring jobs to companies which may not employ local labour can have a damaging effect on the local economy and local people. These matters may be as important to local politicians as the short-term effect of a reduction in the price of services. The Department of the Environ-ment, Transport and the Regions and auditors took a different view of the relationship between competitive tendering and economic policy: demon-strable value for money is a higher priority than policies towards the local workforce. Such practices were made more difficult by the Best Value rules and inspections after 1999, which were designed to make it easier for alterna-tive suppliers to compete.

If the in-house team decides to compete on price, it takes a series of actions to reduce its costs, including staff reductions, changes in employment con-tracts, reduction of assets and changes in working practices.

Competition and privatization

In addition there have been cases where competition and competitive pres-sure was used as part of a process of preparation for privatization, whether explicitly or implicitly. Sometimes, competition simply made organizations more ready for privatization. Post Office Letters was restructured and reor-ganized into more autonomous local units under the management of Bill Cockburn, who then pressed for privatization of the Post Office and resigned to take up a post in the private sector when this did not happen. The reor-ganization could be seen as a preparation for privatization. London Buses Ltd was similarly restructured into smaller companies which were made relatively autonomous. This made the process of privatization simpler although it was not an explicit objective. London Buses' privatization was completed at the end of 1995, raising £218 million net for the Treasury.

Another example was the Government scientific laboratories, which were first made to compete for work, rather than having budgets allocated to them automatically. Competition then caused many to reorganize, 're-engineer' their processes (literally) and make themselves more efficient and competitive. Some were then offered for sale either to private companies or to their own management. The National Engineering Laboratory, in Scotland, was sold to Assessment Services Ltd, part of Siemens. In fact it was sold for a negative price of £1.95 million, the sum which was given to Siemens to take over the laboratory. The Transport Research Laboratory was sold to Transport Research Foundation, a not-for-profit group formed by members of the laboratory and representatives of the transport industry.

Improved management as a preparation for privatization is a confusing activity for workers and managers. There may be a public service ethic, in which the public good is the main criterion. Once privatization is mentioned, the managerial effort is being made for the benefit of the new owners, who may be the managers themselves or an unknown group of shareholders.

Implications for public services

Cost and quality

Surveys of the impact of compulsory competitive tendering suggest that the introduction of competition produces a single reduction in cost. In a comprehensive review of the studies of costs before and after competition, Walsh[10] concluded that competition produces a reduction in direct service costs, especially in relatively simple, repetitive services such as refuse collection. The results vary by service but figures of 20% reduction in the cost of refuse collection were common. This is probably because refuse collection crews were reduced from five people to four and the four had to do the work of the missing crew member. Where it is less possible to make people work harder physically, such cost reductions are less easy to achieve.

The market testing exercise in the Civil Service was mainly for clerical and technical work. Departments were given targets for savings which they mostly met. It was difficult to discover whether the cost reductions represent a cut in unit costs or a cut in volume. However, it is probably safe to conclude that some unit cost reductions were made. Whether they could have been achieved simply by cutting budgets, rather than an expensive tendering exercise, is another matter. During the first round of competitive tendering in local government, managers had an idea of the level of cost reduction which the private sector would be likely to offer, and those figures became a cost reduction target. A similar target could come from a simple budget reduction.

However, reduction in expenditure does not necessarily produce a reduction in unit cost: budget cuts can simply lead to a reduction in volume or quality of service. This is the view expressed by the Parliamentary Ombudsman:

Reductions in staff numbers, organisational changes and new working practices will continue for some time to place individual civil servants under
stress. There is a risk that fewer staff will lead to slower service and to more
mistakes because civil servants will have less time for thought to enable
them to pursue considered and prudent action.[11]

The main difference between budget cuts and competition is that the process of competition forces people to define services and volumes. Budget cutting may change volumes and quality but perhaps in ways which are never
made explicit, other than by the number of complaints and mistakes which
result.

Customer orientation

In some ways, contracted-out public services are less responsive to the public
than directly provided ones. Once a contract is signed, with a specification
attached, it is difficult to change the service. This is probably not important
for services such as refuse collection and street cleaning, while for services
such as homecare or nursing, the details of the service are a result of the
relationship between the service user and the provider, which cannot be described in a detailed specification.

Public accountability and democracy

Accountability to the public can only be achieved in limited ways through the
contracting process. As John Stewart has argued:

> Governing is more than the provision of a series of services on a well-
> defined pattern. Government is the means for collective action in society,
> responding to and guiding change that is beyond the capacity of private
> action. It involves both learning of change, adapting to change and promot-
> ing change. The nature of government does not exclude the use of con-
> tracts, but places limits on the extent to which the governing process can be
> reduced to contracts.[12]

The argument is that contracting makes accountability narrow, concerned
only with service delivery performance, rather than with responsiveness to
changing needs and preferences. It is also narrow in the sense that responsibility for employment practices, environmental concerns and other matters
is irrelevant to the contract and therefore beyond the influence of elected
representatives. At the same time, the process of learning which occurs
when elected representatives are involved in the supervision of service provision is lost when contracts exclude representatives from contact with users of
services.

The growth of public service companies

There is a growing market for companies operating in the public service sector as countries contract out services. Early players include those French companies which were established to provide water and other public utilities in the nineteenth century. US companies are also active in the United Kingdom, as are some home-grown ones. The Department of the Environment (1995) published a survey of 220 companies operating in the local authority sector in building cleaning, refuse collection, catering, sports and leisure and vehicle and ground maintenance. It found that one-third of them were large, with a turnover of £10 million-plus, a third had a turnover of £1–10 million and a third were small. Twenty per cent of the refuse collection companies were owned outside the United Kingdom and one in six also operated in other countries. Meanwhile, some UK companies such as Serco have expanded overseas as well as by taking public sector contracts in the United Kingdom. The Labour government tried to make it easier for such companies to get access to public sector contracts.

Central government contracting for computer services has given a large volume of work to companies such as Electronic Data Services and created a high degree of dependency on those companies in areas such as tax collection. The government's view is that functions such as computing are peripheral, not part of the 'core' business of government. In practice computing is at the heart of tax collection, benefits payments and vehicle registration. Changes in the way these functions are carried out imply changes to computer systems. For example, one of the Treasury's arguments against the introduction of local income tax has always been that the computers could not cope with it. As computing is privatized, it will be the computing companies who have to assess the feasibility of alternatives, since the expertise has mostly been transferred to them. In these circumstances, it would be rational for companies to argue for systems and procedures which suit them.

Patrick Dunleavy[13] warned that radical contracting out to large companies could result in governments losing their expertise and being unable even to purchase services intelligently. Faced with companies operating in many countries, states would have a reduced role, acting as mediator between citizens as consumers and companies. While speculative, this argument is convincing in those areas in which government has quickly reduced its own capacity among directly employed people as it has done in the case of computing.

The workers

Competition based on price has affected the income of workers, whether the in-house team or a company wins the contract. This applies especially where low-skilled work is involved and where women are employed in areas such as catering and office cleaning. The effect is not always on pay rates but can affect conditions of service such as holiday and sick pay. For example, women working as school cleaners used to be paid during the school holidays and are now generally employed on contracts only during school terms. The result can also reduce the numbers of people employed and the remaining employees have to do more work.

Conclusions

Managers have responded to the need to operate in markets according to how the markets have been established. Where there has been competition they have tried to control and reduce costs. Where public sector managers have lost in competition with the private sector this has resulted in greater private sector involvement in public services. Companies have responded either by expanding or by moving into the United Kingdom from their home countries, especially France and the United States of America.

The other consequences have been to weaken the influence of the trade unions, as wage bargaining was affected by the amount of money available for wages in the contract price. Unions have generally been keen to preserve their members' jobs, although in some cases they have been able to retain members who transferred to private employers.

The other consequence has been that services and organizations have been fragmented: individual services are provided by different companies or by fragmented units of the public organizations. While this may improve the way in which managers can concentrate on a single task, it also makes co-ordination of services more difficult.

When services are subject to competitions or market transactions without competition, they have to be managed through a series of contracts. In the next chapter we look at the nature of the contracting process which this implies.

Further reading

Bartlett, W., Propper, C., Wilson, D. and LeGrand, J. (1994) *Quasi-Markets in the Welfare State*. Bristol: School of Advanced Urban Studies. A series of papers on the markets created in health, education and community care.

Walsh, K. (1995) *Public Services and Market Mechanisms: Competition, Contracting, and the New Public Management*. Basingstoke: Macmillan. An analysis of the impact of markets on management of services.

Notes and references

[1] Klein, R. (1995) *The New Politics of the NHS*, 3rd edn. London: Longman, 213.

[2] HMSO (1994) *The Citizen's Charter: Second Report*, Cm 2540. London: HMSO.

[3] Oughton, J. (1994) Market testing: the future of the Civil Service. *Public Policy and Administration*, 9 (2).

[4] Cabinet Office (1997) *Better Quality Services: Guidance for Senior Managers*.

[5] Audit Commission (1994) Taking stock: Progress with community care. *Community Care Bulletin* No. 2, December. London: HMSO, 11.

[6] *Ibid.*, p.22.

[7] DETR (September 2000) *Modernising Local Government Finance — A Green Paper*.

[8] Porter, M. (1980) *Competitive Strategy*. New York: Free Press.

[9] Department of the Environment (1995) *CCT: the Private Sector View*. Ruislip: Local Government Research Programme, DoE, 49.

[10] Walsh, K. (1995) *Public Services and Market Mechanisms: Competition, Contracting, and the New Public Management*. Basingstoke: Macmillan.

[11] Quoted in *The Times*, 21.3.96.

[12] Stewart, J. (1993) The limitations of government by contract. *Public Money and Management*, July–September, 10–11.

[13] Dunleavy, P. (1994) The globalization of public services production: can government be 'Best in World'? *Public Policy and Administration* 9 (2).

6

MANAGING THROUGH CONTRACTS

Introduction

In the previous chapter we saw that many of the services provided by the public sector are delivered through contracts, which are either internal or with private and voluntary organizations. People have had to learn how to write contracts and specifications for services and how to make sure that services are delivered according to those contracts.

In this chapter we look at how contracts have developed and how they affect the delivery of services. First we find that there are different sorts of contracts in the different parts of the public sector, including the contract period, whether they are let after a competitive bidding process, how detailed the specifications are, and how punitive are the default clauses.

We then try to explain why these differences occur. Explanations include the law and regulations surrounding the contracting process, the structure of the markets in which contracts are made, managers' ideas about what sort of contract is likely to produce efficiency and quality, and the political attitudes of those making the contracting policy. The fact that there are wide variations implies that managers have some discretion. We then look at how that discretion is being exercised. For this we use a framework developed by Mari Sako[1] (1992), who looked at business-to-business contracting in the United Kingdom and Japan. She analysed contractual relationships according to a series of dimensions and proposed two archetypes, an obligational contractual relationship and an adversarial contractual relationship. Her dimensions are used to compare public sector contracts. As well as the nature of the contract, we then consider the nature of the specification, what it contains and who writes it.

Different forms in different sectors

Different parts of the public sector have adopted different sorts of contracts. In the case of local authorities, which were compelled to use competitive tendering, the contract forms have necessarily reflected the competition process: sealed bids are invited; there can be little chance to establish a relationship with the supplier before the bidding process, apart from checking credentials and references; everything required must be specified at contract stage; and the authority must protect its interests with strong penalty clauses and default procedures. At the same time, contracts are for relatively long periods (three to five years for most services) and therefore a relationship with the suppliers has to be developed during the contract period.

In the NHS, contracts were initially for one year between the purchasers and the providers, but there were long-established relationships, the purchasers and providers having been in the same organizations before they were split into the purchaser and provider sides. Despite the short-term nature of the contracts, there was not a great use of penalty clauses and destructive default procedures in the early days of contracting. There was, however, great recourse to details about the processes to be carried out under the contracts, as if the purchaser side did not trust the providers. There were not normally competitions for large blocks of work. There was tendering for some services, but generally trusts did not have to bid for the bulk of their work against other trusts. This lack of bidding would imply the need to establish trust, although the details in the contracts and specifications suggest that this has not necessarily been the case. It is not clear why this was so, but it may simply have been the result of people being put into a new position, that of purchaser, when previously they were managers or planners. We will see later that people tend to try to reproduce older styles of management relationships when they are put in the position of purchaser.

There are some doubts about whether what were called contracts in the NHS were really a contractual relationship at all in a commercial sense. It has long been known that internal contracts are not legally enforceable, because there is only one legal entity.[2] Pauline Allen[3] pointed out that there were several fundamental differences between a contract and the contractual arrangements within the NHS, where there was no freedom not to enter a contract (purchasers and providers were compelled to trade with each other), terms were imposed by a higher authority in the event of a failure to agree, and disputes were resolved by internal administrative procedures rather than recourse to the law or the terms of the agreement. She argued that the NHS contractual arrangements were in practice a series of administrative procedures, rather than a set of contracts, because of the control exercised.

She also argued that there was a potential value in using internal contracts to improve performance, but that improvements would have had to be made to the process. These improvements included that the administrative resolution of disputes should be clarified, that clinicians should be more involved in defining services and allocating resources, that the consequences of trusts 'failing' needed to be spelled out so that they knew how their actions could influence clinicians, and finally that the accountability to end-users (patients) needed to be formally established.[4] When the Labour government cancelled the internal market in the NHS it was not making a strong statement about its lack of faith in markets and contracts. Rather it accepted that there had been no market in any conventional sense and that the administrative arrangements needed to be changed to give more real power to those commissioning healthcare services.

In the Civil Service, different procedures were adopted in different parts of the organization. Negotiations, rather than a strict sealed bid approach, preceded the outsourcing of the major computer contracts, implying the development of a close relationship between the departments and the computer suppliers. Market testing in other areas was done with a bidding process and a series of specifications. The major agreements between the Department of Employment and the TECs started as very detailed and punitive contracts, but grew into more trusting arrangements as the years progressed.

Influences on the type of contract

There are a variety of influences on the type of contractual relationship which people adopt within the public sector and between it and the private and voluntary sectors, including legal requirements, the structure of the market, managers' approach to quality and efficiency, and politics and the administrative rules under which contracting is done.

Law and regulations

A major determinant of the nature of transactions and contracts is of course the rules established by the government. Britain does not have administrative law, as such. There are laws, such as the Competition Act 1982, which apply to public authorities as much as to companies, and European Union laws and regulations and directives on business transactions and on the procurement of goods and services by the public sector in member states, which generally promote competition and therefore militate against the development of long-term and less competitive relationships. While European regulations apply to all sectors, the way in which the contracting process has been organized in Britain has not been consistent across the sectors, with regard to the bidding process, the length of contract or relationship, the mechanisms used for monitoring or the actions to be taken in case of default. In local government, laws about contracting and competition were set out in the Local Government Planning and Land Act 1980, and in Statutory Instruments and Regulations.

In the public services, there are those who believe that contracting is a matter for the law and lawyers. This view is especially held by lawyers, who get involved in writing the contracts and therefore think that they should also be involved in determining the relationships between the parties. They apply the same principles to contracting with civil engineering companies, cleaning companies and the local branch of a charity. While the purchasing side of local authorities needs to be protected, the law is not the only answer. As a standard textbook on the law of contracts says:

> Writers of contract textbooks tend to talk as if in real life agreements are effectively controlled by the law as stated in their books. A moment's reflection will show that this is not so. There is a wide range of transactions where the sums at stake are so small that litigation between the contracted parties is exceptionally unlikely . . . in substantial areas of business, contractual disputes were resolved by reference to norms which were significantly different from the theoretical legal position. The most important single reason for this seems to be that, in many business situations, the contract is not a discrete transaction but part of a continuing relationship between the parties and that insistence on certain legal rights would be disruptive of that relationship . . . In other areas of business, strict insistence on legal rights is common.[5]

It would seem, then, that the law and legal obligations are not the whole explanation for contract forms or sufficient guide to how to contract, except in cases where there are specific legal requirements which they cannot avoid.

Economics

There is an economist's view that the form of contract is determined by the nature of the transaction, including how difficult it is to define and monitor all the obligations and expectations, and the number of potential suppliers of the good or service in the market. Williamson[6] argued that as the transaction becomes more complex and as there are fewer potential suppliers in the market, so the costs of transactions increase. A complicated transaction takes time and effort to complete and therefore if it is done less frequently there are savings to be made. Longer-term contracts are more economical. At the same time, there is more chance of the purchaser doing badly from a contract if there are few alternative suppliers: there is less information about prices in the market and there is therefore a need to know more about the costs incurred by the few suppliers who are available. Small numbers of suppliers may also find it easier to collude to fix prices and may therefore lead purchasers to enter longer-term contracts which express a relationship between the two parties which goes beyond the short-term supply of a particular good or service.

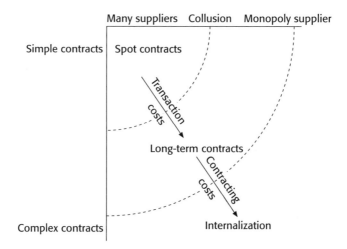

Figure 6.1 Transaction costs and organizational boundaries

In the extreme case where the transaction is very complex and there is only one potential supplier, contracting may be inappropriate: the best way to ensure the supply would then be to merge with the supplier. In other words, there may be circumstances in which a series of employment contracts with people providing the service is the best way to organize supply.

This view is that transaction costs and contracting costs lead people to behave in their relationships with suppliers in an optimal way. Simple transactions which can be entered into with a large number of suppliers can be carried out in a 'spot' way, making a new transaction each time a new supply is required. The further away from these two conditions a market is, the more there will be a tendency for closer relationships, eventually establishing the closest possible relationship, i.e. bringing the supplier inside the organization. The effect of the number of suppliers and the complexity of the transaction is summarized in Figure 6.1.

Quality and efficiency

More recent work on contracting has suggested that there are other factors beside these structural market determinants which can influence the way in which organizations make transactions with each other. For example, Sako found that even where there are a large number of potential suppliers, purchasers may wish to develop a long-term relationship with a small number of them. They do this because of the potential for improved quality and a more economical long-run series of transactions.

Politics

The fourth influence is politics. There is a reasonably close relationship between companies supplying public services and government. For example, the process of developing competitive tendering in local government was informed by advisers drawn from the companies which wished to compete for the local authority work. As well as advisers, working parties were established to allow companies to say how they would like the process to be organized. On the other hand, there were local authority members who did not want to contract with the private sector to carry out functions previously done by directly employed labour. These included Labour-controlled authorities, but there were also Conservative authorities whose members resented being told how to run their affairs by the Department of the Environment. In a survey carried out in 1994,[7] contractors complained that some councils deliberately organized the contracting process in such a way as to frustrate competition. Even among those who had won local authority contracts, 25% were fairly and 11% very dissatisfied with the process (p.92). The reasons for dissatisfaction were that councils did not want private contractors, the documents were too complicated and the procedures too difficult. On the other hand, in central government, work has frequently been awarded to private contractors without a bid from the current employees, as we saw in Chapter 6.

For managers, therefore, there are no simple answers to the question of how to establish and manage contractual relationships. On the one hand, there are market structure considerations and efficiency and effectiveness considerations which would provide some guidance as to the most effective way to do things. In some cases, these might lead to a preference for long-term contracting, in others for short-term. The nature of the market may lead to a desire to establish close long-term relationships with suppliers, or may lead to frequent competitions to keep prices down. Overlaid on these influences on practice are the legal considerations. The law itself and the regulations may force people to behave in a particular way, even though they know that the results will be less good than if they behaved in other ways. There are also more local legal influences. Legal advice may itself lead people to behave in ways which they do not think make managerial or contractual sense. Lawyers accustomed to caution may be more interested in generating apparently detailed and enforceable contracts, which professionals know cannot be enforced in practice. Politics can also determine managerial decisions. While managers may know that it would make more sense to keep a service in-house, they are not able to exercise that choice. The opposite can also be true: managers may wish to contract out but are instructed to retain directly managed provision.

However, there is still some discretion. In the rest of this chapter we look at the elements of the contracting process and ask what would be the best approach to each of these elements in different circumstances.

Obligational and adversarial contracting

Sako[8] has developed a framework for understanding contracting behaviour, setting up two archetypal relationships. At one extreme is the obligational con-tractual relationship (OCR), in which the two parties trust each other, work together for mutual benefit, share risk and do things for each other which go beyond the details in the contract. At the other extreme is the adversarial contractual relationship (ACR), which is based on low trust, the expectation that each side wishes to gain at the expense of the other, and contracts are used to protect each side from the other. Sako breaks down the contracting process into eleven elements: transactional dependence; ordering procedure; length of trading; documentation; the approach to 'contractualism' or contin-gencies; contractual trust; competence trust; goodwill trust; technology trans-fer and training; communication channels and intensity; and risk-sharing.

Transactional dependence

If a purchaser wants to be able to switch from one supplier to another, they will have contracts with a large number of people. They can then use the threat of switching to make suppliers do what they want. On the other side, suppliers may wish to maintain contracts with a large number of purchasers to minimize their dependence. In these circumstances, the relationships are likely to be distant. Under OCR, the purchaser may wish to develop closer relationships with a small number of suppliers and offset the dependency created by fewer closer relationships.

There is a variety of experience with regard to dependency. The large computer privatizations which have occurred in the Inland Revenue and Driver and Vehicle Licensing have made the government very dependent on one supplier in each case. Local authorities which have established contracts for items such as refuse collection have sometimes become completely dependent on a single firm which has won the contract for the whole of that local authority area.

In the case of the contracts between the Department of Employment and the TECs, there was complete dependency, although the TECs themselves had a large number of contractors for different types of work. The NHS had different experiences of dependency, according to the number of potential suppliers a health commissioner has in, or accessible to, its area.

We would expect high dependency to result in a close relationship between the two parties. In practice, the legal constraints and lack of experience on the part of purchasers led to the development of detailed contracts and speci-fications with complicated procedures for coping with default. As time went on, however, both sides realized that the interdependency which comes from having a single supplier and a single purchaser allows a relationship which is closer than those implied by spot contracts or frequent switching of supplier.

Ordering procedure

The stereotype of the adversarial approach to ordering is encapsulated in the compulsory competitive tendering legislation for local authorities: competitors had to bid for the work, the purchaser chose the supplier as a result of the bid, rather than any other aspect of the bidder's work or reputation, and the price was fixed before the contract was let. The opposite, OCR, way of ordering may not involve bidding and if it does, the bid price is not the only criterion for placing an order and prices are finally settled after the decision about who will be awarded the contract. The way orders are placed has an effect on the relationship between the parties. If a long-term relationship is expected, both sides need to decide whether such an arrangement would be beneficial. This requires more than doing some pre-tender checks and then opening sealed bids. When Toyota was setting up its plant in Derby, the process it used to sign up component suppliers started with assessing the management capabilities of potential suppliers, then the manufacturing skills of the workforce. The end of the process was concerned with negotiating price.

Bidding is almost universal in the public sector, for reasons of propriety. Public accountability requires that contracts are awarded fairly, without corrupt favouritism. This is interpreted to mean that the only way to accept bids is through a procedure which keeps the two sides at arm's length. European regulations require that large public sector contracts are advertised in the *Gazette* and bids invited from companies in all EU states. These regulations imply an adversarial style of contract award, rather than the development of a close relationship.

There are occasions on which negotiation about price and quality continue after a bid has been accepted. The most notable of these was the post-tender negotiation for the Inland Revenue computer contract, much to the displeasure of the unsuccessful bidders, who were not given a chance to re-tender. Local authorities sometimes negotiate with the successful bidders for building and civil engineering contracts.

In the United States of America, some public authorities have a system of 'calls for proposals'. In this process, instead of the authority writing a specification and inviting bids to carry it out, it may state a problem, give an indicative budget and ask companies and the voluntary sector how they might solve the problem. This approach has been used in substance-abuse programmes and community care. It allows the suppliers of services to show what they can do, rather than waiting for the public authority to do all the work on service design and specification. It is similar to the system of commissioning buildings in North America, where it is normal practice to specify the required performance of a building and then ask architects to design and organize its building.

The ordering procedure sets the tone for the nature of the relationship between the two parties. If contracts are based on a quotation against a specification which is the same for all bidders, the responsibility for developing the contract and specification rests with the purchasers, rather than being a joint effort between buyers and suppliers. After the contract is let the process of contract management is therefore concerned with ensuring conformance to the specification.

Once a contract is let, purchasers may try to develop a closer relationship than that which existed prior to the award. However, contracts are normally for a fixed term, at the end of which a new bidding process is started. The close relationships are stopped and the distancing implied by fair treatment begins again.

Length of trading

In ACR, the parties expect to trade with each other only for the length of the contract. In OCR, there is an expectation that, if things go well, there will be further contracts and there will be a mutual long-term commitment between the parties. There is the possibility of 'roll-over' contracts in the public sector where contractors are allowed to continue for a further period. However, lawyers say that it is unwise to include clauses in initial contracts which imply that successful completion of a given contract would most likely result in another.

The length of trading can determine the type of company or charity with which the public sector trades. Large suppliers with a variety of contracts in the public and private sectors are more likely to be able to cope with a series of time-limited contracts with any purchaser than are small local suppliers. This applies especially in community care, where small local voluntary organizations become completely dependent on their local authority for their funds. They are, in other words, dependent on the one transaction, the failure of which would result in the end of the organization. In practice, they often lurch from one short-term contract to the next.

Documents for exchange

In ACR, there is an attempt to write all the terms and conditions, including substantive conditions. Every possible item is written down. In OCR, the contracts concentrate on procedural rules which set out how problems would be resolved if they arise and individual issues are dealt with when they occur. Contracts may even be oral rather than written.

In the public sector contracts and their associated specifications have generally been long and detailed. In some cases, manuals of procedure which were in place when the service was directly managed were used as the basis for the contract and specification. For example, the original contracts between the Department of Employment and the TECs were the old department area office programme manuals. Hospital contracts and specifications consisted of a detailed description of existing procedures. However, people have realized that not everything can be written down and that in any case, the fact that the contract contains a long and detailed specification is no guarantee of service delivery. Contracts have become less detailed as people have learned that there are other ways of ensuring quality, such as involvement in the suppliers' quality assurance procedures or talking to the users of the services.

'Contractualism'

Sako refers to the treatment of contingencies as 'contractualism'. A contingent claims contract is one in which contingencies have to be defined, a procedure has to be established to agree whether a contingency has occurred, and the consequences of the occurrence are specified.

Most contracts have contingent elements: exceptional weather can affect highway maintenance contracts; sudden outbreaks of disease trigger health service interventions. The question is whether each possible contingency can be sufficiently defined in advance and whether the recognition of its occurrence can be spelled out in advance. The OCR option is to agree procedures by which both sides can agree on contingencies and what should be done as a result, relying on trust and an expectation that an agreement can be reached. The ACR option assumes that an agreement will not be reached or will be difficult and that every contingency must be defined in advance.

There is a mixture of approaches to this question in the public sector. Attempts to specify contingencies have not always worked. For example, in the care of older people, there are 'tariffs' for the cost of care according to people's degree of dependency, from a range of physical and mental disabilities. Local authorities usually have a 'banding' system in which progressive disabilities trigger progressively intensive care, but there have to be procedures by which the purchasers of care and the provider agree the extent of an individual's difficulties.

Trust: contractual, competence and goodwill

Sako distinguishes three areas of trust: contractual, competence and goodwill. An ACR approach to contractual trust means that suppliers do not do anything without a prior, written order. In an OCR relationship, supply or changes to specification can be started as a result of an oral communication. Competence trust is concerned with the degree to which the purchaser trusts the supplier to deliver the quality of product. If there is low trust, the purchaser will inspect heavily and presume that the supplier will try to skimp. In a high-trust relationship, the purchaser may be involved in the supplier's quality assurance procedures but will not carry out much, if any, inspection. Goodwill trust refers to the degree to which each side is willing to become dependent on the other.

Trust is a very important element in public sector contractual relationships. The degree of trust depends partly on the sort of relationship established during the ordering procedure. If the order is placed on the basis of the bid price only, it is likely that the chosen supplier will be operating on low, or even negative, profit margins. In order to make a profit, suppliers have to shave the quality as close to the specification as possible, if not below it. The purchaser's main function then becomes one of trying to make sure that the specifications are met, requiring inspection and checking. If the winning contractors believe in any case that the purchaser did not wish to contract with them but was forced into it by the legislation, there is no initial basis for establishing trust, and adversarial relationships are probably inevitable.

Trust can develop during the contract period or as a succession of contracts are completed. It is natural for buyers to be wary of new suppliers until they have evidence that they can be trusted. Sometimes the voluntary sector may be trusted more than the private sector, whose profit motive causes immediate suspicion by some public sector managers.

Technology transfer and training

In OCR, the purchaser is willing to help the supplier to develop the best technology and skills. This may involve helping the supplier to organize training or allowing them to join in joint training, which may not be fully costed. In ACR, help is given only when it is fully costed and paid for. One area in which this is important is in the NHS. If purchasers do not fund the development of new technologies, research and development has to be funded in other ways. In practice, since prices are supposed to be equal to cost in NHS contracts, there is no surplus available for research, which is funded through a separate mechanism.

In community care, this is not the case. Providers have to make sufficient surplus from their contracts to fund research and development. This problem was recognized in the joint statement by the Association of Directors of Social Services and National Council for Voluntary Organisations, but there is no compulsion on purchasers to price contracts in such a way as to allow innovation:

> ADSS and Voluntary Organisations jointly recognise . . . that VOs may in-
> clude in the costs of service provision reasonable allowance for indirect
> costs properly associated with the maintenance and development of a cost
> effective quality service, as well as the direct costs of service provision.[9]

It is unlikely that there would be much transfer of technology and training in the mainly adversarial relationships which have developed: public account-ability for funds, which pushes the relationship in an adversarial direction, makes it unlikely that free funding of development would occur as a routine part of a long-term contractual relationship.

Communication channels and intensity

In ACR, the communications channels between the two contracting parties are specified in the contract. Nominated officers on each side are allowed to speak about technical and financial matters, according to their individual competence. In OCR, there are multiple channels of communication as each side tries to understand the other. As with other aspects of the relationship between public organizations and contractors, frequent contact is treated with suspicion, especially informal contact. Lunches are frowned upon as corruption. While there may be some basis for suspicion, it is unfortunate that the need for propriety stops beneficial exchanges between the two sides.

The National Audit Office found that joint working and good communication improved the contracting process in the NHS:

> The National Audit Office surveys of regions and trust monitoring outposts ... showed that both felt that health authorities and hospitals were still mainly concerned with achieving their own distinct objectives rather than coming to a jointly beneficial agreement. Both groups surveyed considered that forming joint long-term strategies and providing comprehensive and timely information as well as maintaining regular communications between chief executives, were most important in achieving good relationships.[10]

Risk-sharing

In OCR, risk is shared, based on principles of fairness. In ACR, risk may not be shared but the acceptance of risk is defined in advance. There are three aspects of risk in public service contracts: risk of price changes, of changes in the volume of demand and the risk that arises from suppliers making innovations.

With relatively low inflation, the risk of price changes turning out to be much different from that predicted at the time of signing the contract is small. However, there are prices which may fall suddenly because of technical changes. For example, the introduction of keyhole surgery or much cheaper computer processing may produce a 'windfall' increase in profits for a supplier. A risk-sharing approach would lead to such windfalls being shared between the supplier and the purchaser.

The second type of risk refers to the possibility that the volume of work predicted will not be forthcoming. The supplier sets up an operation to provide the predicted volume and incurs costs which are not recouped. Again, a risk-sharing approach would involve sharing a proportion of those costs. One way of doing that is for the purchaser to guarantee a certain volume of service will be purchased, even though it may not be required.

The third element comes from innovation; a supplier may invent and offer a new way of providing a service, which turns out to be unsuccessful. Without such innovation, the contracting process will stop the development of new services, as all specifications are based on already accepted practice.

The specification

Inputs, process and outcomes

Sako's work dealt mainly with the supply of components, which could be specified in physical terms. The purchase of services can be more complicated. First, it may be difficult to specify the result required from the service in an unambiguous way. Even in relatively simple, physical services such as grounds maintenance, the results of the work will be hard to describe: what is a well-maintained cricket pitch, or an attractive flower bed, when the answer to the question determines whether a contractor gets paid or not? Attempts to answer such questions have resulted in elaborate schemes of measuring the length of grass and counting the numbers of flowers.

In other services, the problem can be more acute. What is the satisfactory outcome from a process of treating a patient with mental illness, or looking after an elderly person in a residential home? There are ways of defining these things, but if specifications are to be used as the basis for a legal contractual obligation, they are more difficult to define and measure than material things, which can have measurable characteristics and tolerable deviations from them.

Because of this, many specifications rely on describing the processes by which services are provided. If the cricket pitch is mown ten times each summer and rolled before each match, it is assumed that it will be in a good state for cricket. If a patient receives diagnosis, drugs and nursing of a specified quantity, that is enough to ensure that the bill will be paid. If the processes cannot be described in detail, then the specification may rely on the inputs used: the number of hours of a gardener's attention or a psychiatric nurse's visits. The description of the input may include the qualifications and skills of the staff: increasingly National Vocational Qualifications are being used for this purpose.

What is quoted in the specification has a big impact on the relationship between a purchaser and a provider of services. In general the provider has a professional or technical expertise which they are offering as a part of the contract. If that expertise is usurped by the specification, the purchaser has to have all the skills required to write the specification and monitor performance against it to ensure that a good job is done. If the purchaser has to specify the nursing ratio, for example, there is no discretion for a director of nursing services to decide what is appropriate and manage his or her resources accordingly.

The use of outcomes as the basis for a contractual agreement has two implications for the relationship. It assumes that the providers have the expertise to decide on the appropriate inputs and process required to produce the outcome. It also implies that the purchaser trusts the provider to make those decisions in the interests of arriving at the outcome, rather than in the interests of the provider or their profits. The higher the degree of trust, the more possible it is to use outcome specifications.

However, in low-trust environments, the use of inputs and processes as the basis for the contract produces problems of its own. How will the purchaser stay up to date with the best procedures? In services such as building cleaning, for example, technology changes. New chemicals and machines increase efficiency and change working practices: some of the early specifications for floor cleaning in hospitals specified what was meant by mopping floors, complete with diagrams indicating mop direction. In care services, there are developments in best practice for helping, for example, elderly mentally infirm people. Such things as whether doors should be locked or not, or what degree of choice of food people can or should have, have an impact on people's well-being. If contracts for this type of care specify exactly the routines and never change them, best practice cannot be adopted.

As time goes on the purchasers have less direct experience of services. While they may be appointed to a post of purchasing manager with recent relevant direct experience, inevitably they become detached from it over time. As their expertise deteriorates relative to that of the providers it becomes less easy for them confidently to specify inputs and processes.

Who should write the specification?

Therefore, the question 'what is in the specification?' implies another question: 'who should write the specification?' If technical and professional expertise is heavily weighted towards the provider side, then it is sensible that they should at least be involved in writing the input and process part of the specification, the purchasers becoming increasingly involved in specifying the required outcomes.

This brings us back to the beginning of the argument. If the purchasers are to allow the providers to specify the inputs and process, with the intention of providing the best possible outcomes for the money available, this implies a high degree of trust. If the providers are only to be trusted as far as to carry out the letter of the contract, then that letter must contain enough detail to reassure the purchaser that they are getting a good deal. If they are to be trusted to make an impact on the service user and left to decide how to achieve that, then there has to be a high degree of goodwill between the two parties.

There are two separate issues here, which are frequently confused. The first is whether the purchasers have the technical competence to write and monitor an input- and/or process-based specification. The second is whether the purchaser has sufficient trust in the provider to do their best to produce the desired outcomes and therefore have the confidence to write an outcome-based contract.

Learning to manage through contracts

People have learned that adversarial contracting is unproductive and expensive to maintain. The Department of Health began to worry, towards the end of 1995, about the costs which contracting imposed on the administration of the NHS. Contractors for local authorities have complained about over-complicated paperwork and procedures. Local authority social services departments are trying to establish more collaborative relationships with the voluntary sector for the provision of community care services.

However, people have also realized that there are constraints on the development of obligational relationships. Legal requirements to follow procedures put purchasers and providers at a distance from each other and emphasize the elements where interests are opposed.

While the number of actual and potential suppliers varies between sectors, there seems to be a relationship between market structure and contracting style: monopolies or near monopolies in health and employment services have led to the development of longer-term relationships, less reliance on detailed inspections and other aspects of ACR. In the relationship between local authorities and their contractors there are still signs of adversarial relationships.

This may be a result of ownership: the NHS Trusts are still in public ownership and an internal part of the NHS. While training and enterprise councils are legally companies, they are in effect public institutions or quangos funded by public money. It could be that public sector purchasers are more likely to have a trusting relationship with other public bodies than they have with private contractors. After all they have well-publicized reasons not to trust contractors. The first contract between the Prison Service and Group Four for the transport and escort of prisoners to court resulted in escapes and bad publicity for this contract and the idea of contracting in general.

If there is an underlying suspicion of the private sector, it is likely that contracts will remain adversarial. The implication is that there will be a continuation of detailed contracts, harsh penalty clauses, heavy inspection and generally poor relationships.

Expensive failures

The contracting system that was imposed through the imposition of internal markets and enforced outsourcing improved as people, especially in local government and health services, learned how to manage through contracts. Central government has less satisfactory experiences. Defence procurement was one case in which costs got out of hand and delays were sometimes measured in decades rather than years. The Public Accounts Committee investigated 25 major defence procurements contracts that produced £2.8 billion of overspending. The average slippage was 43 months or 27% of the projects' lifecycles. Some were very overdue, such as the Brimstone anti-armour weapon at ten years and Bowman, a tactical communications system, at six years delayed by 2000. One solution to these overspends and loss of control was to commission a Defence Electronic Commerce Service from Cap Gemini Ernst and Young at a cost of £45 million over ten years.[11]

The other was the sad case of information technology contracting. This is a complex area and may be best understood by following through some examples. The biggest contracts concerned large systems to collect national insurance and taxes and to pay out benefits through the Post Office.

Benefits payment card project

In May 1996 the Benefits Agency, the Department of Social Security and Post Office Counters Limited jointly awarded a contract to Pathway, a subsidiary of the ICL computer services group. The benefits payment card project (called 'Horizon') was intended to replace by 1999 the existing paper-based methods of paying social security benefits with a magnetic stripe payment card, and to automate the national network of post offices through which most benefits are paid.

The project was large and complex and estimated to cost £1 billion in payments to Pathway. The contract was awarded under the Private Finance Initiative, under which the contractor designs, builds, finances and operates an asset and is paid for the provision of a service only as it is successfully delivered. Risk was supposed to be transferred to the contractor by the government. The business case for the project was the reduction in fraud in benefits payments.

By October 1996 a trial version of the system was used to deliver child benefit in ten post offices. It was estimated at the time of signing the contract that 24 benefits in 19,000 post offices would be delivered by the new system within ten months. This stage was not reached when the contract was terminated three years later. In February 1997 the project was replanned and all parties agreed to delay the project by three months and each party would cover their own costs.

Although Pathway delivered intermediate releases of the software, by 21 November 1997 it had not completed a live trial as agreed. The purchasers served a breach of contract. Pathway denied liability and asserted breach of obligations by the purchasers. In July 1998 an independent panel of experts concluded that the project could deliver the required results but that it would take until the end of 2001.

In May 1999 the card element of the scheme was dropped and other aspects of automation continued, including the automatic transfer of benefit payments to bank accounts, to be completed by 2005.

The National Audit Office report[12] found:

- The project was high risk. It was feasible, but probably not fully deliverable within the very tight timetable originally specified.
- The procurement method was innovative and since the risk was transferred to the supplier the purchaser was not concerned with the supplier's internal arrangements.
- The department (Social Security) and the Post Office had different objectives for the project.
- The department's business case did not adequately assess the risk and costs of serious slippage.
- The purchasers identified most of the risks of the project, but were less successful in assessing their probability and impact.
- When the contract was signed key parts of the detailed specification had not been finalized.
- More rigorous demonstrations by the bidders might have better highlighted the risks to deliverability and the extent to which new software had to be developed.
- Pathway submitted narrowly the cheapest bid but the purchasers ranked their proposal third on eight of the eleven technical and management criteria.
- A decisive factor in the selection of Pathway was its acceptance of greater risk, making its bid compliant with the Private Finance Initiative.
- The purchasers found monitoring and controlling risks difficult.

Their conclusion was that the project did not fail because of the complexity and scale but because:

- The project was run by two organisations.
- Insufficient time was spent on the specification and on demonstrations by the bidders.
- There was not a shared, open approach to risk management.
- Government does not learn from previous mistakes in IT procurement.

The National Insurance Recording System ('NIRS2')

The Contributions Agency employed 5000 people and collected £45 billion per year in National Insurance contributions, about one-third of national government revenue. The recording system at the heart of the process was a 1960s batch-based mainframe system. In May 1995 Anderson Consulting was awarded a contract to take over the old system, design a new one to provide an on-line enquiry and update service and run it over the contract period to 2004. Anderson chose to design a new system rather than modify the old one using a client/server system based on a Sybase database and Hewlett-Packard servers. The first phase was completed on time in February 1997. The October 1997 release was delayed until January 1998 to reduce the risk of transferring all the work at one time. The April 1998 phase was delayed until July and Anderson paid compensation for late delivery. It then considered that it had fulfilled its contractual obligations.

The National Audit Office estimated that by the end of December 1998 there were still 1900 problems with the system. At the end of January 2000 1 million claims from unemployed people had to be processed with no information, together with 300,000 claims from disabled people. Incorrect calculations resulted in claimants being paid more than £35 million in compensation by March 2000. NIRS2 is likely to become fully operational by June 2001, about three years behind schedule.

In October 2000 the Inland Revenue was given permission to write off more than 1 million tax records from 1997–8 because there was insufficient information to process the tax demands. A *Computer Weekly* investigation showed that there were 7 million records in the NIRS2 system with missing data.

Anderson spent £120 million developing the system for a fee of £19 million. It hoped to recover its investment by selling the system to other national governments. Anderson retains the intellectual property rights (IPR), since it contracted to deliver a service using the software, not to deliver the software. Ownership of the IPR enabled it to put in a low bid, valuing the rights at £100 million.

The Public Accounts Committee concluded that:

- Departments should examine and research the costs, benefits and risks underpinning decisions on ownership of international property rights in major government systems.
- The commercial risk . . . has not sufficiently shifted to the private sector, and has left the government wholly dependent on the contractor.

Electronic data systems and the Inland Revenue

In 1994 the Inland Revenue entered a 'partnership' contract with EDS to provide all its IT services. The contract did not specify in detail all the work to be done, nor was the price fixed. It was a large example of IT outsourcing and transfer of 1900 staff from the employ of the government to EDS. The contract was for ten years and currently is forecast to cost £2.4 billion over the ten years.

The National Audit Office has judged the contract to be successful:

Partnerships like the one between the Inland Revenue and EDS rely on trust and understanding between two organisations, qualities which are particularly important as requirements change and develop. Management of the risks associated with new work is therefore a challenging area for value for money. Much has already been achieved, and the Department must ensure that it retains the capability to manage the relationship and keep its options open for the future. (Auditor and Comptroller General, John Bourne, 29 March 2000)

The areas specifically addressed were:

- Retaining sufficient independent capability in the department to assess projects objectively, so as to avoid becoming locked in the partnership and restricting options to change suppliers at the end of the contract.
- Increasing the rotation of staff in specialist units working in partnership with EDS to address the risk of important skills and knowledge being concentrated in a few key people.
- Exploring how to obtain reliable evidence to enable it to extend its benchmarking of the services offered by EDS.

In October 1999 EDS was awarded the contract to outsource the Department of Social Security's IT services, taking on 1600 staff.

Conclusions

There was still much dissatisfaction with the performance of IT in government. In December 2000, Pensions Minister Jeff Rooker described the computers in Social Security as 'rubbish'. A proposal to outsource the IT function of the Benefits Agency has recently been dropped. Recent examples of embarrassing failures include delays caused by digital scanning of passport applications and delay caused by computerization of immigration control procedures. The government made a commitment to deliver 30% of government services online by 2002.

The combination of a dissatisfaction with the rigid processes of competitive tendering, the failures attributed to the internal market in the NHS and the experience of IT and defence procurement led the search for a less rigid market- and contract-dominated approach. However, the new government was not inclined to go back to a system of trying to improve control purely by improved management of people in public sector organizations. The 'Third Way' approach demanded something different. As with other aspects of the Third Way it contained strong elements of the previous, Conservative approaches, in this case a faith in the capacity of the private sector to deliver results, but in 'partnership' rather than adversarial contracting. At the same time there was to be more partnership between public sector organizations to achieve succesful policy outcomes. Management through collaboration is discussed in the next chapter.

Further reading

A. Harrison (ed.) (1993) *From Hierarchy to Contract*. Oxford, Policy Journals. A collection of articles on the introduction of contracts in UK public services.

M. Sako (1992) *Prices, Quality and Trust*. Cambridge, Cambridge University Press. A comparison of contracting practice in Japan and the United Kingdom. The framework on which part of this chapter was based.

Notes and references

[1] Sako, M. (1992) *Prices, Quality and Trust*. Cambridge: Cambridge University Press.

[2] Harden, I. (1992) *The Contracting State*. Buckingham: Open University Press.

[3] Allen, P. (1995) 'Contracts in the National Health Service internal market', *The Modern Law Review*, 58, May.

[4] *Ibid.*, pp.341–2.

[5] Furmston, M. P. (1986) *Cheshire, Fifoot and Furmston's Law of Contract*, 11th edn. London: Butterworth, 24.

[6] Williamson, O. (1975) *Markets and Hierarchies*. New York: Free Press.

[7] Department of the Environment (1995) 'CCT: The private sector view', Local Government Research Programme Ruislip: DoE.

[8] Sako, M. (1992) *Prices, Quality and Trust*. Cambridge: Cambridge University Press.

[9] Association of Directors of Social Services and National Council for Voluntary Organisations (1995) 'Community Care and Voluntary Organisations: Joint Policy Statement', London: ADSS/NCVO, para 14e, p.7).

[10] National Audit Office (1995) 'Contracting for acute health care in England', report by the Comptroller and Auditor General, London: HMSO, p.19.

[11] 'Engineer', 10.8.00, p.10.

[12] The Cancellation of the Benefits Payment Card Project, report by the Comptroller and Auditor General, August 2000.

7

FROM CONTRACTING TO COLLABORATION

Introduction

One of the negative consequences of trying to manage the public sector through a combination of markets and management is fragmentation. Competitive units looking out for themselves are not likely to search out solutions that might involve loss of resources for themselves. Management systems that emphasize individual and organizational performance defined by units of output and unit costs rather than overall results concentrate the mind on the organization and its products and services rather than social results among the client group or wider population.

The problem is analogous to the business problem of emphasizing vertical integration at the expense of horizontal integration. Vertical integration makes managers and workers concentrate on driving costs down. Production is internalized to make sure that each process is under direct control and management can concentrate on each part of the production process. It may make managers and workers fail to consider either quality or how the product range is seen by the customers. Horizontal integration makes for a positive approach to such things as the customer experience as a whole or to the brand being portrayed by the product range. Whether production is in-house or outsourced is not important, since managers concentrate only on the quality of the end-product and how customers see, buy and use it. The search for efficiency or cost reductions can produce an emphasis on vertical integration, or at least adversarial contracting processes that drive down costs. The search for solutions to policy problems and for better services from the citizens' point of view made politicians and managers look for better ways to achieve horizontal integration.

This chapter looks at the reasons for promoting collaboration and finds that the argument applies both to service delivery and to policy making. It then looks at how managers have responded to the demand for collaboration and finds that there is a spectrum of behaviours, depending on how close the collaboration has to be. It then looks at the case of collaboration between the private and public sectors and looks at some of the companies that have grown as a result of the increasing use of outsourcing as a management tool.

Why collaboration?

There are two main reasons for promoting collaborative working. The first is that the management arrangements that promoted performance orientation for individual units produced unintended negative consequences. Examples include the pursuit of efficiency targets in hospitals: throughput per bed and income derived from procedures performed as targets promote efficiency but do not necessarily make for an allocation of resources that would produce the best health outcomes. Or targets for educational attainment for those who will pass public examinations do not necessarily produce the best overall results for the school population. Collaboration between agencies involved in promoting the health of the population in an area or the educational attainment of the whole school population are one possible solution to this problem.

The second reason is recognition that policy outcomes cannot be achieved by institutions working on their own and therefore nobody can be said to be accountable for results. The police forces are not responsible for many of the causes of crime, schools cannot control the extraneous variables affecting pupils' performance, nobody is solely responsible for controlling the effects of substance abuse and so on. Some of the reasons for policy failure will never be attributable to any organization, such as social inequality, family breakdown or attitudes to authority. In those cases where there are several institutions involved in contributing to service delivery towards a policy objective then some arrangement that encourages them to work together and be accountable jointly for effectiveness would be preferable to them working in isolation.

Collaboration and managerial behaviour

Experience shows that it is not a simple matter to change people from being competitive and concerned with their own organization's success and resources into enthusiastic collaborators. Setting up collaborative structures and co-ordinating mechanisms does not in itself guarantee success. The incoming Labour government in the UK first set about solving the problems of isolated ministries, departments and policy areas with a programme of setting up new organizations and mechanisms for people to collaborate with each other. Some were concerned with joining up policies, such as the Social Exclusion Unit and the new Regional Development Agencies, others were about joining together services, such as Sure Start, the encouragement of prisons and probation to work together. As well as establishing formal mechanisms or

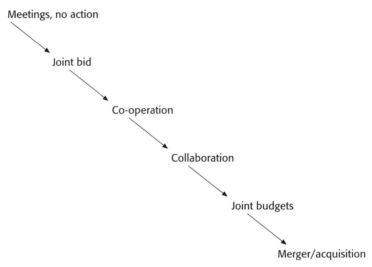

Figure 7.1   Degrees of collaboration

organizations, the main effort went into designing incentives for collaboration. There were many examples of funding being tied to collaborative efforts, such as Health Action Zones and Education Action Zones. Other area-based approaches include economic regeneration, which has been approached through partnership working for at least thirty years under a bewildering variety of titles. The Invest to Save budget was allocated on condition that organizations showed that they were collaborating.

Faced with incentives to collaborate, managers had to work out their strategies, just as they had to work out what to do when they were asked to compete for the first time.

A collaborative spectrum

In practice there has been a wide range of approaches to collaborative working (see Figure 7.1). In many cases collaboration is a requirement of funding. To get funding for a zone and other area-based initiatives, a joint bid is required. Normally there is a lead body responsible for organizing the bid and that body is responsible for calling the partners together and submitting the bid. The government department allocating the funds requires evidence of joint working.

At its worst, the process produces unproductive meetings. People are invited as representatives of their organizations or as tokens of their sector or community. The lead organization proceeds to write the bid document and the criterion by which collaboration is judged is whether the meetings took place, whatever their content or outcome.

A more authentic form of collaboration is a real joint bid. Partners bring their experience and interests to the process and the bid for funding reflects the collection of positions. Meetings to arrive at the bid are real exchanges and joint analysis of problems and proposals is made. There are examples where this is the end of the process of collaboration. Once the bid is made, even if it is successful, people revert to their previous competitive behaviours. The collective agenda is forgotten and people compete for their share of the joint funds. If there was a lead organization putting the bid together it becomes custodian of the cash (for accounting reasons) and thinks of it as its money.

Neither case is real collaboration. The first point on the spectrum that represents real collaboration is co-operative working. Here each organization retains its own specialism, works with the others on projects or programmes but retains staff under their previous management arrangements. They may co-ordinate activities, especially in relation to client contact, but there is essentially no change to the management arrangements resulting from the co-operation, although there needs to be agreement about the objectives and values of the project.

Collaboration involves a shared task with shared management and supervision of staff. People move from their parent organization and become attached to the collaborative venture. If they come from different professions they find they have to adjust to others' professional values and ways of working. In a collaborative venture people may become more attached to the collaborative activity than to their parent organization, especially if they are seconded full-time to the venture.

Legal problems have hindered the development of joint budgets for collaborative efforts. It took years to develop joint community care budgets between health and social services. Very often, budgets are the reason for the behaviours that contradict collaboration. Hospitals discharge elderly patients because they cost too much to keep in a hospital bed and thereby transfer the responsibility to social services. If the budgets were combined there would be no such incentive and the most efficient solution could be pursued by both heath and social services. The same applies to the funding of nursing provision and care provision. Frail and sick old people are subject to the definitional niceties about the boundary between nursing and social care because they come out of different budgets and different rules apply. The almost theological debate about these definitions went on for many years because they were part of the definition of the state's liability to older people: 'healthcare' was part of it, while 'personal care' was not. In Scotland the state was more generous and abandoned the distinction.

An extreme form of collaboration is the merger. Mergers of public organizations have happened for a variety of reasons, whether rationalization and economies of scale in management or service synergies. Over the years the functions of helping people to find jobs and paying benefits have been merged and demerged. Ministries split and fuse like cells as fashions for large and inclusive and small and specialized come and go. Local government reorganization sometimes involves previously independent authorities merging and sometimes involves authorities taking on functions previously the responsibility of another tier. Single-tier government, which is now in place in many towns and cities, is an example of a multi-functional merger.

Take-overs have been fairly common in recent years. There were cases of NHS Trusts, training and enterprise councils and further education colleges in which take-overs were seen as the solution where individual institutions have failed and been taken over by others considered more capable. The education Green Paper of 2001 allowed for similar things to happen in schools, failing schools being taken over by successful ones. This use of merger to solve the problem of failing institutions comes from private sector practice in which an ailing company is bought by a successful one and 'turned around'.

Conditions that promote successful collaboration

Guy Peters studied co-ordination at national government level and concluded that 'The first lesson is that mere structural manipulations cannot produce changes in behaviour, especially if the existing behaviour is reinforced by other factors in government'.[1] Eugene Bardach[2] looked at case studies of inter-organizational collaboration between public agencies in the USA. Various studies have also been made in the UK following the government's espousal of what became known as 'joined-up government'. Reports by government departments in England and Scotland also looked for the factors that make collaboration work. Lessons about collaboration had also been learned in the private sector. Towards the end of the 1990s collaboration became fashionable among business writers and apparently among businesses as a source of competitive advantage.

While the contexts for co-operation and collaboration varied greatly in the private sector, from joint ventures to enter new markets to synergies between technologies and sharing of distribution networks, there are some general lessons from both the public and private sectors about what helps collaboration to work and what inhibits it.

Bardach proposed a model of what he called 'platforming', building 'inter-agency collaborative capacity' on twin platforms of trust and creative opportunities. His model is summarized in Figure 7.2.

The main conclusion is that the two, or more, collaborating organizations have to start their collaboration by jointly defining the opportunity and learning how to work together, rather than starting with operating systems and rules.

A similar analysis was made by the Manchester Business School[3] study of collaboration in health services in Britain. It concluded that collaboration required a 'nurturing environment', including:

- a synergy of interests between management and practitioners and therefore between 'quality' and financial objectives;

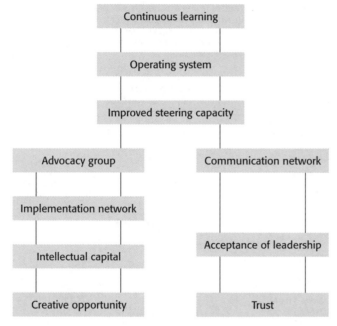

Figure 7.2 Developing Inter-agency collaborative capacity

- an organizational system which encourages active communication with users and front-line staff;
- a cohesive senior management team;
- the involvement of committed medical staff;
- performance and measurement systems sensitive to emergent practice and staff learning.

In other words, the collaborators need to work on the processes required as well as the structural and formal arrangements for collaboration to work. That is not to say that systems are unimportant. At the least collaborative end of our spectrum, it is likely that there are few incentives or rewards for people to really collaborate, whereas if there are joint budgets, performance systems that measure and praise the achievement of joint targets and an accountability structure that makes it clear what is expected of the partnerships, success is more likely. The systems need to be congruent with the development of attitudes and behaviours that are needed to make collaboration work.

Conditions that inhibit successful collaboration

It is not always the case that this alignment exists. Experience of collaborative efforts shows that there are many things that inhibit them. A review of

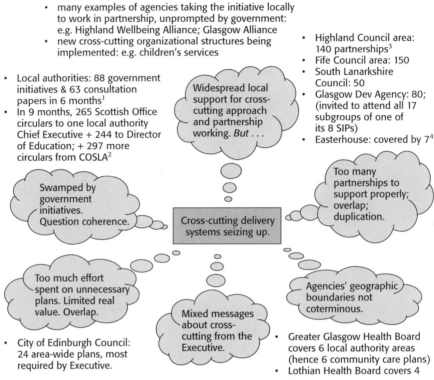

- many examples of agencies taking the initiative locally to work in partnership, unprompted by government: e.g. Highland Wellbeing Alliance; Glasgow Alliance
- new cross-cutting organizational structures being implemented: e.g. children's services

- Local authorities: 88 government initiatives & 63 consultation papers in 6 months[1]
- In 9 months, 265 Scottish Office circulars to one local authority Chief Executive + 244 to Director of Education; + 297 more circulars from COSLA[2]

Widespread local support for cross-cutting approach and partnership working. *But . . .*

- Highland Council area: 140 partnerships[3]
- Fife Council area: 150
- South Lanarkshire Council: 50
- Glasgow Dev Agency: 80; (invited to attend all 17 subgroups of one of its 8 SIPs)
- Easterhouse: covered by 7[4]

Swamped by government initiatives. Question coherence.

Cross-cutting delivery systems seizing up.

Too many partnerships to support properly; overlap; duplication.

Too much effort spent on unnecessary plans. Limited real value. Overlap.

Mixed messages about cross-cutting from the Executive.

Agencies' geographic boundaries not coterminous.

- City of Edinburgh Council: 24 area-wide plans, most required by Executive.

- Greater Glasgow Health Board covers 6 local authority areas (hence 6 community care plans)
- Lothian Health Board covers 4

- rarely given credit for partnership working in performance management systems
- not included in corporate contracts
- unclear about priority between initiatives

[1] *Audit of Government Initiatives and Consultation Documents* (SOLACE), 1999. Study period: October 1998–March 1999. The Scottish Executive has not verified the figures, but a research study being carried out by CRU on behalf of the Development Department will provide baseline data about the demands placed on local authorities by summer 2000. In addition, COSLA and the Accounts Commission also made demands of local authorities in the same period.
[2] Time period: July 1998–March 1999.
[3] NB: the methodologies used to calculate numbers of partnerships vary by agency. They do, however, give an impression of the scale of activity involved.
[4] Specifically: Priority Partnership Area; Social Inclusion Partnership; Glasgow Alliance; Employment Zone; Communities that Care; Working for Communities; New Community School.

Figure 7.3 Cross-cutting policy in Scotland: the view from delivery agencies
Source: Hogg, K. (2000) *Making a Difference: Effective Implementation of Cross-cutting Policy*, A Scottish Executive Policy Unit Review

collaboration in Scotland from the point of view of people in agencies delivering services produced a fairly negative picture, as summarized in Figure 7.3.

The Manchester study produced another list of inhibitors, mostly the opposites of the factors that encourage collaboration but also including the continuation of a competitive culture in which collaboration was seen as the threat of a take-over, and a political environment that demanded results faster than they could be produced.

Some of these inhibitors and those illustrated in Figure 7.3 reflect the fact that a hierarchy was seeking to impose itself on top of a network of collaborating agencies. The Scottish Executive tries to impose its will on the service delivery organizations by issuing directives and calling for plans. The other category of mistake is the number of joint efforts and the amount of time and work involved for people in going to collaborative meetings. Together these are enough to cause the systems to 'seize up'.

Collaboration between the public and private sectors

While collaboration between public agencies has been an important development in recent years, the involvement of the private sector in the provision of public services is growing rapidly. While, as we saw in Chapters 5 and 6, compulsory competition and market testing have waned, the private sector's involvement now occurs through the Private Finance Initiative and Public–Private Partnerships. The difference is partly a matter of the extent to which services are handed over to the private contractors and the length of the agreements. PFI contracts are generally for the estimated life of the building or plant that is involved. PPPs tend to be longer than the previous tendering arrangements allowed for. The market for providing public services has brought rapid growth in turnover and profits to the companies involved. One of the major players is Capita, a company that was set up by the Chartered Institute of Public Finance and Accountancy (CIPFA) in 1984 as CIPFA Computer Services. A management buyout led by managing director Rod Aldridge in 1987 created the Capita Group. Aldridge became chairman and CEO of the new company, which continued providing outsourcing services to the public sector, particularly in information technology. The company went public in 1991.

From 1992 to 1996 Capita more than doubled its number of employees every two years while consistently winning management contracts outsourced by the British government's privatization spree. After the Labour Party victory in 1997, Capita saw no decline in business from the public sector, with 75% of its contracts coming from government agencies. It secured the payroll and pension administration for the Metropolitan Police (London) in 1998 and acquired some of its competition in 1999, buying Oldham & Tomkins (information technology) and MPM Adams (project management). In late 1999 and early 2000, the company bought teacher placement firm Capstan Northern, engineering consultants Edward Roscoe Associates, and teaching placement agency LHR. In 2000 the company continued its buying spree, acquiring IRG, a privately-owned share registration business. The Capita Group also formed an alliance with Microsoft in 2000 to provide more Internet services for the education field. Capita's sales are summarized in Table 7.1.

Table 7.1 Capita sales: 1999 distribution

Sector	% of total
Private sector	34
Local government	30
Central government	19
Education	17
Total	**100 (Total sales £528.9 million)**

Source: Hoover's UK (02/2001) *Hoover's Company Profiles*. London: Hoover's UK

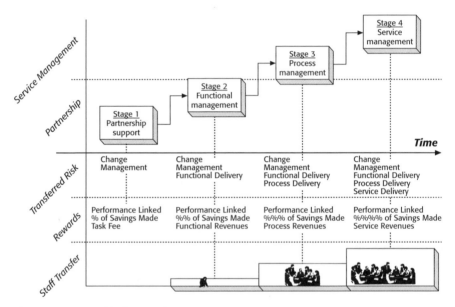

Figure 7.4 Partnership framework
Source: Capita Group plc unpublished presentation

Capita's partnerships with the public sector range from what it calls 'partnership support' to service management. The range is illustrated in Figure 7.4, which shows that the profits increase with the degree of involvement in the services. Figure 7.5 shows Capita's interpretation of the relationships structures in outsourcing, partnership agreements and joint ventures or the establishment of new companies in partnership.

Another firm that has benefited from outsourcing is Serco, a company that dates back to the 1930s but went public in 1998. It has a history of facilities management for government, including running the Fylingdales missile early warning radar, the national rail enquiry system and the Docklands Light

Features	Outsourcing	Partnership Agreement	Joint Venture NEWCO
Client Drivers	• Cost Reduction • Service Improvement	• Cost Reduction • Service Improvement • Additional Benefits • Flexible Relationship	• Cost Reduction • Service Improvement • Sharing of Additional Profits • Statutory Company Position
Control	• Service Control	• Partnership Rule Book • Management Board • Joint Decision Making • Joint Change Control	• Company Law • Declaration of Holdings • Named Company Directors
Financial Management	• Output Prices	• Management Accounts • Baseline Measurements • Books of Account/ Record	• Statutory Accounts
Profit Management	• Open Book	• Base Returns • Profit Shares	• Shareholder Dividends
Investment Management	• Contractor's Responsibility	• Partnership Agreement – Contractor Managed	• Shareholder Resources
Risk Management	• Contractor's Responsibility	• Partnership Agreement – Contractor Owned	• Shareholder Liabilities
Asset Management	• Contractor's Responsibility	• Partnership Agreement – Contractor Owned	• Shareholder Owned
New Business Management	• Contractor's Responsibility	• Partnership Agreement – Joint Incentives	• Shareholder Driven

Figure 7.5 Relationship structures
Source: Capita Group plc unpublished presentation

Railway. When large-scale activities were up for outsourcing or privatization, such as the Air Traffic Control sale and the Future Strategic Tanker System it was well placed to bid for the contracts. Sixty per cent of Serco's £430 million turnover is in the United Kingdom and 65% of that comes from government contracts. Another company benefiting from government service contracting is WS Atkins, which has grown from a base in engineering to provide a wider range of contracted services, including part of the privatized Property Services Agency and documentation for a national motorway control system.

It moved into education management, taking over the education department of the London Borough of Southwark in 2001 and entering various contracts and joint ventures in education services. The Southwark contract is worth £28 million per annum from September 2001 and involved transferring 700 of Southwark's staff.

The Labour government is keen for schools to involve the private sector in building and other capital projects. It encouraged Public–Private Partnerships both for complete new schools and for refurbishment and rebuilding. By the beginning of 2001 there were 34 school PPP projects in England and some major school building projects in Scotland.

Conclusions

Collaborative working as a way of managing public services was a central part of the agenda of 'joined-up' government. In most cases what was asked of managers was that they should collaborate while still being competitive. Competition with collaboration as a way of managing public services has not yet produced universally good results. The behaviours that managers and other workers exhibit are conditioned by their environment and especially the rules, motivations and incentives under which they work. In the case of the collaborative way of working that the government has been pushing in many sectors, these are confused. The rules based on a hierarchical system are still in place: the 'centre', whether the Scottish Executive, the NHS Executive, the DETR or other central government departments both issue a multitude of instructions and try to devise systems of incentive and reward for their constituent service delivery agencies.

The development of contracting companies and their growth in size is making an imperfectly competitive market for service providers available to public authorities. For very large ICT projects there are a very small number of credible contractors. For outsourcing routine operations, a small number of companies are available. In these circumstances, the mechanisms of adversarial contracting we saw in the previous chapter are not feasible: the threat of switching from one supplier to another is credible only if alternative suppliers are available. Rather, obligational-style contracting or collaboration is preferred, the purchaser having good access to the supplier's costs and other information, and a collaborative attitude to problem solving. The same applies to the process of collaborating between public authorities, where information sharing and compatible values are important elements of the collaborative process.

Further reading

Catherine Alter and Jerald Hage (1993) *Organizations Working Together*, Newbury Park, California: Sage.

Ernest R. Alexander (1993) Interorganizational coordination: theory and Practice, *Journal of Planning Literature*, Vol. 7, No. 4, 324–43.

Eugene Bardach (1998) *Getting Agencies to Work Together: The Practice and Theory of Managerial Craftsmanship*, Washington: Brookings Institution.

Yves L. Doz and Gary Hamel (1998) *Alliance Advantage*, Boston: Harvard Business School Press.

John Child and David Faulkner (1998) *Strategies of Co-operation*, Oxford: Oxford University Press.

B Guy Peters (1998) *Managing Horizontal Government*, Canadian Centre for Management Development, Research Paper 21.

Performance and Innovation Unit (2000) *Wiring it Up: Whitehall's Management of Cross-Cutting Policies and Services*, London: Cabinet Office.

Notes and references

[1] B Guy Peters (1998) *Managing Horizontal Government*, Canadian Centre for Management Development, Research Paper 21, p.47.

[2] Eugene Bardach (1998) *Getting Agencies to Work Together: The Practice and Theory of Managerial Craftsmanship*, Washington: Brookings Institution.

[3] Su Maddock and Glenn Morgan (1999) *Conditions for Partnership*, Manchester: Manchester Business School.

8

CONTROL THROUGH AUDIT AND INSPECTION

Introduction

The public sector audit function has a long history in checking the books of public bodies and making sure that fraud is detected. Governments have used the audit bodies in their efforts to gain control and to improve performance. Some have gained high profiles as their reports make headlines about poor performance of local authorities, health authorities and hospitals. Inspectors have similar long histories and a similar recent public presence, especially in relation to institutions such as schools and prisons. In this chapter we look at how inspectorates and audit bodies are used to change management practices and how managers respond to these efforts.

Audit and inspection

The National Audit Office and the Audit Commission have attained a central position in assessing efficiency and evaluating effectiveness on behalf of the government. The Audit Commission has also become a management consultancy with powers to impose management methods on local authorities as well as assessing and reporting on their performance.

This role is different from the traditional, narrow audit function. Audit is concerned to look at processes and procedures in areas such as ordering materials, signing cheques and handling cash to make sure that money is handled honestly. Audit as an effort to stop fraud and waste has a very long history. It also checks that accounts are produced in the correct way and produce a 'true and fair view' or some equivalent phrase of the organization's financial position. If the accounts are not satisfactory they might be 'qualified'. Such work is carried out by trained staff following procedures clearly set out in audit manuals.

Measuring and comparing unit costs is not a big step from traditional audit. It uses accounting techniques to establish costs and is concerned with measurable things. Value for money work by the Audit Commission and the NAO is based on a foundation of comparative cost performance.

Inspection is a different sort of function. There are 27 inspectorates in the UK,[1] including independent arrangements for each country, employing 2300 people. The biggest is in education, where about 1200 people are employed in the UK, followed by the Social Services Inspectorate with 321 people.

Governments have used inspectorates to keep an eye on public employees for centuries. In Britain, such bodies as Her Majesty's Inspectorates of Prisons and of Schools have long traditions. They are charged with making sure that employees are doing what they are supposed to do: that standards are maintained and that results are acceptable. The Office for Standards in Education was established in 1993 to take over the schools inspection function and was made responsible for four elements:

- the quality of education provided in schools;
- the educational standards achieved in schools;
- the way in which financial resources are managed;
- the spiritual, moral, social and cultural development of pupils.

OFSTED inspects processes, outputs and outcomes, defined as the impact of the education process on pupils.

The Social Services Inspectorate is concerned with a similar range of matters, inspecting how services are delivered and assessing their impact on the users of the services. Largely as a result of scandals involving abuse or loss of clients, the Labour government strengthened the social services inspection arrangements, through the Care Standards Act. The National Care Standards Commission was established from April 2002 to regulate and inspect residential and nursing home care for adults and children and domiciliary care, fostering and adoption services. All care sectors were, for the first time, regulated within the same framework.

'Best Value' inspections of local authorities by the Audit Commission[2] are very different from audits and are conducted by different people. They are based on a model of management practice, especially in relation to benchmarking, competition and continuous improvement. The process is illustrated in Figure 8.1.

One characteristic of inspectors is that they are generally recruited from the profession or occupation of the people they are inspecting. There are some exceptions, whereby lay people are included in inspection teams to bring a dispassionate view. Some of the inspectors' experience of doing the job may be in the distant past, and that has proved to be a problem especially for school and social services inspectors, whose relevance to current conditions is sometimes questioned by current practitioners. However, in principle they have relevant experience. This may not be the case for the auditors,

National Focus   **Local Focus**

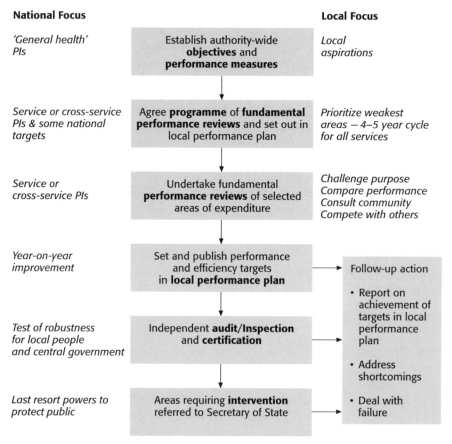

'General health'	Establish authority-wide	*Local*
PIs	**objectives** and	*aspirations*
	performance measures	

Service or cross-service **·** Agree **programme** of **fundamental** **·** *Prioritize weakest*
PIs & some national **·** **performance reviews** and set out in **·** *areas — 4–5 year cycle*
targets **·** local performance plan **·** *for all services*

Service or · Undertake fundamental · *Challenge purpose*
cross-service PIs · **performance reviews** of selected · *Compare performance*
· areas of expenditure · *Consult community*
· · *Compete with others*

Year-on-year · Set and publish performance · → Follow-up action
improvement · and efficiency targets ·
· in **local performance plan** · • Report on
· · achievement of
· · targets in local
Test of robustness · Independent **audit/Inspection** · → performance
for local people · and **certification** · plan
and central government · ·
· · • Address
· · shortcomings

Last resort powers to · Areas requiring **intervention** · → • Deal with
protect public · referred to Secretary of State · failure

Figure 8.1   Best Value inspection
Source: Audit Commission (1999) *Best Value*, London: HMSO. 'General health' = an Audit
Commission expression, along with 'corporate health', to describe the adequacy of
management arrangements

although as they have expanded their role they have tried to recruit people
with direct experience of managing the services they are inspecting.

The consequence of this shared experience is that there can be a shared idea
about what is good practice and at what level standards should be set. This
might not be the case when what is being inspected is management processes
on which there may be no consensus. The distinction between auditors'
inspection of management arrangements and the inspection of professional
practice is not absolute. In the case of schools inspections, there are differences
between teachers about how to teach and teachers may not have the same
ideas as inspectors about what is best. But the notion that an inspector or an
auditor can claim to have a superior grasp of management to that of the people
being inspected is in principle different from an inspection of professional
practice such as providing teaching, prison custody, residential care and so on.

The managerial consequences of inspection

The two main audit bodies have expanded well beyond traditional audit into work that cannot be done following a set manual of procedures. When the Audit Commission was established by Michael Heseltine to improve 'value for money' in local government it set about trying to find a framework for its analysis and recommendations. Its first framework came from McKinsey, probably because the director was an ex McKinsey employee. The '7 Ss' framework (structure, strategy, systems, staff, skills, style, super-ordinate goals) was modified slightly and taken around the country in the auditors' briefcases. It was uncomfortable for some of the people who had spent their career in audit. Following an audit trail and looking for errors or fraud was a very different task from looking for 'style'. What were they supposed to do if they found a lack of 'style'? It did not matter which managerial template was used, the problem was that this outside body had its own ideas about what constituted good management practice (and later, good political practice) and was expected to impose those ideas on independent local authorities. The job was not made easier by the fact that the authorities had to pay the fees for this work.

Unlike both audit and professional inspection, inspecting for the quality of management and, in the case of local government, the quality of the political decision-making processes requires special skills and a report that is different from the report on the inspection of lessons or what goes on in a prison. Prison inspection reports are full of details about what the prisoners do during the day, how much time they spend out of their cell and how useful or productive the activities are. They also report on how clean or otherwise the toilets are, and other easily observable things. Descriptions of 'strategic direction' by a local education authority or the 'leadership qualities' of a management team are harder to formulate and adduce evidence for.

The different traditions and the variation in services provided have produced a varied set of inspections and inspection reports. The different inspection regimes also have incorporated in them different powers for the inspectors and different consequences for those they inspect.

The Prison Service has been the subject of every government initiative to improve performance. It has been made into an executive agency. It has had a geographical management structure imposed with hierarchically set and monitored targets (see Box 8.1). It has been subjected to market testing and privatization. It has a robust regime of inspection and has had a series of outspoken inspectors. It has been forced to manage certain aspects of its work in collaboration with others. Despite all this managerial effort, many prisons are a disgrace to a civilized society, variously plagued by unsanitary conditions, inhuman routines, brutality and suicide, widespread substance misuse, racism including racist murders, and very poor efforts at education and rehabilitation.

Box 8.1   Prison governors' guidance

Prison governors will find their work constrained and directed by the following:
- Government's Crime Reduction Strategy
- Criminal Justice System Strategic Plan 1999–2002
- Criminal Justice System Business Plan 1999–2000
- Home Office Business Plan 1999–2000
- Home Office – Aim 4 Business Plan 1999–2002
- Home Office Public Service Agreement
- Correctional Policy Framework
- Prison Service Framework Document
- Prison Service Corporate Plan 1999–2000 to 2001–2002
- Prison Service Business Plan 2000–2001
- Prison Service Vision
- Prison Service Aim
- Two Prison Service Objectives
- Six Prison Service Principles
- 15 Key Performance Indicators
- 42 Key Performance Targets
- 67 Performance Standards

Source: Bryans, S. (2000) (Governor, Her Majesty's Youth Offenders Unit, Aylesbury) The managerialisation of prisons – efficiency without a purpose? *Criminal Justice Matters*, 40, 7

The Chief Inspector of Prisons who retired in August 2001, Sir David Ramsbotham, continued his predecessors' tradition of publishing damning reports if he found cause. In January 2001 he said that Brixton Prison had been in decline for four years and was 'failing', with no workshops, no education centre and a gym outside the perimeter walls. In 1999 he described Feltham, Europe's largest youth jail, as 'rotten to the core and unacceptable in a civilised society'. He supported a Children's Society report that recommended that 15- and 16-year-old offenders on remand should not be held in prison custody.

In an interview in January 2001 he expressed doubts about the purpose of inspection. 'I have never seen an organisation with so many rules, operating standards, instructions, visions and mission statements. You name it. It is a horrendous amount of bureaucracy, it is not hands-on management. In the Army, the purpose of inspection was to ensure that the organisation being inspected was ready for its operational purpose. If not, you asked why not. This presupposed that someone was listening, which is not always the case in Whitehall'.[3] Extracts from one of Sir David Ramsbotham's inspection reports, on HMP Wandsworth, are shown in Box 8.2.

Inspection reports on prisons are based on either planned or unannounced visits and include physical inspection, and interviews with prisoners, staff, the governor and prison visitors. They are very detailed and include

Box 8.2 Extracts from HM Inspector of Prisons report on Wandsworth, October 1999

'... invariably, I find myself asking how Prison Service line management, with its Visions, Statements of Purpose, Prison Rules, Operating Standards and so on, quite apart from all that it publicises about its aims and performance – all of which profess exactly the opposite of what we have found – can have allowed such treatment and conditions to exist, let alone become established in the first place....

I am saddened at the number of times I and my teams go into prisons, and find practices which are far removed from what the Prison Service itself preaches, about which, when they are exposed, the Director General expresses surprise. This appears to be not because he does not know what he wants prisons to deliver, but because the information that he is given about them is not about the quality of outcomes for prisoners but about budgets, Key Performance Indicators and measurements of the quantity of laid down processes. In other words I fear that the agenda on which I and my team are required to report to Ministers, based as it is on an Act of Parliament, and the Prison Service's own Statement of Purpose that lays down how prisoners should be treated, is far removed from one governed by budgets and Key Performance Indicators and processes, which concentrate on completely different outcomes....

Regrettably I have to report that, in no prison that I have inspected, has the 'culture' that we found caused me greater concern than that in HMP Wandsworth. This is not just because of the grossly unsatisfactory nature of the regimes for many different types of prisoner that are described in the report, but because of the insidious nature of what the 'Wandsworth way' – as the local 'culture' was described to us – represents, in terms of the attitude of too many members of staff to prisoners and their duty of care for them. What we observed, and learned, confirmed that too many staff do not seem to think that the phrase 'look after prisoners with humanity', enshrined at the heart of the Prison Service Statement of Purpose, applies to them, and continue to pursue an agenda which, if it ever was authorised, is not only long out of date but far removed from current and acceptable practice.

There can therefore only be one "way" in prisons, and that must be the "Prison Service way". Those who think, or presume otherwise, preferring such as the "Wandsworth way" should get out, or be got out, of the Prison Service now, and leave it to the decent minded majority, who hate what is happening, but feel, or have been rendered, powerless to do anything about it....

This may suggest that I envisage a long haul, but I would be wholly wrong if I suggested that anything approaching a 'quick fix' was either possible or appropriate.

Sir David Ramsbotham
Her Majesty's Chief Inspector of Prisons
October 1999

recommendations about detailed arrangements and routines. Often the reports produce improvements that are acknowledged in subsequent inspections but sometimes, as in the case of Brixton, inspection reports simply plot the decline of the institution.

School inspections have more clearly laid out consequences. While the inspections involve observation of teaching, they also take account of the management of the school, the role of the governors and the general ethos of the school. A report on a well-run inner city school, which was previously not doing well, includes the following general statement:

> Queensbridge School is well led by the Headteacher, the Deputy Headteacher and members of the Senior Management Team, working with a committed and active Governing Body. The Headteacher has . . . gradually brought about a marked change of emphasis in the management of the school in order to address the complex and varied learning needs of the pupils in a corporate manner. Since the last inspection, the school has improved in identified areas of its life and work, although significant aspects require further attention. Both pupils and staff are proud of and dedicated to their school. There is a strong and caring ethos, in which pupils feel valued and which supports their progress and attainment. Behaviour in lessons and around the school is usually good. Relationships and support for individual pupils are a particular strength of the school community, recognised in full by the parents who attended the meeting before the start of the inspection.[4]

The report contains assessments of the quality of lessons in all subjects, standards at Key Stages 3 and 4, public examination results, spiritual, moral, social and cultural development, and the management and efficiency of the school. In the case quoted above, the management is given a favourable report: the development plan is said to be

> clear and explicit about the priorities facing the school and is under-pinned by extensive documentary support for staff. Consultation processes are full and involve governors, committees and the school's middle managers. . . . structures and procedures provide a model of management that gives all staff clear roles and responsibilities.

There was a suggestion that the devolution of responsibility to what is described as 'middle managers' requires more attention. At the end of the report there is a list of five 'Key Issues' that should be addressed 'in order to raise further standards of attainment'.

This style of inspection report is helpful and supportive of the school and is designed to find things that have made a good impression and those that still need to be put right. It was presumably not too stressful an experience for either the inspectors or the school.

When a school is not in such good shape, inspection is not such a happy experience. In November 1999 there was an OFSTED inspection of Kingsland School in Hackney. The inspectors managed to find two positive things to say, that there is 'harmony between pupils from different races, nationalities and creeds' and that there are 'pockets of good teaching, especially in music, business studies and Turkish'. The report then lists fourteen weaknesses:

I.   Standards of attainment are low particularly at Key Stage 3.
II.   Pupils make unsatisfactory progress overall.
III.   Attitudes to learning and relationships are unsatisfactory; behaviour overall and personal development are poor.
IV.   The leadership and management of the school are poor.
V.   There is some poor teaching, especially at Key Stage 3, where one in five lessons is poor or very poor. The arrangements for the professional development of staff are unsatisfactory.
VI.   Attendance is poor at school and at individual lessons; pupils are often late to school. Although most pupils arrive to lessons on time, a substantial minority arrive late.
VII.   The curriculum is unsatisfactory with several gaps which are breaches of statutory requirements.
VIII.   Procedures for assessing pupils' progress are unsatisfactory and little use is made of the results of assessment.
IX.   Provision for the spiritual and social education of pupils is poor.
X.   The monitoring of good behaviour and the health and safety of pupils is poor.
XI.   Partnership with parents and with the community is unsatisfactory.
XII.   The accommodation and learning resources are poor and have a negative impact on the quality of education.
XIII.   Financial planning and control are inefficient; the school offers poor value for money.
XIV.   Existing systems and structures for running the school are unlikely to ensure improvement.[5]

The inspection resulted in 'special measures' under the School Inspection Act 1996. Under this the governors had to produce an action plan detailing how they intended to put right the list of matters that were unsatisfactory.

Reports on education authorities have similarly clear consequences. A report by OFSTED and the Audit Commission on Brighton and Hove LEA in June 2000 had some very specific recommendations for improvements in areas such as funding, school improvement, support, monitoring and challenge, use of performance data, ICT support for schools, special needs provision, contracted-out services, admissions planning, exclusions and attendance.

In contrast, a report on Hackney LEA in 2000 found that despite the efforts of the education department's management team to provide stability and protect it from the damage caused by budgetary and management failure in the rest of the authority, the performance of the LEA was unsatisfactory:

> ... the corporate context still does not provide conditions which are sufficiently stable, secure or supportive to education. This is dramatically illustrated by the current circumstances in the authority. Sudden and unpredictable budgetary constraint across the council has created nervousness and insecurity among teachers. Poor handling of issues, such as those which led to the resignation of the director of education, who was the principal architect of improvement and who had won the trust and confidence of the schools, officers and elected members, impedes progress and undermines schools' confidence. Too much of the time of senior management in schools is still spent in attempting to compensate for poor performance in some services. The morale of some headteachers is consequently very low, and the recruitment and retention of teachers create significant problems for many. This situation is all the more injurious to morale, because the education department's current senior management team has provided effective leadership and has successfully brought increasing discipline and stability, together with pertinent and rigorous analyses of the problems. More than that, the team brought a degree of hope to Hackney schools that the LEA was in the process of becoming a source of support, rather than a burden. Elected members and schools had begun to trust the senior officers and had more than a glimmer of the benefits which a successfully functioning partnership could bring. What should be a period of stability and consolidation of improvements has become a time of further turmoil. The agenda for improvement set by the previous two inspections has been immense. We found evidence of progress which has been hard won. That progress is not sufficient to enable us to conclude that the LEA is now functioning effectively overall. Nor do we believe that the progress made can be sustained. The resignation of the director of education and her senior colleagues is only the latest in a series of crises resulting from the continuing ineptitude of the corporate management of the council. We do not believe that Hackney LEA has the capacity to provide a secure, stable context for continuous educational improvement. The time has come for radical change.

The radical approach was to outsource the management of the LEA to a private company. This option is also open, in principle, to the Prison Service. The Minister for Prisons in the Labour government, Paul Boateng, made a reputation for threatening privatization if standards in individual prisons did not improve. The opposite threat, bringing the service back into public management, was the solution for one prison, Blakenhurst.

The Home Secretary does not have the option of privatizing the Police Service in England and Wales as a consequence of an adverse inspection, although proposals published in 2001 included the use of private security firms for patrolling. Inspections of police forces are mainly concerned with reporting the achievement of statistical targets, for crime detection, call management, traffic, public order and community relations. Inspections also include a management element, which is very specific in relation to the Best Value regime in the police service. While the 'challenge' part of Best Value, in which every service has to be considered for outsourcing, does not apply to the Police Service, the rest of the process does and the police were involved in the pilot efforts to implement Best Value.

An example of an inspection report that criticized the lack of consultation as part of the management process was the report on Greater Manchester Police published in 1999.

> Her Majesty's Inspector understands the difficulties of consulting (and communicating) within a large organisation and he accepts that the Force is making efforts to improve the situation. Based on his discussions with staff, he urges the Force to focus those efforts at section, unit and relief levels to engage supervisors in the process to generate involved discussion and interest from 'front line' staff. If these staff can be made to feel genuinely included, with feedback and clear signs that they can make an impact, then he believes that business plans will be more effective working documents and performance review of progress will be positively accepted rather than disdainfully received. The issue of internal consultation is closely linked to that of internal communication. Again, systems are in place but effort is needed to make them work. A large amount of information is passed down the hierarchy but little appears to be read or listened to. Meanwhile, the voice from the 'front line' reported difficulty in making itself heard (i.e. 'bottom up') and again a question is raised as to who listens actively rather than merely hears passively.[6]

This was an explicit endorsement of a consultative style of management and a criticism of the lack of enthusiasm for the style in this particular force. An inspection report on the West Midlands Police Force in the same year found that consultation was satisfactory:

> A clear priority is also given to internal consultation . . . The consultation involves OCU[7] commanders and focus meetings based on OCU. It is encouraging to note that the Chief Constable or the Deputy Chief Constable attend each one of these focus group meetings, a fact that is well received.[8]

The West Midlands inspection report also commented favourably on the force's use of a small number of performance indicators, and on its successful partnership meetings with other statutory bodies.

The style of reports in these different services varies. School inspection reports are evaluative, lessons scored on a three-point scale, judgements made about management style. Prison reports have detailed descriptions of what is observed as well as recording the performance indicators. Police force inspections are mainly concerned with indicators but also comment on what officers say about management style. Best Value inspections are mainly concerned with procedures and with service standards against comparators. The assessment of teaching quality in universities is based on assessing the paper evidence of procedures of student feedback and interview opinion from students, resulting in an overall score, also on a three-point scale. The inspection processes have developed independently and were introduced for different purposes. They are also carried out by different sorts of people. Schools, police forces and social services departments are visited by full-time inspectors who have previously worked in middle to senior management positions in the services that they are inspecting. The same is true of prison inspectors, apart from the Chief Inspector, who is not always a prison professional. Best Value audits are done by people who may have had management experience, although for any one service, only one auditor will be from the service being looked at. University inspections are done by 'peers', a team of teachers from other universities who teach the subjects they are inspecting.

One explanation for the differences in style may be that there is a variable degree of consensus about how things should be done between the inspectors and those being inspected. If inspection is used as a way of changing unwilling people's practice, there will be a hostile reception for the inspectors. If the teaching style preferred by the staff of a school is challenged by the inspectors, then the process is not one of scoring performance against an agreed set of criteria.

The exasperation that Her Majesty's Inspector of Prisons exhibits comes from a frustration with the inertia of the system. Standards and procedures are agreed formally but repeated inspections of the worst jails show little improvement. Diagnosis includes the powerlessness of governors, the quick turnover and short tenure of governors and other senior managers, and the power of the Prison Officers Association, the trade union of the prison workers. There is not much the inspector can do about these causes of bad performance or, apparently, about their effects.

In the case of local authorities, the diagnosis of the problems of the performers produces a set of detailed recommendations in a letter to the authority. There are powers, not necessarily in the hands of the inspectors, to intervene if the problems persist. The same is true in schools if they are deemed to be 'failing'.

Dealing with scrutiny

Senior managers have to cope with a wide range of scrutiny, whether audit, inspection or someone telling them how to do their management job. While the Public Audit Forum works towards consistency and tries to avoid duplication, from the manager's point of view not all of these interventions are useful, cost-effective or the best use of time. Nobody wants a bad report, which, in the extreme, can lead to a career-limiting intervention and replacement of the local management.

There are differences in approach according to whether the scrutiny is a professional inspection, an audit or a management inspection. While excuses may be found for poor professional practice, the only acceptable argument is a lack of resources, such as cash or trained staff. A standard response to adverse reports on individual prison performance is to use the report to make the case for more money or staff. The only credible response to criticism in an audit report is to put things right, or even better to claim that things have been put right between the audit visit and the report.

Strategies for coping with scrutiny on performance or the quality of management, such as the Best Value inspections, are more complicated. One approach is to join in wholeheartedly with the latest initiative and try to become a shining example, or beacon. This brings prestige and possibly extra resources, and should be good for a manager's career. To achieve this the organization needs to get involved early, become a pilot for whatever the initiative is, and take part in shaping the process. This requires that the existing arrangements are in line with the current thinking and that the existing managers are well connected with the scrutineers.

Less adventurous is a policy of conformance whereby the manuals are studied and the procedures followed in preference to existing ways of managing. In practice this should not be too difficult, as the prescriptions offered are not usually too far removed from existing practices in well-managed organizations. Conformance involves work on presentation, possibly re-presenting existing processes using the new language. For example, local authorities have been doing various forms of performance review for decades and it should not be too hard to present these as the sorts of performance review implied by the Best Value process.

Less submissive is an approach that involves a dialogue with the scrutineers to persuade them that there are viable alternatives to their prescriptions. This requires confident management, and an evaluation process that enables it to demonstrate that its ways of working are producing results. It also requires some political courage if the regime being imposed has strong government backing, but if the local authority members think that what they do has value, they need to protect it from the visitors.

So far, the strategies described have been feasible only for self-confident and well-managed organizations. What should managers do when they know that they are failing, not only by the standards of the latest initiatives but also by other standards of cost and service quality? At the extreme, managers are just overwhelmed by day-to-day events and whatever the scrutineers say, they cannot do any better. This seems to have been the case in Hackney LBC, where the main effect of adverse reports by the Audit Commission was the resignation of most of the senior officers and their replacement by a new team. Cynics in Hackney would say that they have seen all that before as well, and will remember when the failing and resigning team were the new team brought in to fix the problems left by the previous failures.

Less drastic organizations can harness the external influences to help bring about change. Often managers know what should be done but they need help to overcome obstacles to change. An adverse report can be used to get extra resources. When the Benefit Fraud Inspectorate makes a visit it is very explicit about the resources required to combat fraud and specify the shortfalls in staffing. Similarly the capacity of management is a legitimate reason for non-compliance and can be used to strengthen the management team. A report can also be used to gain legitimacy for changes some managers wanted to make in any case. An alliance can develop between like-minded people among the managers and the scrutineers.

Management style and inspection

The degree varies to which the inspectorates comment on management style. The Audit Commission clearly has a codified version of how management should be done, and managers seeking a good report know what they have to do. Benchmarking, outsourcing, consultation, continuous improvement and decisions made in small groups are the words that represent the management style currently in favour. The style should preferably be backed by some externally validated process, whether Investors in People, the Business Excellence model or ISO 9001-accredited quality procedures.

Police inspectors have a view that management style should include devolved responsibility and a consultative decision-making process. This is slightly surprising, since the police have developed as a hierarchical, disciplined uniformed force. Training emphasizes rank and obedience rather than initiative and imagination. At constable level, however, there has always been a high degree of discretion and individual initiative, as officers have to act on their own or in small numbers in response to incidents.

School inspections also favour management devolved to 'middle managers', as subject or year heads are designated. Participation in decision making and clear planning processes and target setting are the aspects of management that inspectors are looking for.

In social services, especially in children's services, and in the Probation Service the emphasis is on following procedures and keeping records. In both cases the purpose of this is to codify and control the behaviour of social workers and probation officers. Children at risk and people on probation are protected by detailed conformity to procedures. Consultation and participation are not a priority.

Conclusions

How successful are audit and inspection as a mode of control of public services? Clearly, well-established procedures for audit provide protection against fraud and corruption. When external inspectors are concerned with service standards and efficiency, different techniques are required. In some cases the technique is to produce a set of comparative indicators and then urge those at the lower end of the comparative tables to emulate the performance of those at the top. The question then arises, what is it that the best performers do that can be transferred to the less good? At this point the inspectors have to take a view about what works best. While auditors can devise procedures for matters such as how cash is handled and payments made, inspectors of management processes have to seek universally applicable prescriptions for a variety of circumstances. At a high level of generality, there can be agreement that managers should know what is expected of them, should be aware of the results of their actions and should have sufficient control of resources to achieve results. Beyond that, solutions may not be so obvious. The problems found by the various inspectors have a wide range. For units that are performing at or near the average, the route to better performance might not be very clear. A standard template to all units is unlikely to cure the variety of problems. The inspection of Kingsland School referred to above found that one of the main reasons for the problems of the school was that a neighbouring school had recently been closed and a large group of boys had suddenly been inserted into Kingsland. It was not at all obvious how the school should have dealt with this problem. The inspection of Wandsworth Prison found such bad practice that the only solution was to get rid of the prison officers who refused to conform to Prison Service norms of behaviour. The inspection of Hackney Council found that lack of political will, high rates of turnover of senior staff, strong and resistant trade unions and cynical staff led to overspending and loss of control. In all these cases the problems were complicated and deep-rooted. In no case was the application of a standard management template likely to solve the problems. If an organization is out of control, standards very bad and finances overspent then probably a period of 'turnaround' management is required. This implies centralization of spending authorization, the imposition of discipline and probably the replacement of staff who are unwilling or unable to change their behaviours. The very opposite prescription may be appropriate for a middling performer trying to raise its standards. Here, a process of quality improvement through consultation and 'empowerment' is likely to improve performance.

The implication of these differences in diagnosis and prescription is that the inspection is not itself a solution. Checking standards and procedures may show some of the symptoms of the problems but the particular solution lies with the organization itself. The experience of the attempts to turn around schools by importing a 'super-head' was informative. The charismatic leader replacing 'failing' management in 'failing' schools in no case produced satisfactory results. Institutions fail for complex and varied reasons. Inspection can identify and define failure, but is limited in its scope for putting it right.

Notes and references

[1] Figures from Appendix II of Hood, C. *et al.* (1999) *Regulation Inside Government.* Oxford: Oxford University Press.

[2] The process is described in Audit Commission (2000) *Seeing is Believing.*

[3] *Daily Telegraph*, 16.01.2001, 15.

[4] From the Introduction to Inspection Report on Queensbridge School, Birmingham, May 1998.

[5] Inspection Report on Kingsland School, Dalston, Hackney, November 1999.

[6] Her Majesty's Inspectorate of Constabulary, Report on Greater Manchester Police 1998–99, paras 2.6–2.7.

[7] Operational Command Unit.

[8] Her Majesty's Inspector of Constabulary, Report on West Midlands Police, 1998–99, para 2.7.

9

SERVICE DESIGN AND CUSTOMER ORIENTATION

Introduction

The purpose of this chapter is to look at ways in which public services can be made more sensitive to the requirements, preferences and expectations of the people who use them. This is especially important if the volume of services is increased without a corresponding increase in funds: a requirement to produce more for less is likely to result in a reduction in quality unless services can be redefined.

Not all users of public services are 'customers' in the normal sense of the word. There are many relationships between public service organizations and those they serve, although managers in many services have decided to use the idea of a customer as a metaphor which staff can easily understand. While perhaps not technically accurate, the thought of claimants of social security, for example, as customers implies that they should be treated with respect, politeness and dignity.

People using public services can be offered control over those services in a variety of ways, from consultation to direct decision making. Managers and politicians have devised a range of procedures to make services more sensitive, including in a limited way the use of vouchers to enhance choice, market research to find out what people think, charters which set out standards and what people can do if those standards are not achieved, making the politicians' task of making decisions about services more meaningful, and a holistic approach to the design of the service delivery system.

While each of these approaches has been used, there remain some contradictions in trying to develop a customer or service-user orientation, including the difficulty of doing more with less and the distancing from the service users which is implied by contracting out service delivery.

Approaches to customer orientation

Customers, voters and citizens

It has become common for managers of public services to try to make them more 'customer-oriented'. This applies both to services which are for the public and to those which are for internal 'customers', such as personnel or accountancy services. A pure definition of customer would exclude many of the relationships between public organizations and the people who use their services. Customers normally have a choice about what to buy and from whom, they provide the revenue which makes profits for the businesses from whom they decide to buy, and they have certain rights as customers. These conditions only apply to a small proportion of public services. There is a wide range of relationships between public services and the people who use them. At one extreme is the prison–prisoner relationship, in which the prisoner is an unwilling user of the service with no option of exit. At the other extreme, users of public sports facilities have many of the attributes of customers: they pay for at least part of the cost, and they can choose to go elsewhere or do something else. In between are relationships with varying degrees of ability to exit: if geography permits, children can change schools, and patients can change general practitioner. In practice choice is limited: inner city areas, for example, have fewer GPs per head of population than the suburbs.

The right to exit is an important determinant of the way in which competitive businesses treat their customers. If they can go to another supplier when dissatisfied, they will. One measure of customer satisfaction is whether they come back or not. Without the option, there is neither the direct incentive to generate satisfaction nor the obvious measurement of whether it has been achieved. That is not the same as saying that competition and a customer relationship are sufficient to produce customer orientation: whole sectors can be equally poor at customer service. Nor does it imply that competition is necessary for customer orientation: there is no reason in principle why monopolies could not be responsive to their customers — in the case of many public services which are a monopoly, this is indeed the management task (Box 9.1).

Box 9.1   Customer orientation in a monopoly

A manager in a social services department was given the task of organizing a meal for frail older people every day in a rural area. The standard solution would have been to have pre-cooked meals delivered (a 'meals on wheels' service). She asked the people what they would prefer and found that social contact was an important element in their needs. She organized a service by publicans cooking and serving meals to those who were able to get to the public house. A London borough with a large number of different ethnic groups among its older people organizes cooking by restaurants and delivers the meals.

The markets which have been established in the public sector have stopped short of making the final users of services customers. A supplier–customer relationship implies that there is some degree of choice (monopolies are rare in practice) assisted by information about prices and options. If a public service organization does not have such a relationship and the service user cannot withdraw from the transaction, the organization needs to find ways of responding to its clientele without their threat of going elsewhere.

In addition to the question of whether or not there is a choice of provider, relationships vary according to the nature of the service. Some services are protective (fire, child protection) while others are concerned with organizing access to entitlements (social security); yet others are concerned with helping people to have fuller lives (adult education). These services all require different ways of thinking about developing and maintaining a relationship which gives the recipients or users of the service as much control over the service as they want (and can be allowed to have). Willcox and Harrow[1] argue that services can be more responsive if there is a consumer relationship than if the relationship is one of dependency. This is not necessarily the case. A consumer relationship might be unresponsive if there is a monopoly (the only library in the village, the only golf course) or very responsive if there are empowered and sensitive managers.

The question is how to organize the process of listening to the service users and responding to their needs and preferences in each of these different relationships. Even the most coercive services such as the prisons can respond to needs and preferences in areas such as education and training.

Responsiveness can occur at different levels. At its most trivial, a customer care approach is limited to providing a welcoming attitude, including a smile and a presentable reception area. While this may be pleasant it makes only a small contribution to the service. A more responsive approach would be designed to 'deliver' the service in a way which reflects people's wishes. For example, whether they have to travel to get it or it is delivered at home, whether transactions are carried out by letter or by telephone. Even greater responsiveness would give the service user control over the level of service they can receive, such as the frequency of home help services.

Chris Skelcher[2] has argued that there is a spectrum of degrees of power for consumers/citizens. His categories are shown in Figure 9.1. He argues that agencies are less willing to devolve power about fundamental or strategic questions. Once the organization goes beyond the more trivial degrees of responsiveness, the difference between public services and private services becomes apparent: choices have to be made about what services are provided and who should be eligible for them. Fundamental decisions such as these are made through some sort of democratic process, rather than through a market. Democratic decisions, whether at local authority level or at the level of parliamentary legislation, are not then negotiable with individuals or groups of citizens. The boundary between negotiable and non-negotiable is not always either clear or fixed, however. Some managers use the fact that a service is

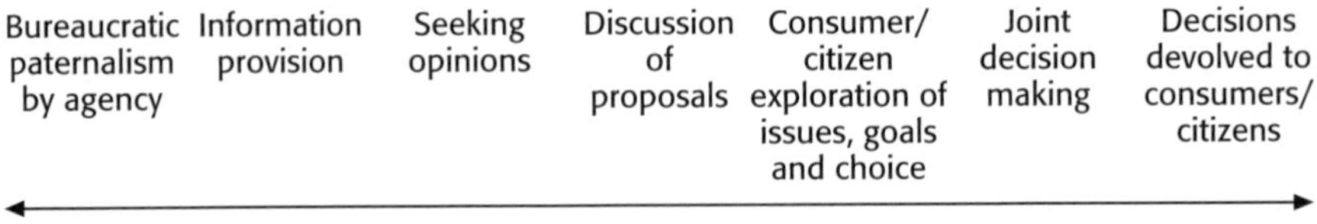

Bureaucratic paternalism by agency	Information provision	Seeking opinions	Discussion of proposals	Consumer/ citizen exploration of issues, goals and choice	Joint decision making	Decisions devolved to consumers/ citizens

Figure 9.1   A spectrum of consumer/citizen control
Source: Skelcher 1993, p.14

'statutory', or defined by law, as a reason for not allowing the users of the service to have a choice.

Given this variety of relationships and degrees of responsiveness, managers of public services have a subtle job to do in making their services responsive. Sometimes they have no control over the fundamentals of the service: managers in social security offices do not decide the level of benefits and teachers do not choose the national curriculum. The fundamental decisions are made in some part of the political process, while informed by managers.

Citizenship and entitlements

T. H. Marshall[3] argued that citizenship has three elements: civil rights (liberty, freedom of thought and speech and religion, the right to own property and make contracts, etc.), political rights (to participate in the exercise of power) and social rights (the right to economic welfare and to participate in the prevailing level of civilization). Social rights could be exercised either by working, through the family or by state provision for people who could not work. If it is the case that people have a right, as citizens, to a certain level of access to income and services, this places a duty on the state and its workers to seek out citizens and help them to exercise their rights.

This argument emphasizes rights rather than duties and to an extent leaves the definition of the citizenship rights in detail to the people running the institutions of the state. Individuals as citizens cannot individually define and exercise their rights, other than by voting. Citizenship rights are very different from consumer rights. Consumers exercise their entitlements by spending money and by invoking the law. Citizens have recourse to law, to rules and norms occasionally defined by the state and to those elements of redress laid down in the various charters.

There have been legal cases to test the degree of entitlements that people have to community care. It seems that if a local authority assesses an individual as being in need of help because of a disability then they have an entitlement to some service. Given that budgets are cash limited, this has made authorities nervous about making assessments for services which they cannot fund.

The whole question of rights is confused and covered by many different pieces of legislation, for example in education, where children have a right to education which is not very closely defined; and in housing, where there is an obligation on local authorities to house homeless people but not a guaranteed source of funds to do so. The lack of definition leaves discretion for managers to interpret what entitlements mean in detail.

Vouchers, cash and customer control

There have been examples of the use of vouchers and/or cash to give service users customer control of their services, such as the allowance for people with disabilities to buy their own vehicles, the disability living allowance, or vouchers for homecare, which are offered in some local authorities. Representatives of people with disabilities argue for the extension of such schemes, rather than the need to choose services which have been designed and provided by somebody else. An Act was passed in 1996 to allow local authorities to make direct payments to people assessed as needing community care.[4]

At various times there have been arguments for vouchers for education, and they were finally introduced for nursery education in 1996. Voucher schemes or cash allowances work if certain conditions apply. First, supply has to be available in a way that offers choice. Without that, the voucher is simply a token of funding. For example, if there is one nursery school in an area, the introduction of vouchers simply adds form filling and paperwork to the previous process of applying for a place. Second, for equity the voucher must be adequate to cover the cost of the service. If vouchers require additional payments, services are available according to how much money people have, rather than to need. Third, people should be both willing and able to organize services for themselves, researching the options, making choices and entering agreements. Tradition and familiarity play a part here. Not everyone is used to the idea of acting as a consumer in relation to doctors or schools, or home helps or residential homes.

Where these conditions do not apply, other mechanisms are required to enable people to exercise power.

Market research

There is now widespread use of market research to find out what users of public services think of them. Local authorities regularly research both general levels of satisfaction and attitudes to individual services. Various agencies also conduct research to find out how to improve satisfaction. For example, the Benefits Agency commissions national opinion polls every year to find out what its customers think of its services and how they might be improved (see Box 9.2).

Market research allows people to express their preferences and reactions to services. It can be done by survey, by focus group or by interview with service users. Without market research, approaches to customer satisfaction or quality are likely to be based on managers' ideas about what is important, rather than service users'.

> **Box 9.2**   Benefits Agency customer survey: reasons for dissatisfaction with outcome of interview at local office
>
> | | |
> |---|---|
> | Claim refused/couldn't help | 47% |
> | Query not answered | 30% |
> | Length of time taken | 26% |
> | Wanted more money | 13% |
> | Incorrect payment/calculation | 13% |
> | Staff unknowledgeable | 12% |

Source: Chandler, P. (1994) The Changing Public Sector, *Economist* conference presentation

Charters and standards

In the mid-1980s several local authorities, such as the city of York and the London borough of Islington, took an interest in service design and the specification of service standards. They published the standards by which services should be delivered, which were expressed as a 'contract' between the local authority and the citizens.

In 1991 the government published the Citizen's Charter. In the Preface, John Major was careful to point out that the charter was not simply a statement of entitlements:

> The Citizen's Charter is about giving more power to the citizen. But citizenship is about our responsibilities — as parents, for example, or as neighbours — as well as our entitlements. The Citizen's Charter is not a recipe for more state action; it is a testament to our belief in people's right to be informed and choose for themselves.[5]

The charter was not only about accountability and standards. The principles of public service set out consisted of seven items: standards, openness, information, choice, non-discrimination, accessibility and redress. To implement these principles, the government decided that there should be nine mechanisms: more privatization, wider competition, further contracting out, more performance-related pay, published performance targets, publication of information about standards achieved, more effective complaints procedures, tougher and more independent inspectorates, and better redress. This list illustrates the range of ideas about the use of the public sector. Privatization and contracting out are seen as positive in themselves whether or not there is competition. Standard setting is purely a matter for the service providers: they will set standards, an inspectorate will monitor them and the citizen may receive redress if they are not met. As the charter initiative developed, more attention was paid to service users' expectations and preferences.

As well as the principles and mechanisms, the charter initiative included the introduction of the Charter Mark, a competition in which public service providers who could demonstrate their quality of provision would be awarded a certificate (and plaque).

Following the publication of the overall charter, individual charters were produced for services. These are published and in many cases, such as at service points for the Employment Service and Customs and Excise, they are on public display. The idea was that the charters would focus managers' and workers' attention on service standards and draw citizens' attention to what they could expect. On occasion, the publication of standards seemed to be directed towards depressing expectations: for example the NHS standards published for 1995 stated that all patients should be admitted to hospital within eighteen months of a referral and that people could expect coronary artery bypass grafts within one year.[6] The Labour government continued the use of charters and standards, together with awards. Some of the names were changed, such as the establishment of 'Service First', but the principles remained the same.

Standards and charters may or may not be customer-oriented. They can be based on service users' expectations, or they can be devised in isolation. Customer satisfaction occurs when the service as perceived matches the customer's expectation. Meeting standards which do not themselves match expectations will not produce satisfaction. Parasuraman et al.[7] investigated where customer satisfaction and dissatisfaction came from. They argue that dissatisfaction arises from a gap between the expectation of a service and the customers' perception of it. The expectation comes from a range of sources: past experience, word of mouth, need, and the advertising which the service provider produces. The managers' task is to find out what the expectations are, produce a specification which matches them, and then organize service delivery according to the specification. They found that dissatisfaction was as likely to be caused by misinterpretation of the expectations as by the failure to produce the service according to the specification. The performance element of the Citizen's Charter and the related departmental charters started with standards devised internally, but many have progressed to include customer expectations.

There are three aspects of charters which would make them an effective method of ensuring satisfaction:

1. The criteria by which services are judged should be those of the service users. Response times, convenience, privacy and politeness may all have different weights in different services. One example is response times in social security. In practice some benefits can be slower than others and still meet expectations. Pensioners are not concerned with the time taken to process their pension as long as it is available on the day they retire.
2. The judgement of performance against those criteria should also include the service users. User representative groups or surveys can be used to see whether the objective measures match people's experience. If charters are to be used to improve anything other than the most superficial aspects

of customer care, they need to include the fundamentals of the service as well as the peripheral items. The Patients' Charter, for example, contains pledges about waiting times but nothing about recovery rates from procedures.

Democracy

A more difficult managerial task is to assist the political process to make the big decisions about what services to provide and to whom. This is especially difficult at times when funds are being cut: decisions about what to subtract are harder than those about what to add.

The elements of support for the political process are an evaluation of services and their impact, rather than only budgets and the way in which they are spent; distributional impact of changes in services (geography, gender, age, race); and options between which political choices can be made. The elements which make the process more difficult for politicians are shroud waving, a process by which managers tell of the worst consequences of changing or withdrawing a service; recourse to untrue legal advice, in which managers speak of 'statutory responsibilities' which are in practice vague; and professional obstacles, in which reference is made to professional judgements which override political choice.

Customer-oriented service design

European service companies thought carefully about their service design during the mid-1980s. Competition and over-capacity in the airline industry made companies such as British Airways and SAS try to attract and retain passengers by improving services rather than cutting prices. Similar attempts were made by banks, holiday companies and car hire firms. People realized that designing and delivering services had special characteristics which made service management very different from manufacturing management.

Services are intangible and therefore quality standards can only be measured by the customer's perception. While standards of manufactured products also have to meet customer requirements, once that requirement has been defined there are objective measures of whether they have been met. This is true of services only to a limited extent, through measuring response times, for example. In fact response times and waiting times are a common element of all charter-type standard setting, precisely because it is something that can be measured. Other aspects of the service experience, such as the degree of anxiety caused, the confidence the customer has in the abilities of the service provider, and the politeness or empathy level during the transaction, are all important parts of customer satisfaction but cannot be measured continuously. Because of that, people designing and managing services have to find ways of

Box 9.3   Redefining the customer

A dog warden service in a London borough was unpopular and expensive. Children threw stones at the wardens' vans and dog owners resented having their dogs picked up as they roamed the streets. The managers decided to orient the service towards the dogs as customers, rather than the general public. The service concept became one of secure and happy dogs, rather than protection for the public. The delivery system was changed from catching dogs and taking them to Battersea Dogs Home to finding the owners, or a substitute owner. Owners were offered counselling in how to look after dogs. As a result fewer dogs were destroyed, costs were therefore lower, grateful substitute owners made donations to the service, and the children stopped stoning the vans.

ensuring that the exchanges take place in a consistent way without being able to check on every member of staff all the time.

The second main difference between services and products is that services cannot be stored but have to be made available when the customers want them. Matching the timing of service availability with customer preferences sometimes requires work outside 'normal' hours and often requires seasonal variation in supply. More recently, people have come to realize that most industries have a service element to them, whether this consists of after-sales service or the service elements of the process of buying a product, and many of the ideas of service management have been applied in sectors which are not service industries at first sight.

These developments have been commented on and supported by academics and consultants on service management and service marketing. They need careful interpretation in public services because of the different relationships between the organizations and their service users and because of the frequent need for equitable treatment and the exercise of entitlements which derive from citizenship rather than the market.

Who is the customer?

The first aspect of service design which managers in the public sector have had to cope with is the definition of the 'customer' (see Box 9.3). While the people who receive the services are the most obvious customer, public services have other people to satisfy. For example, the Benefits Agency decided early that claimants of social security benefits should be called customers and treated as such. Managers argued that the customer relationship was an appropriate one as a model for the way in which claimants should be treated, even though some of the features of the supplier–customer relationship were absent. They said that the respect, politeness and concern which good customer service implies were appropriate and would be well understood by staff dealing with members of the public. They also had to acknowledge the interest in the service relationship of ministers, the Treasury and other parts of government.

Similarly, the Probation Service has a relationship with offenders which has elements of a customer–supplier one. At the same time, the service is reliant on magistrates to give non-custodial sentences. The service has also had to respond to the Home Secretary's ideas about what probation orders are, as we saw in Chapter 4. Service design therefore has to take account of the expectations and preferences of a range of 'stakeholders' or people who have an interest in and influence on the organization.[8]

Service concept

Different stakeholders have their own ideas about the benefits of the service being provided. While people on probation may see the service as an intrusion, magistrates see it as a way of preventing reoffending and the Home Secretary sees it as a punishment. The service concept is defined by Normann[9] as the benefits of the service as defined by the customers. Clearly the public sector, with its multiple stakeholders, has to design services for many different definitions of benefits.

Market segment

As well as having multiple stakeholders, public services have service users with different characteristics. One of the dilemmas which managers face is how to meet the different expectations of different types of service user while maintaining equitable treatment. Should doctors give as much time to people with minor ailments as they do to people with serious complaints? Fairness would suggest that everyone should have the same time spent on them, while creating an equal outcome would dictate that the serious cases get more time. In social security, should all claimants have the same access arrangements or should routine enquiries about pensions and child benefit be dealt with differently from Social Fund applications? Should gifted children receive more attention from teachers than children with difficulties?

Service delivery system

Once the service concept has been defined, and differences between groups of service users identified, the service delivery system can be designed. The delivery system has many elements: physical things, such as buildings, vehicles and telephone systems; staff; processes of access and rationing. Most services can be seen as having 'core' and 'peripheral' elements. The core is those parts of the service without which the service would not happen at all, while the peripherals may be designed to make the services attractive or accessible.

In the private sector, a lot of the competition between service organizations is based on the quality of the peripherals. Airlines, for example, have similar service cores: aeroplanes, which take people from one airport to another.

They differentiate themselves from each other partly by their schedules, so that people can go where they want at the time they want, and partly by the peripherals. The booking system can be very easy or tortuous. Treatment on the ground can vary: some airlines provide business class passengers with chauffeurs from their office to the airport; and they build special lounges at the airports. Treatment in the aeroplane can also vary, with different grades of food and drink and entertainment.

The public sector attitude to the peripherals is somewhat different, especially in periods of budget cuts. Managers and professionals defend the core services more than the peripherals against cuts. So, if there is a choice between reducing the number of staff and delaying redecorating the waiting area, the core service is preserved.

Where there is competition for customers, these attitudes change. Schools which have to attract pupils to maintain their budget often concentrate on the attractive peripherals, as well as the core service of teaching and learning. Uniforms, school plays and music lessons may not be essential to the core service but they differentiate one school from another in the eyes of parents and potential pupils. In the Netherlands, such competition on the peripherals extends to free logo-printed T-shirts for potential pupils at open evenings.

The call centre is a cost-effective way of providing access to services. It represents a relationship with the customer that is in practice entirely impersonal, although it has some superficial aspects of real human contact. Call centres handle calls for a range of businesses, and workers access information on customers and services through databases during the conversation. Banks, utilities, cable companies and many others operate their customer interface through this method. The first Blair government saw call centres as the 'modern'[10] way to provide services. It established NHS Direct, a way of accessing advice from the NHS over the phone as an alternative to visiting primary care providers.

The government has also set targets for the proportion of services that can be accessed through the Internet. This is illustrative of the Labour government's approach to management. Rather than think through in detail the best service design to help people get access to services, it imposes an arbitrary target for one particular method, available, of course, only to those with access to computers.

Customer co-production

All services involve a partnership between the service provider and the service user. In fact the expression 'service delivery' implies that the user of the service is a passive recipient who has the service delivered to them. School children have to participate in the education process, doing most of the work, or the service will fail. Medical services also require active participation by patients to effect a cure. The degree to which service users wish to participate varies, and sensitive service design and management will take this into account.

Image

The fourth element of service design is how the organization is to present itself to the outside world. In private services, designers work on the whole set of ways in which an organization communicates with its customers, from the appearance and attitudes of staff, through the colours used in the premises, to the organization's letterheads.

Many public sector organizations have had similar design make-overs. The creation of NHS Trusts, grant-maintained schools, competitive white-collar services and executive agencies has promoted the flourishing image management industry, producing logos, 'corporate dress' (staff uniforms), glossy brochures and repainted signs.

Just as the other elements of design need to be interpreted in a public sector context, so does image management. The reasons are also similar: different messages may be appropriate for different stakeholders. Even glossy brochures may give the impression of profligacy to funders while instilling confidence in service users. The police have a particular problem in projecting a consistent image to members of the public, transgressing drivers and criminals.

Values

There is a debate about the role of values or organizational culture in service design and management. Normann, for example, argues that without shared values, service delivery cannot be of high quality and consistent. If there is to be discretion at the point of contact between the organization and its customers, that discretion cannot be exercised by reference to a rule book, rather to the customer service ethos of the organization. When the airline SAS transformed its customer service, the managers symbolically threw away the rule books.[11] When price competition called for cost reductions, rule books about the limits to customer service were introduced.

The opposite view is that if there is a high turnover of staff and especially if they are poorly paid and uncommitted to their organization, staff cannot be expected to use their discretion and express the organization's customer service values. Rather they can learn routines of behaviour which match most customer expectations. This is especially true in services which are relatively routine and where little discretion is required. Operatives in fast food outlets have not internalized an ethos of desiring general well-being when they tell us to 'have a nice day'. They have learned a routine, in which communication with customers is as regimented as portion size and uniform clothing. Such routine service produces customer satisfaction because it matches expectations.

In the public sector, there may be values and a collective ethos which are more than a desire for customer service: many public sector workers say that their motivation for working is to provide a service for people, to high standards and with equity. If, together with these values, they also have the necessary skills, then the service management process can rely on their appropriate use of discretion.

However, if the people in contact with the service users are not inspired by a desire to serve the public but regard the work as 'just a job', and a low-paid one, managers have a dilemma. Do they try to engender an appropriate set of values, perhaps through a training programme, or do they design a set of behavioural routines which simulate a good ethos? Approaches such as quality circles, in which people collaborate to find better ways of doing things, rely on the willing and perhaps enthusiastic participation of people in service improvement. If willingness is in doubt, such approaches are a failure.

Once these elements are put in place, they reinforce each other. The delivery system reinforces customers' expectations. The image reinforces staff attitudes to the organization. Different segments have a modification of the delivery system. In well-managed services there is consistency between the elements.

Quality

Public service organizations have all had initiatives about service quality. There are two main approaches to quality, implied by two definitions of it. One is that quality is defined as 'conformance to specification', a definition clearly derived from manufacturing. Management's main effort, using this definition, is to make sure that the specification is met, either by employees or contractors. Quality control, through inspection and monitoring, will ensure conformance.

Another definition is 'fitness for purpose', which implies that it is the person using the service who makes the judgement about what would make it fit for the purpose and whether that has been achieved. This approach implies that service users are involved or control the quality assurance process, reacting with those providing the service to ensure that it does what it is supposed to do. This further implies that the specification may be ignored or modified to make sure that the service is what the user wants. Inspection of conformance to specification would not achieve this.

Quality assurance is an approach to quality which emphasizes the importance of making sure that all the processes and activities involved in producing services are working properly, from planning to delivery and feedback. There are certification procedures, such as the international quality standard ISO 9001, which check whether all the right sorts of procedures are in place. Many firms and public authorities will only deal with organizations which have such a certificate. The Charter Mark initiative is something like this sort of certification.

Another approach to quality is to start quality improvement programmes, sometimes by setting up quality circles, which are groups of workers who make suggestions about how things might be done better. This idea is based on the view that however well things are working, there can always be improvement.

Citizen-oriented service design

We have already seen that a private sector service design and management model cannot be applied directly to the public sector without interpretation. The underlying reason is that people who use public services are citizens as well as customers. Their access to services is frequently a right which derives from meeting eligibility criteria or simply from being a citizen, rather than from the ability to pay.

There are several implications of this. First, overstretched services may not wish to make themselves too attractive, because they cannot cope with existing demand. On the contrary they may want to engage in 'demarketing' their services, especially to those in least need. Second, in those services which are available as a right, the organization cannot decide that they do not want to provide a service for a particular individual or group. Airlines can decide not to participate in the package holiday market, or pubs can decide that they are not in the 'lads' night out' market. Public services are not in this position. Inclusiveness may obstruct good service design and delivery. Third, decisions about what to produce, in what quantity and for whom are not in the hands of the managers. All public services are ultimately under the control of politicians, whether directly or indirectly. A pure customer orientation is affected by politicians' attitudes.

In addition, accountability is more diffuse in the public sector. Managers of private services are accountable to shareholders for attracting enough customers at the right price to make a profit. Public sector service managers are accountable, ultimately, to their customers through the political process. They are also accountable to people who are not customers but taxpayers, and to their elected representatives.

Contradictions in customer/citizen orientation

Budgets and quality

These special characteristics of public services present managers with dilemmas. One is the balance between service quality and cost. In private services, generally, a higher-quality service can command a higher price and stay profitable. In the public services, high quality does not necessarily generate more revenue, but may be more expensive. If there are insufficient resources to meet overall demand, there is a temptation to provide a mediocre standard of service to as many people as possible, rather than a high standard to a few. An example is the homecare service, through which people with disabilities or infirmities are helped with certain tasks at home. With a given budget for this service, the options are to give as many people as possible a small amount of help (a relatively low quality of service) or concentrate the service on those in greatest need and give them a high quality. Politically, withdrawing small amounts of help from large numbers of people is unpopular.

Politicians, citizens and consumers: limits of arm's-length control

The relationships within public services involve at least three participants. Politicians vote the funds, decide what services should be provided and take decisions about the nature and style of service delivery, as representatives of the electors. At the same time there is a direct relationship between the service providers and the users, which can itself change the nature of the services. There can be tensions between decisions made by politicians and decisions made by managers.

The problem is even more complicated when contractors are involved in service delivery. Politicians do not have direct control over the operations of contractors, which are managed through a series of contracts and specifications. Contractors have to refer to the specification and the purchaser before changing a service in response to a service user's preferences or requirements. It is more difficult to have a responsive service in these circumstances.

Equity, equal treatment and customization

Another serious dilemma is that between equity of treatment and customization. Private sector services can be customized, as long as the customer is willing to pay and is satisfied with the result (Box 9.4). If the service design is to recognize and respond differently to different sorts of people, the implication is that managers and workers respond in different ways to each group, or even to each individual, which implies a greater degree of discretion than standard, routine treatment. Some people have described the process of designing

---

Box 9.4   Customer service, choice and rationing

At a seminar for managers of community care services, the proprietor of a private homecare service said that one of her workers had arrived at a client's house to carry out her normal routine of work. The client said that she would rather use the time, and money, being assisted to go to a bingo game. The worker agreed. The public sector homecare managers said that this could not have happened in the public sector. The client could not have been assessed as 'needing' a bingo game. Such use of funds and time would be depriving someone else of their service. In any case, had she won the jackpot, her ability to pay for the service would have to be reassessed. The reason that it could happen in a private transaction was that the client was paying for herself.

services for individuals, rather than producing a standard service, as 'post-Fordism', an analogy with flexible production methods making manufactured products more individual.

It is possible to overstate the existence of such individual treatment. An example sometimes quoted is the creation of 'packages of care' in community care. The range of alternatives to residential care is in practice not large: the combinations may be individual but the services are quite limited in scope. In other services there does not seem to be a trend towards customization. Standardization through national standards and procedures leads to less individual treatment and the growth of contracting leads to less flexibility.

Conclusions

The relationship between public service organizations and their users can be more complicated than that between a company and its customers. People have rights as citizens as well as customers, and in any case may be unwilling users of the services. There is a choice of ways of making services more sensitive. Managers are sometimes asked to use many methods at once, if their organization decides that customer service should be the subject of some sort of initiative. However, good service design is an important element of the manager's task and can make the difference between satisfied and dissatisfied customers, even when resources are limited.

One of the differences between managing public services and managing a business is that the business has an obvious measure of customer satisfaction, which is repeat business and profitability. These factors are rarely available or appropriate in the public sector as neither the health nor prison services, for example, are pleased to see their customers again. Other performance measures are required, and how managers are measuring and managing performance is dealt with in Chapter 10.

What is clear is that creating customer satisfaction with public services does not happen automatically by target setting or by setting up market-type mechanisms. Targets only reflect managers' views about the service, and virtually all the markets established stop short of giving customers power. Service design and delivery require a close relationship with the service users, whether through real empowerment or just by consulting them through market research.

Further reading

Normann, R. (1991) *Service Management*, 2nd edn. Chichester: Wiley. An analysis of the elements of service design. Mainly based on private sector experience.
Prior, D., Stewart, J. D. and Walsh, K. (1995) *Citizenship: Rights, Community and Participation*. London: Pitman. A review of the exercise of citizenship in public services.

Notes and references

[1] Willcox, L. and Harrow, J. (eds) (1992) *Rediscovering Public Services Management.* London: McGraw-Hill, p.116.

[2] Skelcher, C. K. (1993) Involvement and empowerment in local public services. *Public Money and Management,* July–September.

[3] Marshall, T. H. (1963) *Sociology at the Crossroads.* London: Heinemann (originally published 1950).

[4] The Community Care (direct payments) Act, 1996.

[5] HMSO (1991) *The Citizen's Charter,* Cm 1599. London: HMSO, p.2.

[6] Department of Health (1995) *Fit for the Future: Second Progress Report on the Health of the Nation.* London: HMSO.

[7] Parasuraman, A., Zeithaml, V. A. and Berry, L. L. (1985) A conceptual model of service quality and its implications for future research. *Journal of Marketing* 49, Fall, 41–50.

[8] For an analysis of the stakeholder approach to public services, see Bryson, J. M. (1995) *Strategic Planning for Public and Not For Profit Organizations,* 2nd edn. San Francisco: Jossey-Bass.

[9] Normann, R. (1991) *Service Management,* 2nd edn. Chichester: Wiley.

[10] I asked a senior manager of a major outsourcing company if it ran call centres. 'Ah,' he said, 'you mean the modernization agenda.'

[11] Carlzon, J. (1987) *Moments of Truth.* Cambridge, Mass.: Ballinger.

10

MANAGING PERFORMANCE

Introduction

Performance measurement and management are important both for the accountability of organizations and individuals and for managers to produce better services. Accountability is more than a process of showing how money is spent; it also involves demonstrating that money has been used efficiently, effectively and for the purposes for which it has been allocated. Who benefits from services, the question of equity, is also part of the accountability process. In this chapter we see how performance is measured and how that measurement is used.

The argument is that while effectiveness is difficult to measure, unless performance management systems can show how well services are achieving what they are supposed to, they will be of limited value. The systems must include the evaluation of effectiveness as well as the more narrow idea of efficiency. Different stakeholders have different ideas about both what services are supposed to achieve and how they should achieve it, and managers have to balance their requirements.

In addition, public services are supposed to be flexible and responsive, attributes which may be lost in the search for efficiencies. Sometimes redundancy and spare resources are necessary to achieve flexibility.

Why measure and manage performance?

Accountability

Public sector organizations are in principle accountable to the public for three things: that money has been spent as agreed and in accordance with procedures; that resources have been used efficiently; and that resources have been used to achieve the intended result. At the same time politicians are supposed to be accountable for the policy decisions they make while holding the management of the organizations to account for their actions.

Both sets of accountabilities require ways of measuring performance. Accounting for how money has been spent is relatively simple despite the mysteries of accountancy. We will see that this measure, how much money was spent and on what, is still an important part of managers' lives, however sophisticated the other types of accountability become.

Whether resources have been used efficiently is a question which requires some measure of the output or value of services provided, which can then be compared with the cost of provision. Here the problems of measurement begin: how to measure the outputs of schools, hospitals, prisons and so on.

The third question, did the service achieve what it was supposed to, requires an assessment of what works best in the particular service, or indeed what works at all. Here the relationship between management and professionals or experts is important. One aspect of the specialized occupations in public services is that people claim to know what works and what does not, without necessarily being able to explain or demonstrate it. Day and Klein[1] found that doctors, police and teachers all made such claims. While not certain of the explanation for this, they tentatively conclude that 'we may be getting a hint that where a particular occupational group dominates a service, its ability to appropriate the language of evaluation may derive from its power as an organised interest group or trade union'.[2] Day and Klein also refer to occupations engaging in 'mysteries' or secret, enigmatic rituals which exclude non-members from scrutinizing their activities. Measurement of effectiveness, as part of the process of accountability, has to overcome these obstacles.

Performance measurement for political accountability is a different problem. If we assume that there is a hierarchy in which politicians state unambiguous goals which can be disaggregated into measurable objectives for managers to achieve, the process of performance measurement is simple. In real life, politicians' goals are often neither unambiguous nor measurable. Such clarity would enable failure to be revealed as clearly as success. The 1997 Labour government was brave enough to make specific electoral promises, using targets whose achievement could be verified in areas such as class sizes in primary schools. It took the work of the previous government on target setting through the Citizen's Charter initiative and made 'Service First' an important part of its toolkit for delivering measurable improvements in public services. The government's critics from the Left dismissed this attempt as 'managerialism', using methods derived from management rather than politics to run state services. Rather than electoral accountability through local government and parliamentary elections, it chose the methods of 'management by objectives' to make and monitor promises. There is no doubt that the government had a belief that management methods could improve the standard of public services. Specific targets for the level of attainment in literacy and numeracy in schools were set, backed by a measurement system, given priority through the literacy and numeracy hours in schools. The test results suggest that the intervention is working. The same may be true of the campaign to reduce the numbers on waiting lists for surgery: simple targets, made a priority and given resources, can usually be achieved. The question is whether the overall standard of services can be improved by using multiple targets, some of which may conflict with each other.

Stakeholder expectations

Public services have a variety of constituencies to whom they have to answer and it is unlikely that all will be interested in the same results. For managers this presents a dilemma, especially when satisfying one stakeholder will upset another. In most circumstances, managers are able to work out which stakeholder is most powerful and satisfy them, while making efforts not to upset the less powerful. This does mean, however, that performance measurement and management can be complicated by having to devise measures which reflect the interests of many groups.

For the Labour government this problem connected with its political desire to present itself as occupying a 'centre' position or the 'Third Way'. This applies especially to Home Office services. Evidence-based approaches to the measurement of effectiveness lead to the conclusion that the current performance of the prison system is very poor. Recidivism rates are very high, indicating that outcomes are bad, and many inspection reports show that there is very little rehabilitation, education or training going on inside the prisons. And yet, the centre of the Home Office's crime strategy is the biggest prison-building programme of any government. 'Prison works' was a slogan adopted by Michael Howard when he was Home Secretary and despite the evidence, Jack Straw continued the sentiment, presumably for political rather than 'managerialist' reasons.

Management for results

Managing a budget and accounting for expenditure is less demanding than managing people to produce a defined and measurable result. Performance targets enforced by a system of sanctions and rewards, whether moral or material, focus managers' and workers' attention on achievement rather than conformity with rules and procedures. But because of the fact that the simplest form of accountability, for money spent according to procedures, still applies, managers face another dilemma: what if the most effective way of achieving this result implies breaking the rules and procedures for handling public money? There are numerous examples. Competitive tendering has meant that managers of competitive units have adopted the faster commercial practices of the private sector and failed to follow financial regulations. There have been cases of people being dismissed, not for dishonesty but for failing to recognize the dilemma between speed and public accountability. The search for efficiency savings through outsourcing has meant that some contracts have been negotiated rather than subjected to a visible tendering process.

The dilemmas are caused by the fact that managing for results has not replaced the need to account for public funds but rather been added to that need. The need for probity in the use of public funds is in principle no greater than that in the private sector, but in practice the fact that taxpayers are concerned with how their money is used is different from the concern of shareholders with the preservation and growth of their wealth. Audit and inspection organizations have to combine a concern for probity with a desire for 'value for money'.

Individual and organizational performance

Almost all public servants have an appraisal process through which their individual contribution to their organization's performance is assessed. While the appraisal process has other objectives, such as to identify people's training and development needs, the emphasis is normally on individual performance, sometimes with an element of performance-related pay. In principle, the targets which individuals are assessed on should aggregate into the perform-ance targets of the organization as a whole. In centrally managed services there is a direct relationship between targets set by ministers and the targets in individuals' work plans, targets and assessments. Sometimes the individual targets are not related to those of the organization itself, especially if managers are free to decide their own priorities.

The Labour government tried hard to link individual targets and rewards to performance indicators for services. In the case of education targets, it introduced a system of performance pay for teachers, who would be paid up to £2000 per year extra if they crossed a 'performance threshold'. At the same time schools had to install performance management arrangements with targets for pupil progress and the professional development of staff. Annual appraisals include setting targets for each teacher in line with the school's targets for the coming year.

This is a clear example of the replacement of management by professional methods including peer judgement, and autonomous teachers setting their own priorities, by management by objectives. The same approach was at-tempted right across the public sector. The emphasis was on the achievement of results, wherever this was possible.

What is being managed?

Both the Treasury and the Audit Commission encouraged the achievement of the 'three E's': economy, efficiency and effectiveness. Economy is about the cost of the inputs used, and making economic use of them. Efficiency is concerned with the cost of producing outputs. Effectiveness is defined as producing results. People concerned with equality of access to services have talked of a fourth 'E', equity, and argued that it should be included in any scheme of performance measurement.

In economics there are two definitions of efficiency. Productive efficiency is measured by the average cost of producing goods and services. Allocative efficiency is measured by the extent to which the economic system produces that mix of goods and services which reflects people's preferences as expressed by their consumption decisions. We saw in Chapter 5 that there is an argument that markets promote both types of efficiency. Competition between producers generates the need for producers to reduce their prices to that of their competitors. Choice allows consumers to influence producers in their decisions about what to make: if nobody wants what is on offer, producers have to make something else.

In those parts of the public sector in which there are markets, it could be argued that measures of economy and productive efficiency are taken care of: competition eliminates those producers whose costs are too high, or forces them to reduce their costs. There is no need for any independent measurement or analysis of their costs. There may be targets and measurements related to resource use, such as return on capital employed. Where there are no markets, public accountability for the use of resources would require that those given stewardship of public money demonstrate how well they are spending it. Measurement and reporting of efficiency is an essential part of public accountability and needs to be independently validated.

The most important aspects of performance management are not technical issues divorced from the real world of politics. Managers operate in a political environment and ignore politics at their peril.

Economy

At its simplest, performance measurement looks at how much money was used up by the organization over a period. At first sight this might seem trivial and say nothing about managerial or organizational performance. In practice such measures are given importance by the dominance of the budget process. Budgets are cash-limited and in many cases are projected from one year to the next with the expectation of an 'efficiency saving' of a certain percentage of the last year's budget. The notion of the annual efficiency saving relates to a general expectation that productivity, especially labour productivity, increases constantly. Technology changes, improvements in work organization and enhancement of skill levels all contribute to a trend improvement in the value of output per worker. Even if outputs cannot be measured, because these processes of improvement are going on in the public sector, it can be expected that productivity will improve every year. Hence budgets can be reduced in real terms without loss of outputs. In those cases where the output cannot be measured or where the quality varies with cost, what this means in effect is that the main performance target is staying within the budget.

Staying within budget means both not spending too much and not spending too little. The fact that budgets have normally to be used up in a financial year (with some exceptions) means there is sometimes a need to stop spending in the tenth or eleventh month, while in other cases, there is a rush to ensure that money is spent at those times to ensure that budget targets are met. This necessity overrides other, more sophisticated aspects of performance management. A manager who can demonstrate that the services were effective, the service users were delighted and the other stakeholders were satisfied will not last long if the budget is consistently overspent.

Reporting systems reflect this. Financial management reports of actual expenditure against the projected spend are sent out, usually monthly. While there are variations between sectors and within them, there are two remaining problems even with this most simple measure of performance. The first is that the details of the projected spend are sometimes produced after the year has begun, which means that managers are not sure against what figures they are monitoring the spending. The second is that monitoring systems are still often based on cash outflows in each period. In many services, a decision taken in one month may represent a commitment to spend money for many months or even years. For example, if a social services department assesses a child aged 12 as needing residential care, it undertakes a potential commitment to looking after that child in a residential home for four years. A monthly financial report which says that this month £4000 was spent on the child does not give a picture of the continuing commitment.

Productive efficiency

A more sophisticated view of how well money is being used is to ask how much was produced in exchange for what expenditure. For most services, it is possible to devise a measure of volume. Universities can measure the number of hours of student contact the staff have or the hours of staff contact the students have, hospitals can measure the throughput of patients, libraries the numbers of books issued and reference materials referenced, pest control the number of rats captured or cockroaches killed. All that remains to produce a measure of efficiency is to find out how much each one cost. For example, we can measure that collecting council tax costs £6 per house in Barnsley and £63 per house in Tower Hamlets and that educating a primary pupil costs £2639 in Lambeth and £1346 in Rochdale. In themselves, these comparisons might be useful: it could be that council tax collectors in Tower Hamlets could learn something from those in Barnsley. In a mood of helpfulness and collaboration, the tax collectors of Barnsley may even be willing to help.

Such comparisons have to be interpreted with care. The accounting mechanisms used to make the calculations have to be the same: the allocation of overheads, for example, may be made using different methods. The nature of the 'product' may also vary: the fact that Rochdale educates primary pupils for half the cost of doing the same thing in Lambeth may be because the education system is twice as efficient there or because the quality of the education is half as good, or some position in between.

A different consequence of such comparisons might be that those with high costs will concentrate on finding reasons for the differences: council tax is harder to collect in areas where there is a high turnover of population, for example. Such comparisons should be used to raise questions about apparently poor performers, rather than be accepted simply as a certain indicator that one organization is performing better than another, and the factors affecting the comparative figure should be looked at.

Barzelay[3] has argued that the emphasis on measuring and improving efficiency has been a mistake. He argues that the scientific management approach to performance improvement is based on how manufacturing is managed, where the product is easily defined and measured, whereas public service 'products' are not so easily measured:

> Since it excluded the concept of product, reformers' influential conception of efficient government was trouble waiting to happen. It encouraged the notorious bureaucratic focus on inputs to flourish and it permitted more specialized functions to become worlds in themselves. More specifically, an increase in efficiency could be claimed in government whenever spending on inputs was reduced, whereas it was much easier to argue in an industrial setting that cost reduction improved efficiency only when it led to a reduction in the cost per unit of output.[4]

While progress has been made in the definition and measurement of outputs, it remains a problem for managers to be able to demonstrate whether reduced budgets result in reduced output, or that productivity has increased.

Allocative efficiency

The other definition of efficiency is whether the organization produces the range of services which reflects the preferences of citizens or their representatives. At an aggregate level, this is a question of the distribution of resources among the main services: defence, social security, education, health and so on. The notion of Pareto optimality is that there is an allocation of resources which produces the most possible benefits. To move resources from one activity to another would diminish the total of benefits. Classical economists would argue that the market achieves precisely this optimal position: the sum of individual purchasing decisions and the response by producers will produce the best allocation of resources in this Pareto sense.

However, the question of allocative efficiency poses a different problem. If there are markets in which consumers have a choice of what to buy and from whom, it might be argued that there is an automatic process of matching supply to demand or even need. But what if there is no choice? Political processes of resource allocation substitute for the market. How do we then know whether those choices reflect demand, preferences, or even need? We shall see in Chapter 12 that the process of allocating public money to services is hardly likely to lead to a reflection of collective preferences among, say, school buildings, military hardware and social security benefits. If the ballot box is the only mechanism for expressing an opinion, it is a very remote and imprecise way of influencing such choices.

In practice, allocative efficiency is never measured: there are no mechanisms for measuring whether the result of the resource allocation processes reflect either any individual's set of preferences or any sense of a set of collective preferences. In any case different classes of people have different preferences. As we saw in Chapter 5, the markets which have been introduced into public services do not allow citizens a great deal of choice within the services which are offered. They certainly do not offer people the choice of how their tax contributions should be spent.

Effectiveness

But what of effectiveness? Given that the success of the allocation process is difficult to measure, is it possible to measure the degree to which those resources which are allocated to services produce the desired results? Progress is being made towards measuring effectiveness in those areas where there is agreement on what a desired outcome is, such as improved health status or acquired knowledge and skills. The issues about measuring effectiveness are partly technical. There are two broad categories of outcome. One is a change in *state*. The purpose of the service might be to improve the quality of a person's health, the durability of a road, or the cleanliness of water. While there may be arguments about what to measure, there are numerous examples of how to measure. The second sort of outcome is a change in *behaviour*. The criminal justice system aims to change the offending behaviour of people convicted of crimes. Interventions by social workers are sometimes intended to change the behaviour of parents or children. Such changes may be more difficult to measure than changes in state, although offending rates and rates of abuse can be measured and monitored.

Measuring effectiveness is concerned with finding out which services produce the desired outcomes. The outcomes of services may be different for different stakeholders. As Peter Jackson says:

> Because different stakeholders have different interests in the performance of public sector departments, the stakeholder approach helps to force the question 'whose value for money is being considered?' Value for money will mean different things for different individuals. Often these different perspectives will come into conflict and will need to be resolved. This is the business of politics. Value for money is not a technocratic value-free concept.[5]

There are many examples of the differences in opinion about what outcomes are desired from services. For example, applicants for planning permission want to be able to carry out their developments, while neighbours may not.

The Labour government was very keen on the idea of specifying outcomes and measuring their achievement. The Introduction to the Public Service Agreements for 1999–2002 said:

> The amount spent or numbers employed are measures of the inputs to a service but they do not show what is being achieved. While the number of new government programmes established or the volume of legislation passed are often critical milestones on the path to achieving change, they are only a means to delivering the real improvements on the ground that this Government wants to see. What really matters is the effectiveness and efficiency of the service the public receives. That is what makes a difference to the quality of people's lives.
>
> The targets published in this White Paper are therefore of a new kind. As far as possible, they are expressed either in terms of the **end results** that taxpayers' money is intended to deliver — for example, improvements in health and educational achievement and reductions in crime — or **service standards** — for example, smaller class sizes, reduced waiting lists, swifter justice. The Government is therefore setting specific, measurable, achievable, relevant and timed (i.e. SMART) targets, related to outcomes wherever possible. Moreover, as experience of this new approach develops, it hopes to further refine and improve future target-setting.

As we saw in Chapter 2, there are political differences about what public services are for and even what they should consist of. There are many examples of changes in the outcomes expected of services. They have developed over time and may have transformed themselves several times in the process. The home help service was developed initially for mothers at home who had recently given birth: the home help would help with the baby and the domestic work during the first few weeks. It then developed into a domestic help service for older people unable to look after themselves without some assistance. It then changed again into a personal care service for people who otherwise might have to have care in an institution outside their own home. The last transition was difficult: withdrawing the domestic help service from a large number of voters has a political impact.

The Citizens' Advice Bureaux have also been through a transformation in their desired outcome. Originally established to help rehouse people whose homes had been destroyed during the Second World War, the service transformed itself into a legal and welfare rights agency, largely funded by the state, providing accessible advice to individuals about a range of different problems. The Crown Agents were originally established as a supply agency for equipment for offices in the colonies, became a trader on the money markets and then a management consultancy. The Home Office decided to transform the Probation Service into an agency which delivers punishment in the community. The British Council was established to combat the rise of fascism in Europe and became an agency providing English language teaching, cultural diplomacy and a range of other services throughout the world. The intelligence agency MI5 was established in 1909 to gather military and political information from enemies and potential enemies. The decline in overtly hostile attitudes to Eastern Europe meant that it needed new work, which it found in part in Northern Ireland from 1992. When the truce was signed in 1994, MI5 decided to diversify into countering organized crime under legislation introduced by the Home Secretary in 1996.

What these examples show is that organizations can change their objectives, or that governments can change them for them. Hence the first question 'what does the organization exist to do?' may have changing answers. Further, different people may have different ideas about what the organization exists for. Politicians and professionals may differ, politicians will disagree and managers and professionals may not always have the same definition of purpose. The disagreement may go as far as the issue of whether the organization should exist or not. There was a process in the Civil Service called 'prior options', which was originally designed to happen before an organization was considered for agency status. The questions asked under this process included whether the function was necessary, if so should the state be involved, and if so could the work be done by a company. Only when these had been answered could the managers consider whether to become an agency. In many cases the managers thought that their organization should survive and stay in the public sector, in contradiction with ministers' ideas. Even such obviously 'public sector' functions as the Public Records Office were considered for privatization. The process continued as a part of the Comprehensive Spending Reviews under the Labour government.

Once the decision to continue to exist has been made, there can also be differences about the purpose and therefore what should be measured. The first task of a performance management system is therefore to reach agreement on the overall purposes of the organization.

Public Service Agreements

Public Service Agreements are concerned with outcomes, improvements in efficiency or productivity, and contain performance indicators. The elements are set out in Box 10.1.

The emphasis on efficiency and effectiveness varies according to how difficult it is to measure these things. In the case of education, standards, measured by items such as class sizes, and achievements, measured by test scores and examination results, are both included in the PSA, as shown in Box 10.2. The targets include outcomes of the New Deal approach to job placement by the DfEE.

Box 10.1   Elements of Public Service Agreements

- an introduction, setting out the Minister or Ministers accountable for delivering the commitments, together with the coverage of the PSA, as some cover other departments and agencies for which the relevant Secretary of State is accountable;
- the aims and objectives of the department or cross-cutting area;
- the resources which have been allocated to it in the CSR;
- key performance targets for the delivery of its services, together with, in some cases, a list of key policy initiatives to be delivered;
- a statement about how the department will increase the productivity of its operations.

Source: Public Service Agreements 1999–2002

Box 10.2   Public Service Agreement, Department for Education and Employment

(i)   an increase in the coverage of nursery places for 3-year-olds from 34% to 66% by 2002, focusing on the most deprived areas of the country;

(ii)   the number of pupils aged 5, 6 or 7 in infant classes of over 30 to fall from 477,000 to zero by September 2001 at the latest;

(iii)   an increase in the proportion of those aged 11 meeting the standard of literacy for that age (level 4 in the Key Stage 2 (KS2) test) from 63% to 80% by 2002;

(iv)   an increase in the proportion of those aged 11 meeting the standard of numeracy for that age (level 4 in the KS2 test) from 62% to 75% by 2002;

(v)   a reduction by one third in school truancies (from 0.7% to 0.5% half days missed a year through unauthorized absence) and exclusions (from 12,500 to 8,400 permanent exclusions a year) by 2002;

(vi)   an increase in the proportion of those aged 16 who achieve one or more General Certificates of Secondary Education (GCSEs) at grade G, or equivalent, from 92% to 95% by 2002;

(vii)   an increase in the proportion of those aged 16 who achieve five or more GCSEs grades A*–C from 45% to 50% by 2002;

(viii)   an increase in the proportion of those aged 19 to have achieved National Vocational Qualification (NVQ) Level 2 or equivalent from 72% to 85% by 2002;

(ix)   by May 2002, to get 250,000 under 25-year-olds off benefit and into work by using money from the windfall tax (shared with HM Treasury target (xvi));

(x)   targets for the New Deals in 1999–2000, published each April, including the New Deals for lone parents and disabled people for which DfEE and DSS are jointly responsible, the figure to be updated annually for each succeeding financial year; (1998–99 target for New Deal for 18–24s placings was 100,000);

(xi)   a target for placing unemployed people into work in 1999–2000, published each April, including within it individual targets for the number of JSA claimants unemployed for more than six months placed into work and those with disabilities, the figure to be updated annually for each succeeding financial year (1998–99 targets included unemployed placings 1,300,000; long-term unemployed (6 months or more) placings 250,000; people with disabilities placings 80,000).

The Best Value arrangements for local authorities and other parts of the public sector such as the police have a similar range of indicators. The outcomes are related to the overall purposes of the organization and there are also indicators of outputs or service standards. Box 10.3 shows some of the Best Value performance indicators for the criminal justice system.

While the PSA and Best Value targets are subject to influence by variables outside any department's direct control, such as the state of the labour market or the effect of changing levels of unemployment on crime, they do focus on the purpose of the various parts of the public sector and provide tangible measures of improvement. Not all the changes in outcomes, positive or negative, will be attributable to the organizations' success, but the indicators at least make clear to managers and workers what the targets are.

Performance management and policy evaluation

Once it has been decided that a set of outcomes is the objective of the organization, the next question is how their achievement is to be measured. There are two approaches to this. One is to search for some global indicator, such as the quality of life changes as a result of a service, such as a health intervention, or an environmental improvement. Employment policy may be measured by the level of unemployment in an area. This is essentially a top-down approach in which the change in the state of a person or a population is defined by the organization and then measured.

The other approach is to start with the individual service encounter and start a discussion between the service provider and the service user about what outcomes they expect from the service. A good example of this has been the health authority in east London which developed outcome measures for the treatment of leg ulcers by asking nurses and patients what results they expected from treatment. Or the employment service can measure the numbers of people with whom it deals who find employment, rather than measuring the level of unemployment in its area.

Once the problems of defining the desired outcomes have been solved, there is then a third question: the organization needs to evaluate how best to achieve those outcomes. Here the distinction between policy and management is not clear. Politicians may decide on the services to be provided, such as sentencing policy on criminal justice, that education should take place in particular sorts of institution, or that health treatment should take a particular form. After those decisions have been made, managers implement them. However, the policies themselves may have as big an impact on the outcome as the way in which the service is managed. Even the best-managed workhouses probably had negative effects on their residents.

This aspect of performance management is the process of policy evaluation. This might involve scientific studies of the impact of medical interventions, teaching methods, or treatment of people convicted of crimes. It also involves dealing with the opinions of politicians about what works and what

Box 10.3   Best Value performance indicators, crime

STRATEGIC OBJECTIVE

Level of crime (using British Crime Survey)

Fear of crime (using British Crime Survey)

Feelings of public safety (using British Crime Survey)

Public confidence in the criminal justice system or its component parts (using British Crime Survey).

SERVICE DELIVERY OUTCOME

Total recorded crimes per 1000 population and percentage detected

Domestic burglaries per 1000 households and percentage detected

Violent crimes per 1000 population and percentage detected

Vehicle crimes per 1000 population and percentage detected

Number of offenders dealt with for supply offences in respect of Class A drugs per 10,000 population

Number of public disorder incidents per 1000 population

Percentage of all full files and percentage of full youth files provided to the Crown Prosecution Service both within pre-trial issue time guidelines and which are fully satisfactory or sufficient to proceed; percentage of all expedited/remand files and percentage of expedited/remand youth files which are fully satisfactory or sufficient to proceed

Number of road traffic collisions involving death or serious injury per 1000 population.

QUALITY

Percentage of responses to incidents requiring immediate response within local target response times (appropriate to rural/urban areas)

Percentage of 999 calls answered within local target response time

Percentage of persons arrested for notifiable offences who were charged/reported for summons or cautioned

Percentage of persons arrested referred to drug treatment programmes as a result of arrest referral schemes.

FAIR ACCESS

Number of Police and Criminal Evidence Act (PACE) stop/searches of white persons per 1000 population and percentage leading to arrest

Number of Police and Criminal Evidence Act (PACE) stop/searches of minority ethnic persons per 1000 population and percentage leading to arrest

Number of substantiated complaints under Police Act 1996 by detainees per 10,000 people detained

Percentage of reported racist incidents where further investigative action is taken and percentage of recorded racially aggravated crimes detected

Percentage of reported domestic violence incidents where there was a power of arrest, in which an arrest was made relating to the incident

Percentage of victims of reported domestic violence incidents that were victims of a reported domestic violence incident in the previous twelve months

Percentage of domestic burglaries where the property had been burgled in the previous twelve months.

does not work. It may be politically attractive to favour harsh treatment in prisons even if criminologists can show that rehabilitation produces lower recidivism rates. Mixed ability teaching may be shown to produce better overall educational outcomes but some politicians believe in streaming. Low public transport fares may reduce road congestion and improve passenger movement, but politicians may prefer balanced budgets for transport operators.

Evaluation has two aspects. One is to find out what works best in producing the desired outcomes: this may indeed be technocratic. Although professionals may continue to claim that only they know what works, because only they have the training and experience to make judgements, empirical scientific methods can produce results which allow people other than professionals to use their own judgement about policy choices. Such science is normal in the medical professions, where blind testing of drugs and treatments gives a good idea about the effectiveness of different approaches to diseases. In other services, such an approach may be less appropriate if the outcomes are less measurable, although if outcomes are definable, it ought always to be possible to see whether they have been achieved. Indeed, it could be argued that if outcomes cannot be identified, the service has no purpose and should not be provided.

The second aspect is the preferences which service users have for different services. For example, police forces claim that deploying their resources into 'rapid response' units with cars produces higher rates of crime detection and solving than using foot patrols. Surveys have shown, however, that visible police have the effect of reassuring people about their safety. The same is true for certain aspects of school education: parents have preferences for styles of discipline, uniforms and teaching methods which are not scientifically based judgements.

The Labour government's pragmatism to some extent promoted the idea of policy evaluation. The idea that ideology or populism should not distract services from 'what works' was widely promulgated. 'Evidence-based' practice was to be preferred to prejudice. The nature of the evidence on which practice was to be based was contested. The government's view was that evidence was represented by a national view of all evidence, rather than local experience, and that 'what works' should be defined from above and handed down. National service frameworks for treatment in the NHS are an example, as are the guidelines for probation services. Centralized interpretation of policy analysis became another way of controlling the organizations delivering services.

Customer satisfaction

Once these measurement issues have been resolved, there is a situation in which services of a certain kind are allocated, within a budget, to a set of service users. There remains another aspect of service delivery which managers need to address: given the resources allocated, are people satisfied with their contact with the people delivering the service? We saw in the previous chapter that the service experience is hard to control and measure but efforts are made to find out how people feel about their experiences. The Benefits Agency, for example, surveys not only how satisfied its customers are but also what is important to them and the criteria by which they judge the service: the degree of privacy, the speed of service, the courtesy of staff. These surveys of satisfaction are helpful for managers and workers to find out what is important to people and how well they are doing their job. No surveys are done of how satisfied claimants are with the amount of money they are entitled to. The surveys are of customers, in their role as service recipients, not their role as claimants of their entitlements as citizens.

Surveys of service users became more systematic and more centrally directed under the Labour government. Sample sizes and methodology were included in central guidance and surveys were written into the various performance management arrangements.

Equity

A special consideration in public services is the extent to which services are allocated equitably. In markets the idea of equity does not apply. Indeed, products and services are designed to attract different sorts of people. Profit maximization means that people have to be persuaded to pay as much as possible, which implies price discrimination, market segmentation and other methods which are opposite to the principle of equity. The problem for managers in the public sector is that they may have both a requirement to achieve profitability and a requirement to make services accessible equitably. For example, NHS Trusts have to break even. If they can offer higher-priced services to private patients in private beds with faster access and a higher quality of hotel services, they can make more money but discriminate in favour of people with private health insurance.

Flexibility

One advantage of public services is that they offer the possibility of a flexible response to events such as emergencies or disasters. For example, the building and works department of Glasgow City Council used to be able to respond to floods and severe weather, helping and rescuing people. While it may not have been the most efficient building organization, it was at least a group of people who could be called out in such circumstances. Such flexibility is difficult to measure and may not be called on for long periods. It is therefore difficult to contract for and specify if a contractor were to be required to do this sort of work.

Flexibility may also require spare capacity. For example, if all school places are full, pupils will not have the option of changing schools. If all places in children's homes are full at any time, people concerned with child protection

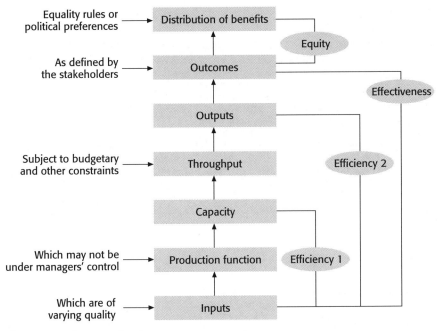

Figure 10.1   Elements of performance measurement

will have that option closed until a place becomes available. This aspect of flexibility is in contradiction with the requirement for efficiency and full use of capacity.

Managerial discretion

Performance information is used for two main purposes: to judge the effectiveness of policy and the performance of organizations and their managers. Managers may also use measurement to judge and improve their own performance. The degree to which measures are able to offer a judgement of managerial performance is partly determined by the degree of discretion which managers have. Figure 10.1 represents a simple flow from inputs to outcomes. The ratio between inputs and outcomes or results is a measurement of a mixture of policy effectiveness and managerial performance. If the choice of outputs to achieve the outcomes is made by either politicians or professionals, then managers can be judged only on the efficiency with which they produce the outputs. If managers have little discretion in the choice and arrangement of inputs, any judgement on their performance is in practice a judgement of how well they manage a given set of people and equipment.

For example, let us consider what is being judged in a league table of school examination results. If a headteacher has no control over which teachers

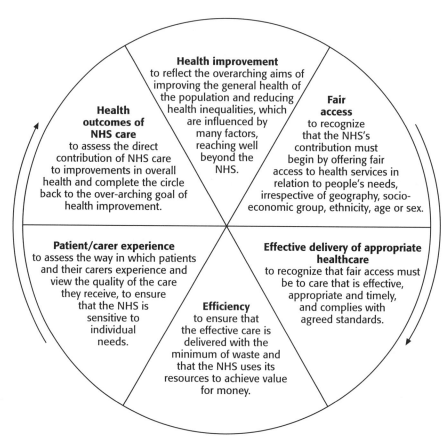

Figure 10.2 The NHS performance assessment framework
Source: Department of Health, NHS Performance Indicators, 2000

are hired, what equipment is purchased and how the school buildings are built and maintained, his or her discretion is limited to the organization of the school and the motivation and skills of the staff. As personnel policy and budgets are delegated to schools, more discretion is given to headteachers and governors about the uses to which the budget is put, and the results achieved are more subject to their efforts.

Satisfactory performance management requires a balance between all of these elements. Organizations that concentrate on a narrow range of targets, especially efficiency targets, are likely to look away from important elements of their work, such as the nature of their relationships with their service users. The NHS performance assessment framework is a good example of a balance between many different types of indicator, including efficiency, outcomes and the patient and carer experience of the service. The framework is shown in Figure 10.2.

> **Box 10.4** Performance targets can change behaviour
>
> Since 1992 the government has produced league tables of schools' performance. One indicator which receives a lot of publicity is the proportion of pupils who receive a grade C or above in five subjects in the GCSE examination. As the *Financial Times* reported (21.11.95):
>
> > Schools have registered a sharp improvement on the 'five Cs' yardstick since the first government tables appeared in 1992, improving from 38.3 per cent then to 43.5 per cent this year... Meanwhile the numbers failing to pass at any grade are rising... Some councils ask teachers to give extra attention to children on the C–D borderline, a practice which seems inevitable while the government continues to express its rankings as a series of thresholds.

Uses of performance information

Performance indicators are now in use throughout the public sector. They are put to different uses by different people. Politicians can pick a crude local authority performance indicator and use it to berate members of another party. Governments can use indicators to show that things are getting better. Oppositions can use them to show that things are getting worse. None of this is useful to managers, although they are involved in the processes.

Performance indicators can have two managerial uses: they can be part of a control system which in some way punishes bad performance and rewards good; or they can be part of a process of finding out better ways of managing. The Labour government used the idea of 'beacons' to promote good practice. A 'beacon' could be a police force, local authority, college or some other institution that scored well on its performance indicators and was given publicity to encourage others to perform as well.

League tables

There are many cases of the publication of comparative performance information. Schools and education authorities have their examination results made public each year (see Box 10.4). The local authority indicators are available to the public. The NHS has produced the health service indicators since 1983. Universities are judged and ranked on the quality of their research and teaching.

The publication of these tables can have two effects. Managers may make efforts to achieve the targets contained in the league tables, to the detriment of other aspects of performance. In practice, there are trade-offs between elements of performance. For example, the Benefits Agency has targets for both the speed and the accuracy with which benefits are paid. Accuracy can take more time. Universities teach and do research. Since resource allocation has been based in part on research output, some universities have recruited staff with a high volume of research output and not asked them to engage in much teaching: results in the research assessment exercise are improved, with a negative effect on the quality of teaching for students.

The second effect is that managers may try to find out how they can improve their performance by looking at how people above them in the tables work. One way of organizing this is through 'benchmarking', the systematic comparison with the best performer in a group. Benchmarking was first used by companies faced with competitors who could achieve much lower costs than themselves. It consists of comparing elements of the production process against a 'benchmark' performer. The benchmark may not necessarily be in the same industry. Benchmarking has grown in the public sector, both internally and using private sector benchmarks.

There is a national benchmarking project, based on the 'business excellence model' of the European Quality Foundation. Public sector organizations can check their performance on a range of criteria against each other and against those private sector organizations that have also signed up to the scheme.

Performance management and organizational culture

At the beginning of this chapter it was suggested that performance measurement can be used to punish or to learn. Which approach is chosen depends on the overall management culture of the organizations involved. We will see in the next chapter that there are two extremes of organizational culture, from extreme control to an approach which emphasizes trust and autonomy. In rigid-control cultures, performance management is achieved through fear of failure on the one hand, and some incentives to do better on the other. In a culture in which people are expected to take initiative and control their own work, performance measurement can be one way in which people learn from others about how to manage.

There is a danger in a rigid culture that 'what gets measured gets done', as Likierman[6] expressed it. This is especially possible when the results of the performance measurement process determine individual or organizational reward. An example is the performance target of answering the telephone after three rings, a 'customer service' performance measure. As an indicator of an organization's responsiveness, the time taken to answer the telephone may be reasonable. Once it is made into a target, all that happens may be that the telephone is picked up and the caller asked to wait. Computer-controlled telephone systems will record a fast response time. Such items as speed of telephone and letter answering are now included in the national standards for central government organizations.

Conclusions

A lot of progress has been made in the development of performance management and measurement. There are still some problems caused by the fact that performance measurement is used for many different purposes. Measures which are appropriate for external accountability may not be the right ones for improving management. Measures which are used to expose poor performers publicly may not be the best ones for helping management to bring about improvements. In any case managers will necessarily become defensive if the systems are used to punish the weak.

Performance measurement and the use of performance indicators are at the heart of the managerial mode of control, especially in the hierarchical form represented by 'management by objectives'. The Labour government's enthusiasm for performance targets both in its 1997 election manifesto and in its management of the public sector shows its belief in this form of control.

If performance measurement is to improve performance, all the relevant measures must be made, not just those that are easy to count. Managers and workers must be consulted about which measures are true reflections of their success; users of services must also be involved in choosing relevant criteria, and managers should only be held to account for those elements over which they have some control. This is quite a list of conditions for performance management to work, and they can be fulfilled only if all those involved in the process are committed to learning and improvement, rather than blame.

Further reading

Day, P. and Klein, R. (1987) *Accountabilities: Five Public Services*. London: Tavistock. An analysis of the historical development of the idea of accountability and an empirical study of accountability in practice in the NHS, police, water (pre-privatization), education and social services.

Jackson, P. (ed.) (1995) *Reader: Measures of Success in the Public Sector*. London: Public Finance Foundation. A collection of articles on performance measurement and management from *Public Money and Management*. Includes articles on particular sectors, such as local government, education and social services.

Notes and references

[1] Day, P. and Klein, R. (1987) *Accountabilities: Five Public Services*. London: Tavistock.
[2] *Ibid.*, p.239.
[3] Barzelay, M. (1992) *Breaking Through Bureaucracy: A New Vision for Managing in Government*. Berkeley: University of California Press.

4 *Ibid.*, p.120.

5 Jackson, P. M. (1995) Reflections on performance measurement in public service organisations, in Jackson, P. M. (ed.) *Measures of Success in the Public Sector*. London: Public Finance Foundation, 4.

6 Likierman, A. (1993) Performance indicators: 20 early lessons from managerial use. *Public Money And Management*, 6 (1).

11

MANAGING PEOPLE

Introduction

The performance of public sector organizations and the development of user-oriented services depend on two other elements: the skills, effort and motivation of the people who work in them and the organizational arrangements to enable them to do their jobs well. In both areas there have been developments in recent years, some of which may enhance performance and some of which seem likely to make it worse. In practice, the two sets of issues are related: if organizations are structured in a hierarchical way and management operates through instructions and discipline, the style of personnel management is likely to be consistent with that. On the other hand, if there are non-hierarchical structures and work is co-ordinated by mutual agreement between equals, this also has implications for the way in which people are recruited, rewarded, developed and promoted.

This chapter looks at how people are controlled, managed and paid in the public sector. It argues that while much has been written about how employees are managed, most of the theories are in practice about two approaches: one in which managers design how work is to be done and organize the management and supervision process to make sure that the workers follow instructions; another in which workers are given a task to do and they work out the best way to do it. The choice of approach is influenced by the nature of the task, the sort of people doing the work, the power relations in the organizations and the preferences of politicians and managers. Some politicians and managers believe that the only way to manage is to be 'tough', by which they mean telling people what to do in a loud and aggressive manner and sacking them when they fail to perform. Sometimes, the toughness is a moral position: no sector should be exempt from the pain experienced by those in sectors where competition is strong.

The chapter goes on to look at changes in employment conditions and pay. It describes how pay bargaining has been devolved to localities and organizations in the Civil Service and the NHS but that in local government a period of local bargaining has been succeeded by renewed efforts to arrive at national agreements, because of the variation in pay which resulted from local bargaining. It also shows that there has been a tendency towards less permanent employment contracts, a move which has been to the benefit of senior managers and to the detriment of the low-paid. In general, the effect of recent changes which have been made to the way people are paid has been to increase the distance between the treatment of those at the top and those at the bottom of the pay hierarchy.

Approaches to managing people: control systems and employment relationships

There have been a few fundamental issues which reappear frequently in the literature on managing people. The first is the extent to which work is divided into small tasks and therefore the breadth of individuals' jobs. Adam Smith observed in 1776 that the division of labour seems to improve productivity:

> This great increase in the quantity of work, which, in consequence of the division of labour, the same number of people are capable of performing, is owing to three different circumstances; first to the increase of dexterity in every particular workman; secondly, to the saving of the time which is commonly lost in passing from one species of work to another; and lastly, to the invention of a great number of machines which facilitate and abridge labour and enable one man to do the work of many.[1]

The whole of the 'scientific management' school of thought was devoted to this proposition. The problem of management was how to arrange the division of labour in such a way as to get the best possible productivity. Mechanization of the individual tasks and a scheme of discipline and reward to make sure that people worked hard were the major functions of management.

The main alternative to this approach is also very old. The Luddite opposition to the factory system, which developed at the beginning of the nineteenth century, was a protest against the impact of mechanization on the independence of artisan producers and their subjugation as hired workers.[2] This is one of the fundamental distinctions in management: whether managers should organize the work in a 'scientific' way, and control the way the workers work, or whether the production process should be organized by the people carrying out the work, possibly supported by technical and organizational expertise. An idea underlying the 'scientific' approach is that the workers themselves should not design the way in which work is done: the design of work should be kept separate and done by different people, the managers.

Weber[3] defined a set of characteristics of a bureaucracy, in which the management arrangements were based on law and rules, including a division of labour, the principle of hierarchy, appointment according to qualifications and a system of discipline and control. Bureaucracy was seen to be an efficient and a fair way of designing and managing organizations. Compared with nepotism and corruption, bureaucracy offered significant benefits.

McGregor[4] called the two approaches 'Theory X and Theory Y', the former being the approach to management based on the assumption that workers do not want to work and therefore have to be controlled, the latter based on the assumption that people are self-motivated and get satisfaction from work. Numerous other people have written about similar distinctions. Ouchi and Johnson[5] defined ideal types 'A' and 'Z' in which 'A'-type organizations have specialized jobs and careers and detailed evaluation, while type 'Z' have non-specialized careers and a holistic concern for people.

These alternatives can be applied to the management of public sector organizations. One approach is to organize the work by managers designing the tasks in a way that individual workers carry out their part of the work according to a set of detailed instructions, often set out in manuals of procedures which have to be learned. Supervision consists of making sure that they conform to the instructions. The opposite approach is that people are expected to understand what is to be achieved, are given the resources and support to get on with the job and organize themselves, either individually or in groups. Devolved management, in which units have autonomy over their use of resources, normally involves some operational freedom about how to manage, subject to strict targets and performance measurement. The emphasis of the bureaucratic way of controlling is more on the rules, procedures and hierarchy. Controlling by managerial methods emphasizes the achievement of results with varying degrees of freedom to decide how to achieve them.

As well as these two types of control mechanism, the second issue is the choice to be made about the nature of the employment relationship with the organization. At one extreme, people are employed for life, subject to satisfactory behaviour. They enter at an early age and make a career by progressing by qualifications and/or seniority. Their terms and conditions are negotiated collectively and are the same for all employees. Pay is based on grade and is known to everyone. An alternative is that each employee has an individual contract for a specific job. Entry may be at any point in the organization and is based on entrants having the skills and experience relevant to a job. Pay is based on individual negotiation and on market conditions for people with that particular skill.

Control systems

What determines the choice of control system? One factor is the nature of the task to be performed. There are some routine tasks which lend themselves to the division of labour and mechanization. There are sections in the Benefits Agency offices which have many of the characteristics of a factory system. People processing child benefit applications, for example, sit in groups, under the direct supervision of a slightly more senior person, dealing in a routine way with files of forms which are delivered to their desks on a trolley and then removed to be delivered to the next part of the process. Other jobs are less like that. Although there is some specialization in schools, teachers do not have their work divided into very small segments as on a production line.

The second factor is the power relationships which exist within the organization. A workforce which is in a strong position because of its trade union strength or its profession is able to organize work in a way which suits itself rather than which suits management. Managers who try to change work processes learn how strong the workforce is.

A third element is politics. We saw in Chapter 2 that management style and approach is itself a matter for political preference. For some on the Left, the organization of work in self-managing groups is preferred to hierarchy. On the Right, there are those who believe that public servants should be directly supervised and subject to a disciplined regime. More fundamentally, the ideology which expresses itself in the public choice literature suggests that public servants are motivated only by self-interest and therefore need to be controlled if they are to act in the public interest. Hence the preferred way of managing people is itself a philosophical problem about human motivation as much as a technical problem about which methods produce results.

A fourth determinant is management's preferred style. Some managers are only happy if they can issue orders and expect them to be obeyed. Others prefer a consultative or consensual approach. Preferences are not independent of the task. Senior fire-fighters, for example, may be happy with a participative style of management but cannot operate with it at a fire-ground, where orders have to be given and obeyed. Conversely, headteachers may like to be authoritarian but cannot be in every classroom supervising teachers directly. Managers' preferences are really a result of a combination of their own previous experience and training and the nature of the task. But there is no doubt that certain types of managerial style find political favour and are good for people's careers. A manager who can be authoritarian, take little account of people's feelings and adopt a 'tough' tone will certainly be popular with politicians who believe that public servants are workshy and self-seeking. Conversely, managers who are used to working through consensus building and consultation, a method many social work managers prefer, will be less popular with such politicians.

Another factor is the nature of the workforce. If the workers are relatively untrained and only stay in their jobs for a short while, it is less likely that they will work well with a high degree of discretion. If the task has to be constantly reinvented by new recruits, it is likely to be reinvented badly. An example of a low-discretion operation is the call centre. Here the staff are relatively poorly paid, typically earning £11,000 to £14,000, they have to learn routines for their conversations with callers and their performance is measured by the machines they use and tightly supervised. Turnover of staff in UK call centres is 20%.[6]

The other important aspect of the workforce is the degree to which they belong to a profession which governs itself. People such as doctors, lawyers, engineers and accountants have working practices which are governed by their training and codes of conduct, whatever organization they work in. Management regimes which attempt to contradict those working practices are faced with resistance. Some of the reforms are designed exactly to change the supervision regime for professionals, introducing 'management' as a substitute for professional self-regulation.

Finally there are equity considerations: if a service has to be provided in the same way and with the same eligibility criteria in all locations, discretion must be minimized. Lower discretion means more routine and codification of procedures in manuals. This tension, between discretion and uniformity, has been felt especially in the social security service. When the Benefits Agency was first established, for example, there was an attempt to increase managerial and worker discretion, to make the service more sensitive to the customers' requirements. 'A bias for action' was promoted as one of the valued behaviours in the organization. Many managers took this seriously and took local initiatives to improve service delivery in their areas. These actions soon came into conflict with the national targets for speed and accuracy. While local managers might be responding to local needs, which may not have had speed and accuracy as a top priority, their contribution to the achievement of the Secretary of State's targets was held to be most important.

Employment relationships

What determines the employment relationship? In some countries, the employment of public servants is governed by laws which define the tenure of positions and the rights of employees. In the United Kingdom, employment practices in the public sector are covered by general employment law and it is possible for managers and politicians to change or attempt to change them without legal constraint. Because of this, employment practices are subject to negotiations whose outcomes depend on the relative strengths of the parties. Bargaining takes place about wage and salary levels and about all aspects of the employment contract. In recent years, teachers, doctors, dentists, civil servants and nurses have all gone through changes in their employment conditions and contracts.

While each of these changes was different, a common theme runs through the changes in conditions: the employment contracts are more explicit about what the workers have to do to earn their money, and where possible, volumes of work are defined, either expressed as hours worked or work done. In other words, the employment contract is no longer a contract to 'occupy a position', with the work content of that position settled by the organization as a whole or the profession. Work content and volume are increasingly part of the employment contract.

Table 11.1 Average earnings, Great Britain, 1995 = 100

Index at July	Whole economy	Private sector	Public sector
1996	103.7	103.8	103.1
1997	108.0	108.7	105.0
1998	114.1	115.3	109.0
1999	119.3	120.7	113.6
2000	123.9	125.5	117.5

Source: HMSO (2000) *Economic Trends*, 565, Table 4.6

Pay

Level

Trinder[7] showed that public sector pay increases were lower than private pay increases between 1982 and 1990, caught up somewhat between 1991 and 1993 and lagged behind after that. Table 11.1 shows the different rates of change of pay in the private and public sectors from 1996 to 2000. It shows that between 1997 and 2000 public sector pay rose by 12%, while private sector pay rose by over 15%.

One of the results of the process of competitive tendering has been that at the very bottom end of the pay scales, cleaners, messengers and other relatively unskilled workers have been transferred to the private sector. Some local authorities had what was known as a 'low-pay policy', designed to protect low-paid workers from low wages. Such policies are not possible under a regime of competitive tendering. The low-paid were also affected by the abolition of the wages councils in 1993, and the Trade Union Reform and Employment Rights Act 1993. The wages councils had existed since 1909 and were designed to protect the worst-paid workers from low pay. The Labour government's introduction of the minimum wage offered a substitute for this protection.

Performance-related

If public servants are motivated by self-interest then it is obvious that they can be managed through performance-related pay (PRP). The government promoted performance-related pay through the Citizen's Charter, among other initiatives:

> The Citizen's Charter contains a firm commitment to establishing a regular and direct link between a public servant's contribution to establishing the quality of service actually delivered and his or her reward. Performance-related pay is an important element in the more results-oriented culture that is being developed in our public services.[8]

Elements of PRP have been introduced for all civil servants, for managers in the NHS, for teachers and in the upper grades in local authorities. So far there has been no general evaluation of the effectiveness of the introduction of PRP, although an early study of the Inland Revenue[9] found that it had some impact. Other studies[10] have shown that PRP can have some impact on performance but mainly through the process of improving understanding of what is expected from a worker and which elements of performance are important.

Whether or not PRP improves organizational performance, it does have other effects. First, it emphasizes individual contribution rather than team or group effort. While team-based PRP is used in other sectors it has not been widely used in the public sector. The emphasis on the individual has implications for management style and working style, promoting individual rather than collaborative work. Second, it potentially reduces the total pay bill. We have seen that pay rises are financed in part by improvements in productivity and that progression up scales has been made less normal. PRP allows a direct link to be made between productivity and the total pay bill. It may be seen as a way of keeping pay down overall as much as a way of promoting performance.

The Labour government favoured performance-related pay. It introduced a scheme of performance management and performance pay for teachers from September 2000. The scheme was designed to do two things, provide a higher level of pay for teachers who stay on the main grade and encourage a standard level of performance, known as a 'threshold'. The performance criteria are set out in Box 11.1.

Teachers and their unions were not in favour of the scheme. A survey by David Marsden[11] showed that teachers did not believe in performance pay in principle. When asked whether they agreed that 'The principle of relating teachers' pay to performance is a good one', 63% disagreed, 12% were neutral and 24% agreed. The introduction of performance pay in the education sector came as the enthusiasm waned for individual performance pay in the rest of the public services. An Incomes Data Services report[12] on pay rises in 2000 found that the emphasis had shifted towards salary progression and less priority was given to performance rises. It also found that many organizations were looking for ways of paying team bonuses rather than individual ones.

Pay determination: decentralized bargaining

The Major governments' policy on public sector pay was to use the overall level of public spending as a control on the size of the pay bill. From the 1993 Budget the intention was to freeze the public sector pay bill. Increases in pay levels had to be financed by increases in productivity and reduction in staff numbers. In 1996, the Prime Minister reconfirmed his policy, stating that public sector pay was expected to rise by 4% but 'increases should be offset by efficiencies and other economies to help deliver improved efficiency from the public sector'. The Labour government initially maintained the pay freeze, in line with its policy of continuing with previous spending plans, but by

> **Box 11.1   Threshold standards for teachers**
>
> **Knowledge and understanding**: Teachers should demonstrate that they have a thorough and up-to-date knowledge of the teaching of their subject(s) and take account of wider curriculum developments which are relevant to their work.
>
> **Teaching and assessment**: Teachers should demonstrate that they consistently and effectively:
>
> - plan lessons and sequences of lessons to meet pupils' individual learning needs
> - use a range of appropriate strategies for teaching and classroom management
> - use information about prior attainment to set well-grounded expectations for pupils and monitor progress to give clear and constructive feedback.
>
> **Pupil progress**: Teachers should demonstrate that, as a result of their teaching, their pupils achieve well relative to the pupils' prior attainment, making progress as good as or better than similar pupils nationally. This should be shown in marks or grades in any relevant national tests or examinations, or school-based assessment for pupils where national tests and examinations are not taken.
>
> **Wider professional effectiveness**: Teachers should demonstrate that they:
>
> - take responsibility for their professional development and use the outcomes to improve their teaching and pupils' learning
> - make an active contribution to the policies and aspirations of the school.
>
> **Professional characteristics**: Teachers should demonstrate that they are effective professionals who challenge and support all pupils to do their best through:
>
> - inspiring trust and confidence
> - building team commitment
> - engaging and motivating pupils
> - analytical thinking
> - positive action to improve the quality of pupils' learning.

2001 the Treasury had relaxed its controls slightly. Pay rises in 2001 ran at about 3.7%, or 1% higher than the rate of inflation, although budgets were still set after making allowance for a percentage 'efficiency saving'.

Within the overall financial constraint, pay is either determined by a pay review body, for nurses, doctors and teachers; by an indexing formula (police and fire services); or is subject to bargaining whether at national or local level. Since April 1996, Civil Service pay determination has been devolved to departments and agencies, an arrangement which brought to an end the national pay agreement for civil servants. In the NHS there are both national and local agreements: the national bargain sets a minimum pay rise and additions are determined locally.

In local government there are national changes in rates but a great deal of local discretion about what grades people should be on for particular jobs. The variation in pay reflects difficulties in recruiting for particular occupations in different parts of the country at different times. Once pay for a group is increased, however, it is rarely reduced again when the shortage is over. At the end of the 1990s many local authorities were developing harmonized conditions for all their employees, out of a belief in equity of treatment and as a way of attracting and retaining staff.

The rationale for local bargaining is that pay rates should reflect local labour market conditions. It is expected that pay will be lower in areas of high unemployment or in skills for which there is an excess of supply. The evidence suggests that local bargaining does not always finely tune the rates of pay to local conditions. In local government, for example, the Audit Commission[13] found: 'There is a variation of up to 50 per cent in the pay rates for similar staff groups. This is true even of authorities which are geographically close, which operate in similar labour markets, and which use consultants to help them design their pay structures' (p.24). Partly in response to these wide variations, the Local Government Management Board and the local authority trade unions signed an agreement in 1994 to return to national bargaining from April 1996, while recognizing that there will continue to be local variations on the national agreements.

In the NHS, trusts negotiate their pay locally, although within a national agreement. In 1995, a national two-year agreement was made whereby trusts which failed to meet the national pay rise in the first year would have to make up for it in the second. This agreement was a compromise between national and local bargaining. It seems to have the disadvantages of local bargaining, which still takes up a large amount of time without the flexibility implied by such an arrangement. Since then, national pay bargains have been made for the main groups of workers in the NHS.

Local bargaining also occurs in further education, where the college principals have formed an employers' organization but make local settlements in about 50% of colleges. By October 1995 the lecturers' union, the National Association of Teachers in Further and Higher Education, estimated that 47% of its members were on locally agreed contracts, 29% on personal contracts and 23% on national terms and conditions. Once an employer enters personal contracts with employees, it is difficult for the union to bargain on their behalf even at local level: by definition, collective bargaining involves a contract for a collection of employees. All the unions can do is offer individuals representation at the negotiation, an expensive process.

While the new contract was imposed on all new recruits, colleges had difficulties in imposing it on existing staff. A variety of tactics were used to persuade them to sign (Box 11.2), from pay freezes, refusal to promote people on the old contract and a £500 bonus for signing.

The growth of local bargaining has meant that many more managers and employee representatives are involved in the process of pay determination. In the early days, both sides lacked the skills and knowledge of employment law which were necessary to be able to carry out this work, and many negotiations resulted in a referral to ACAS. As well as managers needing skills, the unions in the public sector also had to adjust to the new bargaining regime. This

> **Box 11.2**   Local bargaining
>
> Comments by two further education college principals on local negotiation of the new contract with their staff:
>
> When they realise that they are not going to get a pay rise – ever – and that refusal to sign puts them at the top of the list for redundancy, they might think again.
>
> We have them by the toenails. If individuals think they might be better off not signing, and working fewer hours than their colleagues, I would urge them to think about their pensions since there will be no further pay rises.

Table 11.2   Determination of pay for non-managerial employees by sector

	% of employees	
	Private sector	Public sector
Multi-employer collective bargaining	5	35
Single employer collective bargaining	14	16
Workplace collective bargaining	9	3
Management at higher level	28	8
Management at workplace	37	3
Individual negotiation	2	0
Set by some other method	4	35

Source: Cully, M. *et al.* (1999) *Britain at Work: As Depicted by the 1998 Workplace Employee Relations Survey*. London: Routledge, Table 5.6, p.108

adjustment took place at a time when union membership was falling and the finances of the trade unions were poor. The result has been that public sector trade unions have merged to form stronger organizations to cope with the devolved bargaining process. The public sector has a less decentralized process of wage bargaining than the private sector, as illustrated by Table 11.2. Multi-employer collective bargaining still determines the pay for 35% of employees, and for only 3% of workers is pay determined by management at the workplace.

The difference in pay bargaining is reflected in the relatively high level of trade union recognition by public sector employers. In the private sector only 25% of workplaces recognize trade unions, while the figure for the public sector is 95%.

Pay and grading reviews

In the Civil Service there have been moves away from uniform pay schemes, agencies designing their own pay and grading schemes under detailed instruction from the Treasury. The purposes of these reviews are to make pay more aligned to the actual job, rather than a position on a pay scale, and to try to avoid a pay system which generates an automatic pay rise each year as people progress up incremental scales.

The Civil Service has also been subjected to a senior management review in every department. The objective of this was to reduce the number of civil servants in the core departments at a senior level. Cuts of about 25% of posts were made during 1996. The senior management reviews were carried out in a fairly arbitrary way, with a target staff reduction figure in mind. The Labour government was less interested in a cut in numbers for its own sake.

Pay review bodies provide an independent assessment of public sector pay awards. They were not always welcomed by the Conservative governments, which were sometimes unwilling to fund pay at the levels recommended. Labour took more notice, and even extended the process to pay in the Prison Service.

Conditions

Casualization: part-time and temporary work

Because of the expectation of cuts in spending and the continuing search for efficiency savings, managers are increasingly reluctant to hire permanent full-time workers. Even at the level of counter clerk or administrative assistant, civil servants are being employed on temporary contracts.[14] In places where there is competitive tendering, employment contracts are often offered only for the duration of the services contract: employers cannot guarantee to be successful in the next tendering round. Part-time working has increased as a proportion of total employment in the public sector. For women, part-time employment made up 45% of the jobs in 1985 and 51% in 1995, while for men the proportion rose from 4 to 7% over the period.[15] (Central Statistical Office 1996, p.15). In 1998 30% of jobs in the public sector were part-time, compared with 22% in the private sector.[16]

The use of fixed-term contracts is also more common in the public sector than in the private, as illustrated in Table 11.3. Other 'non-standard' employment practices have the same prevalence in the two sectors, other than home working, which is rare in the public sector.

While these effects are gradual, there being many people still employed on older-style contracts, there is an impact on the attitude of new recruits to the prospect of a public sector job: the old trade-off between the security offered by a public service job and the low probability of earning a very high salary has been broken. The security has been removed and at the top levels, such as chief executives of NHS Trusts or local authorities, salaries are comparable with those in the private sector.

Table 11.3 Subcontracting and use of non-standard labour, by sector

	% of workplaces	
	Private sector	Public sector
Subcontract one or more services	91	88
Temporary agency workers	29	26
Fixed-term contract employees	34	72
Freelance workers	16	7
Home workers	8	3
Zero-hour contract employees	6	2
None of these used	5	6

Source: Cully, M. *et al.* (1999) *Britain at Work: As Depicted by the 1998 Workplace Employee Relations Survey*. London: Routledge, Table 3.6, p.35

Classes of people and types of treatment

One impact of this process is that the difference between the top and the bottom of the earnings scale has grown. There is a trend towards senior managers in the public sector being recruited on short-term contracts. Chief officers and chief executives in local government, NHS Trust chief executives, executive agency chief executives and other senior managers in these organizations commonly have a three-year contract with a performance-related element of pay, sometimes 15% of the total pay. The theory is that a short-term contract is likely to make the management more effective. What happens in practice is that managers concentrate on short-term results, naturally choosing to achieve those results to which pay is attached. For their employers, the short-term contract is not necessarily an advantage: removal of the manager before the term of the contract is completed can involve substantial compensation payments.

As well as the short-term performance-related contracts, some pay and conditions schemes have been designed to compete with those in the private sector. One NHS Trust, for example, included in the conditions for its chief executive a car for his spouse as well as one for himself. At the other end of the scale, people on a series of short-term contracts with a variety of employers have no protection against redundancy and little compensation for the uncertain nature of their employment position.

The impact of competition and contracting

Competition has changed the relationships between employers and employees, especially in local government. The IRS survey of local authorities showed that compulsory competitive tendering had made trade unions more 'realistic', promoted local bargaining and resulted in 'a tendency for pay and other financial rewards such as sick pay, bonuses and allowances to be lowered'.[17]

Competition has affected women's pay and conditions especially. The jobs which have been tendered and lost to private companies are predominantly done by women: in cleaning, catering, NHS ancillary staff. While they are still done by women, the terms and conditions either with the winning companies or with the in-house employer have been lowered as a result of competition.

This tendency makes a contribution to the general trend towards more inequality in income distribution. The pay rates of the unskilled workers have stagnated, while those of skilled and professional workers have grown in real terms in recent years, partly because of increased competition from low-wage countries for the products of low-skilled workers. The public sector is no longer a place where low-skilled people can earn reasonable wages, because of the policy of employers to pursue efficiency through poor pay and conditions. Trinder has warned about the effects of this:

> ... there are special problems at the bottom of the pay range. Because of the effects of structural change and global competition in the traded goods sector, the demand for people with limited skills has fallen throughout Europe, irrespective of cyclical factors, and they have faced deteriorating pay prospects and growing unemployment ... The managers of services which are not subject to it [global competition] should take account of the social and financial consequences of adding to long-term unemployment ... Where they can and there is a clear need and demand for improved services, they should as far as possible put the emphasis on output-efficiency (better service from the same staff) rather than merely going down the cost-cutting input-efficiency route.[18]

While managers may heed this exhortation, it is really a matter for politicians. Compulsory competition under rules which do not allow protection of workers leaves managers with no choice. The only protection which workers have is the European Union rules, and this applies only in the short term.

Conclusions

We have seen that there have been fundamental changes to the ways in which people are managed in the public sector: the idea that a public service job provided stability of employment in a relatively easy environment no longer applies, if it ever did. Automatic progression through grades has been mainly replaced by progression as a result of appraisals sometimes accompanied by a performance-related pay scheme. National scales have been replaced by national guidelines and local bargaining. These changes have been the result of two beliefs: that people will work hard only if they have incentives to do so; that the market is the way to set pay, rather than national collective bargaining. This has taken place within a framework of an overall pay bill freeze. While the bargaining has been localized, the amount to bargain over is under Treasury control.

Such an approach to pay has mainly been accompanied by control systems which are based on set ways of doing tasks, rather than a high degree of discretion. Both are valid approaches to management as opposed to a pure bureaucracy, in which people occupy positions and follow rules. This chapter has shown that there is an emphasis on control over work processes, backed up by the inspection and audit regime we saw in Chapter 8.

Further reading

Kessler, S. and Bayliss, F. (1995) *Contemporary British Industrial Relations*, 2nd edn. Basingstoke: Macmillan. A description of the legal and institutional framework of industrial relations.

Corby, S. and White, G. (eds) (1999) *Employee Relations in the Public Services*. London: Routledge.

Incomes Data Services (2001) *Pay in the Public Services 2000/01*. London: IDS.

Notes and references

[1] Smith, A. (1776) *An Inquiry into the Wealth of Nations*. London: Straban (1976 edition, Oxford: Clarendon Press) Book 1, ch. 1.

[2] Thompson, E. P. (1963) *The Making of the English Working Class*. Harmondsworth: Penguin, ch. 14.

[3] Weber, M. (1947) *The Theory of Social and Economic Organization*. New York: Oxford University Press.

[4] McGregor, D. (1960) *The Human Side of Enterprise*. London: McGraw-Hill.

[5] Ouchi, W. G. and Johnson, J. B. (1978) Types of organizational control and their relationship to emotional well being. *Administrative Science Quarterly*, 23 (2).

[6] Incomes Data Services (2000) *Pay and Conditions in Call Centres*. London: IDS.

[7] Trinder, C. (1995) *Medium Term Strategy for Public Sector Pay*. London: Chartered Institute for Public Finance and Accountancy.

[8] HMSO (1994) *The Citizen's Charter: Second Report*, Cm 2540. London: HMSO, 117.

[9] Marsden, D. and Richardson, R. (1992) *Motivation and Performance Related Pay in the Public Sector: A Case Study of the Inland Revenue*. London: Centre for Economic Performance, London School of Economics.

[10] E.g. Torrington, D. (1995) Sweets to the sweet: performance related pay in Britain. Mimeo, Manchester School of Management, University of Manchester Institute of Science and Technology.

[11] Marsden, D. (2000) *Teachers before the threshold*, Centrepiece, Centre for Economic Performance, London School of Economics, May 2000.

[12] Incomes Data Services (February 2001) *Pay in the Public Services 2000/01*. London: IDS.

[13] Audit Commission (1995) *Paying the Piper: People and Pay Management in Local Government*. London: HMSO.

[14] The extent should not be exaggerated. In April 1995, 18,244 civil servants, from 516,893, were employed on casual contracts (see HMSO, 1995 *Civil Service Statistics*. London: HMSO.)

[15] Central Statistical Office (1996) *Economic Trends* No. 508. London: HMSO.

[16] Cully, M. *et al.* (1999) *Britain at Work: As Depicted by the 1998 Workplace Employee Relations Survey*. London: Routledge, Table 3.5, p.33.

[17] IRS (1995) *IRS Employment Trends* 594, October, p.8.

[18] Trinder, C. (1995) *Medium Term Strategy for Public Sector Pay*. London: Chartered Institute for Public Finance and Accountancy, 22.

12

MANAGING MONEY

Introduction

In this chapter we see how financial management has changed in line with other changes in management. The desire to get away from bureaucratic management concerned purely with rules and probity led to an emphasis on the efficiency with which public money was deployed. This has meant that budgets and financial controls were based on outputs and costs, not just on the money spent on inputs. Later an emphasis on management for results has led to the search for outcome measurement and for budgets based on results. The emphasis on collaboration and joint working has produced a need for joint budgets and collaborative financial management.

The chapter looks at the budgeting process at both national and local government levels. It shows that while the budget process is designed to allocate resources to priority areas, it is also a political process. At central government level, the Comprehensive Spending Review is used to challenge activities, services and methods of service delivery and financing.

The chapter then turns to financial control and describes recent changes to the control of capital and current spending, which have been rationalized at central government level to make choices between capital and current expenditure more sensible. It also shows the tendency to decentralize financial control. Despite all these efforts, spending can still get out of control and the chapter describes how this can happen.

Finally the chapter looks at a relatively recent innovation in financing, the Private Finance Initiative and Public–Private Partnerships. These are ways of combining public and private money, changing the way of accounting for capital spending and in principle transferring risk to the private sector.

Management and financial control

Changes in financial control follow the changes in the approaches to management identified in the Introduction to Part Two. There are ways of managing money that reflect both the bureaucratic and professional modes of control. Changes to financial management have occurred because of the attempts to change the overall methods of management control.

Under the classical bureaucratic way of working, financial control is exercised through rules and through hierarchy. Money is allocated to departments, sections and units in a hierarchical way, subdivided as it moves down the organization. At each level an individual is held accountable for certain items in the budget. The more significant the sums, the more likely it is that a senior official will be allocated the funds and be held accountable for them. So in a school, for example, run as part of a bureaucracy, the headteacher might be given the budget for heating costs and the purchase of teaching materials but the budget for staffing, by far the biggest item, is likely to be held at a higher level.

In the bureaucracy, budgets are made and managed line by line, under what is known as 'subjective headings', for each individual sort of expenditure, such as salaries, overtime, fuel, travel and so on. Once such items have been allocated, the manager needs to apply to a superior level in the hierarchy for permission to switch money from one category to another, a procedure known as virement. At the end of the year, officials will be held to account for the money they have spent and be required to show that it was spent on the items for which it has been allocated.

The drawbacks of such a system of financial management have been apparent for many years. Money is allocated to inputs by someone working at a level far removed from where operational control is exercised and is therefore likely to be allocated without the benefit of detailed knowledge of the best way of spending the available money. For this reason, budgets are likely to be backward- rather than forward-looking: budgets are based on last year's allocation and adjusted slightly in the light of last year's experience. Since the incentives are all designed to make people spend the money as allocated, this is what they will do, so experience is not captured to make a better allocation for next year. Money is allocated to buy inputs rather than to achieve results. The financial control mechanism is designed as if the purpose of the organization were to spend money and acquire inputs, rather than achieve results.

In organizations managed in the 'professional' mode of control, there is more trust of the professionals and a greater emphasis on areas of work rather than inputs. So a hospital run in a professional mode will have an allocation for each medical speciality, and the head of each speciality will decide how that money is to be used. Sometimes the bureaucratic and professional modes will both be present in the financial control system: allocations made to professional areas but also subdivided into subjective headings. This way of working gives more control over resources nearer the front end of the organization, but the emphasis is still on the allocation of cash and control, and accountability over how it is spent, rather than on what the money is expected to produce, defined as outputs or outcomes. Professionals have traditionally been reluctant to involve themselves in financial management.

The managerial mode of control tries to solve this problem through the financial system by allocating money to outputs, rather than inputs. For two decades managers and financial controllers have been defining outputs and trying to calculate unit costs. In the Civil Service the early attempts to do this were called the Financial Management Initiative and caused great pain to those used to operating hierarchical, input-based budgets. People were asked to define their jobs and accountabilities in new ways, measuring their efficiency in using resources to produce services rather than simply counting the resources consumed. There were some technical difficulties with this movement as well. One problem is that many services are produced by one set of people in one building. How much of the cost of an area office shared by housing, social services, environmental health and housing benefit should be allocated to the children's services? How much of an individual's cost should be allocated to each individual service? The answers to these questions may involve a very expensive exercise in measuring and allocating time and money to services.

The allocation of costs to individual items of service was not easy in a centralized bureaucracy: if a manager cannot move the operation to cheaper premises, can he/she be held to account for accommodation costs? If salary scales and numbers employed at each grade are set centrally, how can the local manager be held accountable for staffing costs? Similar questions apply to central purchasing of equipment and materials. If the local manager cannot control any of these items of expenditure, how does calculating unit costs help the individual to manage or help senior management to make a judgement about his or her skills and efficiency achievements?

The financial management system can only reflect the rest of the management system and structure. The move to a managerial mode in which people were held accountable for results at a relatively low level in the organization produced a wave of decentralization of financial management. Budgets were devolved to individual units, whether schools in the 'Local Management of Schools' initiative, local offices in the Employment and Social Security agencies, hospitals, police divisions, probation services, magistrates courts, and so on. The purpose of such a management approach was to achieve greater efficiency: the remote budget setting and control of the bureaucratic system was seen to be insensitive to the possibilities of efficiency improvements at local level. At the same time, devolved budgets gave the possibility of devolving accountability: individuals could be held to account not just for the money they had been allocated but also for the product and its unit cost.

This approach produced its own problems. First, managers had to be trained to run their own financial control systems and spend time on this aspect of their job. Oversight that was previously done by a few people at a high level now required many people at a low level. Schools needed bursars, hospitals needed many more financial administrators. Financial control and responsibility also brought with it the requirement to negotiate over pay and grading at a local level, again requiring managerial skills previously not needed.

There was also a problem of knowing what should be regarded as an efficient operation — how low should unit costs be? Calculating unit costs alone does not reveal the answer; they are only helpful if they can be compared with some standard. Unit cost calculation only helps management to manage if such comparisons are available and if they also have the power to change costs to match those of the better performers. In the early years of devolved financial management the temptation for senior management was simply to cut budgets, measure outputs and call for 'efficiency improvements' each year. Such improvements had to be made by the managers further down the line by 'improving productivity', and could be said to penalize good performers in the same way as poor performers. Such targets were still in place in the 1999 Spending Review, which set out a 3% per year value for money improvement in the NHS and a 2% efficiency target for the police, for example. In later years, league tables called for improvements to meet the levels of the best performers.

In one sense, management through the use of markets solves this problem of knowing what the desired cost should be: they can be set as prices in the market. In fact the market mode of control changes the emphasis of financial control from inputs to outputs and from target costs to market prices, assuming that there is a competitive market. If managers have to win the right to produce services through a competitive tendering process, then the main ratio they have to worry about is that between cost and revenue, or profitability. If a unit can keep its costs below its tender price, then managers at a higher level no longer need to monitor the details of costs or resources used. If the unit makes a loss it can be replaced, and the standard cost has been set automatically by the tender process. Unit managers need more frequent cost information than if they were simply managing within an expenditure budget, because their revenue depends on the production of the product or service and their profitability depends on keeping their costs below those revenues. Achieving that balance requires timely and accurate information as well as managerial skills. The financial systems designed to monitor expenditure under subjective headings and produce an annual report on spending were rarely smart enough to provide the information competitive managers needed. This caused tension between operational managers and the people providing financial information. It also caused extra work when the only solution was to keep a set of management accounts in parallel with the financial accounts.

The move to management by outcomes changes the requirements of financial management. While defining outputs and measuring their unit costs caused headaches for managers and cost accountants, defining outcomes takes people into even more painful situations. Budgeting for activities or programme areas assumes that professionals can be allowed to define outcomes and then find the best way of achieving them. Once budgets are based on outcomes, the professionals have to define them in a quantifiable way and then assign costs to them. The Labour government made progress in introducing outcomes to the national budget process, although so far it has proved more difficult at lower levels of management. This may be a lasting technical issue: while money may be allocated at a high level to the achievement of health, educational or criminal justice outcomes, the allocation of specific sums in specific classrooms, wards or prisons to specific outcomes may always remain inexact. The variability among small populations will make local outcomes less predictable than the general level of outcomes in the whole population. For these reasons it is unlikely that budgets will ever be based entirely on outcomes, rather that budgets will have 'bonuses' attached for the achievement of outcomes.

The collaboration agenda also has implications for financial management. Certain budgets have been allocated to groups of organizations, or at least allocated on the assumption of collaboration. 'Challenge' funding, Education Action Zones, Health Action Zones and Lifelong Learning all require collaboration between agencies before money is allocated. 'Joined-up government' implies that departments' budgets are not the best way of allocating money to solving problems that have multiple causes and need collaboration to solve them. Collaborative or shared budgets need collaborative financial management. The most convenient and common solution is to pick a lead organization among the collaborators and give it the accountability for the cash and the job of handling it. If more and more of national and local budgets are allocated to collaborative solutions, then new financial arrangements will have to be found that meet the new accountability and control requirements.

The national budget process

For the last thirty years, the budget process has been an iterative one between a Treasury trying to keep spending under control and departments and ministers pushing their departments' case for more spending. As we saw in Chapter 3, in most years the aggregate outcome of the process was a growth in spending not far from the trend line. Over the years there have been attempts to design a system under which this bargaining can be harnessed to pull in the ruling party's preferred political direction and to make it more comprehensive. Comprehensiveness was required if the individual budget decisions were to add up to the government's priorities. Piecemeal negotiations would produce results that were random with respect to political decisions.

The budget process provides both a planning and a control mechanism. When the emphasis is on reducing or controlling spending, for economic or ideological reasons, the process is more confrontational and consists of finding items of spending that can be cancelled or postponed. At various times governments have wanted to make the process more scientific or rational. In 1961 the mechanism chosen to bring some order to the process was the Public Expenditure Survey Committee, a committee of ministers whose job was to align spending with the government's priorities, take a longer than one year view of spending and think about the affordability of the spending plans. At times of financial stringency the process has been harsh, often involving confrontations between the Chancellor and ministers, who were told individually what their next year's spending limits would be.

While the incoming government of 1997 did away with the PESC it adopted its own version of an oversight and review process, the Comprehensive Spending Review (CSR), a process under which all spending was looked at simultaneously before resources were allocated for the next year with firm projections for some parts over a three-year period. It had many similarities to its predecessor, the Fundamental Expenditure Review, in that it asked basic questions of spending areas, such as whether they were necessary and whether their results could not be achieved in some other way. Doing nothing was not an option in the process. The least that could be done to a service was 'internal restructuring', if alternative forms of provision were not available. This use of the financial planning process as a challenge not just to spending levels but also to the fundamentals of services was an innovation introduced during the Conservative governments.

The CSR was very comprehensive and quite as radical in 'thinking the unthinkable' as previous spending reviews. It sent the message that the new government was not going to be spendthrift; in fact it was used by the Chancellor, Gordon Brown, to hold spending to previously planned levels for the first two years. Ministers knew that their bargaining was for a medium-term pay-off, since in the early years prior commitments to reductions in spending had to be met.

While the CSR was in part an exercise designed to hold back ministerial and departmental ambitions, it also formed the base for the budgets in subsequent years. Since 1993 decisions about spending and taxation have been taken together. The mechanism chosen to bring them together is the pre-Budget report, which appears about four months in advance of the Budget, contains plans about both spending and revenue, and is based on the previous spending review.

In practice, financial planning is mainly incremental. The great bulk of spending in any one year represents commitments from the year before. In both central and local government, the aim of the CSR and the Best Value process respectively is to question the degree of commitment to continuing the same expenditure on the same services year after year. The challenge to the commitment could be to the need for the service to be provided or the way in which it is delivered and the choice of service provider. The solution to the problem of committed expenditure in the NHS is slightly different in that the people commissioning services are not in principle committed to buying next year everything they bought last year. In practice of course the bulk of what was done in the previous year will be required again this year and next.

Budgeting is sometimes presented as a linear process of building up the required level of expenditures either by forecasting totals with marginal changes or by building up from estimates of the requirements to spend on individual services. On the income side, decisions have to be made on taxes, duties and charges to cover the required level of spending. The process may be more or less comprehensive and more or less 'rational' in the sense of trying to fit the money to the needs or demands for services or the outcomes required.

However it is organized, the process is a political one in which interests and power are articulated through formal and informal iterative discussions. The interests represented range from poor children to oil companies and the power sources include electoral support, party funds contributions, bureaucratic authority and closeness to the centre of government. Both interests and power sources are fluid, and the processes through which they are articulated vary over time. To understand the budget process at any level of government requires knowledge of both elements, beyond the official descriptions of the formal procedures.[1]

Some parts of the budget are easier to control than others. At one end of a scale there are demographic factors that determine expenditures: the numbers of school children or pensioners have a big influence on the level of spending on schools and pensions, and while in the long term adjustments can be made to entitlements to education and pensions, in the short term demographic change, whether up or down, triggers a change in the demand for spending. At the other end of the scale there are discretionary expenses. Military and cultural spending are largely a matter of taste and can be varied according to political preferences, subject of course to interests and power. One of the reasons that some items are more easy to change is that they are more invisible than others. This is especially so when cuts in spending are made: some services have more direct contact with the public than others.

On the income side the same is true: the rates of income tax and value-added tax are very visible and sensitive. Adjustments in items such as exemptions in corporation tax payments affect fewer people and are therefore less sensitive for electors. One main determinant of government revenue is the level of activity in the economy, and while this may be affected by policy, the actual amount collected in any year has to be a forecast range in any budget.

Figure 12.1 shows the main components of the central government budgeting process. The idea is that the expenditure and income sides should balance over some period. The Labour government's plan was that income should match expenditure over one phase of the economic cycle. However the budget is made, the process has to be an iterative one between finding an acceptable level of forecast income, with the tax and duty rates implied, and an acceptable level of expenditure.

In central government total managed expenditure is divided into that part that is used to run government and deliver services and collect taxes and that

Expenditure	Income
Departmental expenditure limits (three-year budget) = Previous year's budget adjusted for estimated actuals	Inland Revenue taxes + Customs and Excise taxes and duties, less tax allowances
+ inflation in prices and pay + changes in volume of activities + new outcomes	+ National Insurance contributions + Business rates, council tax, oil royalties, etc.
− productivity improvements − activities abandoned − price and pay reductions	+ 'Treasury' earnings + or − debt repayments or borrowings
Annually managed expenditure (one-year budget)	
Forecast eligible populations Rates of benefits and grants	
= Total managed expenditure	= Forecast income

Figure 12.1   Central government budget making

part that consists of grants and benefits. The running costs are labelled 'departmental expenditure limits' (DELs) and are planned on a three-year cycle. Spending on benefits, grants and other transfers is called annually managed expenditure and because these are subject to changes in the levels of unemployment and other cyclical factors they are planned annually.

The starting point for next year's DELs is last year's budget with adjustments for whatever spending has already been done in the current year. This is then adjusted for the next year by forecasting changes in things such as pay and prices and by making decisions about the volume of activities and what services should be added to or dropped from last year's list. Additions to activities should be defined by the expected outcomes or results of those activities.

Forecast changes in productivity and in pay and prices are a mixture of prediction and ambition. There might be an aspiration to reduce costs by better procurement or higher productivity. Forecasts of changes in pay may be used in the process of bargaining pay changes. In these cases the financial planning process is used as one way of influencing management and of managers increasing their control over staff. If a pay rise can be financed only through productivity improvements, this is a bargaining point for managers trying to get people to produce more.

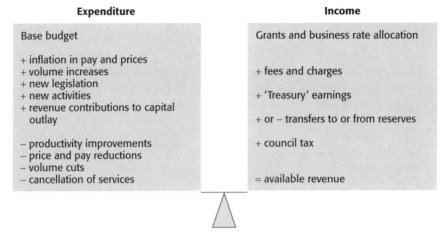

Expenditure	Income
Base budget	Grants and business rate allocation
+ inflation in pay and prices + volume increases + new legislation + new activities + revenue contributions to capital outlay	+ fees and charges + 'Treasury' earnings + or − transfers to or from reserves
− productivity improvements − price and pay reductions − volume cuts − cancellation of services	+ council tax = available revenue

Figure 12.2 Revenue budget making in local government

Budgeting for annual managed expenditure involves forecasting the numbers of people eligible for benefits or grants and the levels at which they will be paid. Some of these are fixed by statute, while others, such as overseas aid and financial support for people with disabilities, are more discretionary.

Meanwhile the Treasury forecasts the government's likely income. Some of this is subject to a decision for the budget period, such as the tax levels or the decision to take on new debt or to repay some of the outstanding debt. Other parts involve making a forecast, such as for the price of oil and its impact on oil royalties or the level of transactions generating value-added tax.

It is unlikely that independent processes for predicting and planning income and spending would produce a balanced budget. Departments are concerned to secure enough revenue to run their services, while the Treasury looks for acceptable tax levels. Guidelines are issued for spending plans so that departments have targets for their DELs. Political guidelines are given for acceptable tax and duty rates. During years when spending is being cut back there is a downward pressure on all the elements of spending.

In local government, budget making is similar but generally less subject to discretion. Figure 12.2 shows the main elements in a local authority budget process. As in central government the starting point for the expenditure side is last year's budget together with what is known so far about the current year's spending. Changes to last year's budget will come from a mixture of changes in activities and changes in costs, whether up or down. Some changes will be the result of new legislation bringing new commitments. Examples would include things such as a new Mental Health Act, a requirement to look after refugees or provide new services for children at risk. Also, as in central government, there may be discretion to cancel or cut back on some services. During times of spending cuts those services that are not prescribed in detail by statute will be cut first. Libraries have been a favourite in recent years, as have youth services, arts and recreation subsidies and other discretionary services. Savings may be found in productivity improvements, in getting lower prices for goods and services bought, as well as in cuts in the volume of services.

Sources of income are subject to central government controls. Each service is allocated a level of spending required to provide a 'standard' level of services, known as the Standard Spending Assessment (SSA). Each authority is then allocated a grant (the Revenue Support Grant or RSG) and a share of the business rate that would allow it to provide a standard level of service if it raised a standard level of council tax. While it can raise more or less than the standard council tax there are reserve 'capping' powers to stop any authority spending what the government defines as excessive amounts.

A local authority's ability to determine its income level is limited to changes in the council tax and its level of fees and charges. These include rents on houses and commercial premises, car parking, commercial waste collection, museum charges and so on. Together council tax and sales, fees and charges add up to only one-third of local authority revenues, as we saw in Chapter 3. Because of this relatively low discretion to vary the revenues raised at local level, the task of balancing the budget at local level is more difficult than at national level. Consider the options if the level of the SSA for all services together is lower than the level of spending the authority thinks it needs to make, or than the level it is currently spending. If it decides to spend at that level, it has to find the money from fees and charges and the council tax, since the level of RSG and share of business rates is fixed.

At times of cuts, some councils have simply found it impossible to get spending down to the level implied by the grant settlement. The combination of the 'negative' elements of the expenditure side of the equation in Figure 12.2, productivity improvements, pay and price cuts, volume cuts and service cancellations, is always hard. In extreme cases the combination can prove to be impossible for managers and politicians.

Meanwhile the government is encouraging local authorities to follow two aspects of its own financial management. Best Value, a process of challenge to current practices of service delivery and financing, emulates the CSR at local level and is backed by an inspection process. The Local Government Finance Green Paper[2] suggests that local authorities should receive a bonus of 2.5% of their 2001 budget over three years for meeting their outcome targets in their public service agreement.

Financial control: cash and resources

Since the 2000 spending review, financial planning in central government has been done on what is called a 'resource basis' or accruals accounting. This means that instead of each department having a cash budget for the coming one and three years, they have a budget to cover the resources used up in providing services, divided into current and capital costs. Capital costs are budgeted through an allowance for depreciation and a capital charge to reflect the costs of using the assets. Together the revenue and capital used to provide services make up the departmental expenditure limit.

This form of accounting and control has some real impacts on management. First, the fact that departments have a budget that covers more than one year and that expenditures can to some extent be postponed or brought forward means that the traditional rush to spend or make arbitrary savings by the end of the financial year to make the cash budget balance exactly is confined to history. It was widely believed that such practices were wasteful.

Second, the new process implies that decisions about whether to spend on capital or current expenditure can now be made more objectively. Since capital spending is accounted for over the life of the project rather than according to the cash consumed each year, real comparisons can now be made of the relative efficiency of current and capital spending. In practice this decision is made less clear by the need to finance capital spending through the Private Finance Initiative and Public–Private Partnerships, which make the accounting treatment more murky. This is discussed later.

Third, the separation of running costs from programme budgets enables financial planning to focus on the two issues separately. While it has always been possible to identify the two, in practice they have been mixed up. When the social security programme budget was growing under the Major administration, for example, the department was expected to make savings in running costs because of a sense of panic about the overall budget. A more calm approach might have suggested that if more cash were being handed out it would cost more to do it.

Decentralized financial management

During the 1980s a belief developed that if financial management were devolved to the operational level, resources would be better used. 'Frontline' managers would be in a better position to make decisions about the fine detail of resource allocation and would be less likely to waste money than remote financial controllers. The idea spread. Area teams in social services, clinical teams in hospitals, individual schools and many other local units were allocated budgets and told to manage them. An early example was the Financial Management initiative in the Civil Service, followed by the Local Management of Schools.

The principle of allocating a budget to a unit had important consequences. First there was an accounting task to be able to break down the budgets. If teachers' pay is to be allocated to the school rather than the education authority, how much cash should be transferred? The average salary multiplied by the number of teachers? What happens if all the teachers move up the pay scale in one year and nobody leaves? Should the school get a bigger allocation to cover the extra cost or should it have to manage within a fixed budget? If it simply gets reimbursed for all the teachers it happens to have, why bother devolving the budget?

The accounting grew more complicated when budgets began to be allocated for the cost of outputs rather than the expenses incurred on the inputs. To recast accounts to include such unit costs is a big job and subject to a different set of errors from a budget based on the cost of inputs.

As well as these technical matters, which took up a lot of management time, there were some real effects of the devolved budgets at local level. Managers who became budget holders for the first time needed to think about finance in a different way. A school head, for example, before the budgets were devolved, would have a real budget only for books, equipment and materials, possibly school cleaning, ancillary staff and other relatively small items. Once devolved, the budget covers everything. Responsibility for overspending or for potential overspending then becomes part of someone's job, whether the head or the governors. This is mainly a positive effect, because the head no longer has to defer to the decisions of a remote bureaucrat and can be more sensitive to his/her own local situation. On the other hand it is an extra responsibility and in most cases incurred extra cost, as schools hired bursars to look after the money.

Another effect was to create larger contingency funds. A central contingency fund in a department or authority is effectively an insurance against unexpected events or natural disasters. The amount that managers will need to hold to cover the same degree of risk increases as smaller units have to provide for their own contingencies.

A third effect of budgets being contained in small units is that uneven incidence of demand can lead to unequal access to services. A good example is the community care budget, money for individuals requiring support services. Since the call on the funds depends on the needs arising at any time, the allocation of the funds to geographical areas is necessarily based on some prediction of those needs. The smaller the areas into which the funds are allocated, the less accurate will be the predictions. To cope with demand that follows a pattern different from that predicted, some financial manager above the area level will have to either claw back some money from 'underspending' units to give to those under pressure, or will have to hold some funds back for allocation later in the year, partly negating the idea of devolved budgeting.

How spending gets out of control

Towards the end of every financial year, NHS Trusts and health authorities issue press releases predicting how overspent they will be by the end of the year. While this is all part of the bureaucratic rain dance to bring a supplementary shower of money, there are some good reasons why budgets might get overspent.

Budgets are almost always set as a cash limit at or near the beginning of the financial year. Inflation is predicted for the budget period, and the cash sums take account of pay and price rises in the forthcoming year. If those pay and price rises happen to be higher than predicted, the extra expense is rarely covered by a supplementary budget. So, in years when nurses get a pay award that is over the average level of inflation, the nurses' employers are likely to overspend if they cannot make savings by reducing other staff costs.

Another cause of overspending is the lack of political and managerial will to make cuts in services or staffing when budgets are cut. During the period of reduced central government grant for local government, many authorities had to reduce expenditure several years in a row. As we saw above, there is a range of ways in which this can be done during the process of making the budget. The problem is that these budgeted cuts have then to be implemented.

A third reason for spending getting out of control is the separation of decisions about how much money can be spent from decisions about what to do. If the admissions manager at a hospital responds to the need for beds and procedures without reference to the hospital's long-term contractual arrangements he/she may well commit expenditure for which there is no budget. Or a social worker may place a child in a unit for disturbed children for an unpredictable period and not consider the budget. A professional decision in the interests of the child might well commit over £100,000 in the current budget year, without reference to the budget. The same can be true for community care. Decisions based on need rather than budget are likely to result in overspending.

The most spectacular overspends, though, happen in big projects. Over 60% of the defence budget, or about £15 billion, is spent on equipment, buildings and stores and services. Various reports have shown some breathtaking overspends.[3] The IT procurement programmes that we also looked at in Chapter 6 are further examples of spending getting wildly out of control.

While less dramatic than either defence or central government information and communication technology overspends, a severe case of a financial situation that got out of hand was the London borough of Hackney. A combination of uncommitted political leadership, turnover of chief officers, cynical staff and budget reductions produced poor services combined with high levels of spending and overspent budgets. The Audit Commission[4] found in November 2000 that it was possible that the budget would be overspent by £40 million or 16% by the end of the financial year and that it might be overspent by up to £67 million in the following year if drastic action was not taken. Despite overspends on street cleaning and refuse collection, budgets that were already very high by London borough standards, service quality was poor. At the time of the Audit Commission inspection there were 17,000 outstanding housing benefit cases that had not been dealt with by ITNET, the company to which that service had been contracted out. The education department was found to be failing in many areas, some of which were attributable to poor financial management and unpredictable budgets by the authority.[5] Panic measures were taken, such as cancelling all new spending late in the year and issuing large numbers of redundancy notices. This level of financial and management breakdown is not common. When authorities overspend, it is normally more a matter of a combination of different factors in different departments, as illustrated by the case of Birmingham City Council described in Box 12.1.

Box 12.1   Why Birmingham City Council overspent in 2000–2001

Birmingham City Council is in danger of spending at least £40 million a year more on services than it receives in income. Rent and tax arrears at the beginning of this financial year stood at £50 million. The council's problems are compounded by one of the worst staff sickness records for any English local authority. Employees ring in sick for three weeks a year on average, costing the council £60 million in lost productivity.

Street services
The problem:
Road repair gangs and bin crews are heading for a £3.1 million budget overspend. Increased staff sickness, higher fuel prices, emergency flood repairs and the cost of dealing with huge amounts of domestic refuse are blamed for the financial problems. More than a quarter of Birmingham's principal roads are designated as sub-standard.

Housing
The problem:
The Direct Labour Organization (DLO), responsible for carrying out council house repairs, is likely to overspend by up to £16 million. Soaring absenteeism among the workforce sent finances deep into the red. An average 12 per cent of employees report sick at any one time, a statistic that prompted council chief executive Sir Michael Lyons to describe the DLO as a 'failed business'. Council house rent arrears cost the local authority £15 million in lost income. Council tax arrears are £38.6 million.

Social services
The problem:
Projected overspending is at least £17 million, although some estimates suggest the figure could hit £20 million by April.

The pressures of coping with the needs of an ageing population combined with a sharp increase in children being taken into care prompted a line-by-line review of social services spending. The budget for placing children in residential care and foster care outside of Birmingham is in danger of being overspent by £6 million. The council cannot find the £30 million needed to bring old people's homes up to modern standards.

Staff sickness levels throughout the social services department are higher than in many other metropolitan authorities.

Source: Paul Dale, *Birmingham Post* 23.01.2001, p.4

Private Finance Initiative and Public–Private Partnerships

The Private Finance Initiative was introduced in the Autumn Statement in 1992 when Norman Lamont was Chancellor. Essentially the idea was that instead of borrowing money for capital expenditure, the government would contract with a private sector firm to provide the services associated with a capital asset and pay a fee for them. So, for example, a road could be designed, financed, built and operated by an engineering company, which would then receive an annual fee for doing so. The advantage to the Treasury was that it would not have to borrow the money and that the capital spending would not appear as public expenditure, thus keeping borrowing and spending low in the year in which the deal was done.

The scheme was accepted enthusiastically by the incoming Labour government in 1997, which commissioned a report on it from Michael Bates within two months of the election. The previous advisory body, the Private Finance Panel, was replaced by a task force inside the Treasury. It is not entirely clear what were the reasons behind the enthusiasm. Once the accounting treatment of capital expenditure was changed to reflect the use of capital rather than the cash expended on it, the impact on the published public expenditure figures was reduced. In any case, as we saw in Chapter 3, the new government had reversed previous policies of cutting capital spending as a matter of principle.

The arguments put forward in favour of PFI and later Public–Private Partnerships were that they might produce better value for money than traditional financing and management and that they could transfer risk from the public to the private sector. Value for money was to be tested by making a comparison with a real or hypothetical public sector comparator and by introducing some competition for the right to participate in a PFI deal. Risk was to be transferred explicitly by calculating the value and likelihood of various contingencies.

The government's position, argued at length with various accounting and professional bodies, was that PFI deals were contracts for the purchase of a stream of services, not for the lease of an asset. If a road, hospital or school were built by the PFI contractor, this was an action prior to the provision of a stream of services, which is all the public sector is interested in. This has implications for the control of the asset, which remains in the contractor's hands, and for the accounting treatment in that the value of the asset does not appear on the government's balance sheet. There were arguments about the accounting treatment, the Accounting Standards Board arguing that the asset and the service stream could be separated and therefore accounted for separately, but the Treasury prevailed and PFI schemes remain off balance sheet for the government.

There were also arguments about the question of value for money. In general governments can borrow at lower rates of interest than companies.

Hence borrowing directly to purchase an asset should be cheaper than leasing the asset (and its associated stream of services) from a company that has to pay higher rates on its borrowings. In addition the company has to make a return to its owners. For a PFI scheme to provide better value for money means that the difference in efficiency between the private management and its public equivalent, plus the value of the transferred risk, outweighs these cost differences. When the argument was applied to the health sector it was found that PFI deals reduced the number of hospital beds available.

For managers the presumption that PFI should be considered for any capital investment scheme implies that the financing method drives the way projects are managed. Since it is generally (not universally) the case that PFI schemes bring with them staffing as well as the building, then outsourcing of basic building services is implied.

Second, the PFI schemes lock up the expenditure for the period of the agreement, which may be up to sixty years. Options to replace or change the service arrangements over that period will be limited by penalties incurred to cancel the service agreements. There is also the question of the extent to which risk is in practice transferred. As we saw in Chapter 6, while IT contracts in principle transferred risk from the government to companies it was the taxpayer who eventually paid for the dire failures.

Conclusions

The budget process has been used to plan and control expenditure and to provide a forum in which allocation decisions can be made and which can challenge existing practices. Developments in financial management have reflected more general changes in the management of public organizations, moving from control over inputs, through a search for efficiency, to the use of budgeting and control as part of the effort to improve effectiveness.

The process is not perfect and there are still examples of spending getting out of control. The collaborative efforts between the private and public sectors are an attempt to change both management and financial control by transferring financing and management of certain aspects of services to the private sector along with some of the risks. It remains to be seen whether this solution produces better outcomes and effectiveness.

Further reading

Lipsey, D. (2000) *The Secret Treasury*. London: Viking.
Wilson, J. (1998) *Financial Management for the Public Sector*. Buckingham: Open University Press.

Notes and references

[1] Lipsey, D. (2000) *The Secret Treasury*. London: Viking. Gives detailed descriptions of the process in central government.

[2] DETR (2000) *Modernising Local Government Finance: A Green Paper*. September. London: HMSO.

[3] See, e.g., National Audit Office (2000) *Ministry of Defence Major Projects Report*, HC 970, November 2000. London: HMSO.

[4] Audit Commission (2000) *Hackney LBC Corporate Governance Inspection*. November 2000. London: Audit Commission.

[5] Office of Her Majesty's Chief Inspector of Schools, in conjunction with the Audit Commission (2000) *Inspection of Hackney Local Education Authority*. November 2000.

13

THE FUTURE OF PUBLIC SECTOR MANAGEMENT

Introduction

This chapter has two aims. It looks for some indicators of whether the efforts that have been made to improve management have been successful. While we might expect all the reforms and changes to be accompanied by reliable evaluation, this is not the case. Each set of management changes is launched in a spirit of optimism and with a big investment of political credibility. Even the major organizational changes such as the establishment of executive agencies or the market in the NHS or competitive tendering in local government were made without an evaluation programme in place. Some evaluation has been done after the event, but without good 'baseline' data about performance before the changes, judgements of success are difficult to sustain.

The second aim is to look to the future. The chapter argues that we need to understand the political, economic and institutional contexts within which public sector management operates to explain why certain approaches are taken, and forecast what to expect in the future. It also asks what managers in the public sector can do to improve services within the sometimes confusing range of initiatives and reforms handed down to them.

How well is the public sector working?

The Blair government presented its modernization programme as if there had been stagnation in management arrangements before 1997. The NHS was as it had been in 1948 and local government worked as it had in the mid-1800s. If this had been true it would be easy to evaluate the changes they made: the baseline would be so archaic that anything would be an improvement. But of course it was not true. As we have seen, there has been almost continuous change in management arrangements in all parts of the public sector.

Unfortunately serious problems confront anyone who tries to evaluate the results of all these efforts. The first is that the baseline from which to judge changes is rarely clear and measurable. When competition was introduced in local government at the beginning of the 1980s the services that were subjected to competitive tendering had never been accounted for separately, using reliable costing. When the direct costs of providing services were compared with those of the private sector during the bidding process, those direct costs were newly calculated and bore little relation to historic costs. The same was true during the brief period of 'market testing' in the Civil Service. Without a baseline, it is a matter of faith[1] to claim cost reductions. The faithful were, of course, only too willing to make such claims, since they knew *a priori* that competition would reduce cost. And then those who were charged with creating costs retrospectively to compare them with bid prices would get caught up in the enthusiasm and produce a measured cost saving. The size of the saving was usually 20%. Eerily, the PFI process has produced similar calculations. The cost of a PFI scheme is not compared with any actual costs but with a hypothetical public sector alternative to any proposed PFI. The hypothetical cost is based on projections of costs long into the future and using discount rates close to current base rates. Values are given to the net present value of future risks. All these hypothetical numbers are then added up and compared with actual PFI costs. And the answer, or at least the one that gets published, is usually 17%, a number close enough to the calculated savings from competitive tendering to give comfort to the faithful and suspicion to the sceptical.

The inability to make accurate measurements of cost savings is a serious shortcoming if the main objective of change is to cut costs. There were other objectives of the reforms we have examined: improving customer satisfaction, making services more sensitive to needs, producing services that solve the problems they are designed to solve. The attainment of these objectives is intrinsically harder to measure and to attribute. Improved service can lead to higher expectations and lower satisfaction ratings. Needs change and may leave services behind. Problems may solve themselves regardless of services. For example, the amount of crime committed by young men decreases as the number of young men in the population declines.

The third evaluation problem arises from trying to find a consistent time series of performance indicators. The executive agencies were established with ambitions to provide freedom to manage and accountability through measurable results. In practice, targets set were changed frequently and agencies' progress along the road of improvement was sporadic and inconsistent. Even when performance measures and targets were consistent, they did not always aim for or show improvement. The Executive Agencies 1999 Report expressed some surprise that agency targets were not set to produce continuous improvement:

> Where targets are comparable year-on-year, in 1998–99 34% were set at a higher level, 50% were the same and 16% were set at a lower level than the previous year. For comparable targets set in 1999–00, 29% were set at a

higher rate, 55% the same and 16% were lower. While this small reduction is welcome (?) it is disappointing that less than 33% of the targets were stretching. (p.16)

What is more disappointing from the point of view of trying to evaluate the whole enterprise of setting up the agencies is that there is no consistent data to trace improvements in performance.

At an aggregate level, there is some data on civil service costs and staff numbers for the last five years of Conservative rule. During this period there was a consistent policy in government of reducing costs and staff numbers. All the controls were in place: the agencies were well established; performance targets, management freedoms, new accounting systems, reformed pay scales, performance pay instead of automatic progression, and annual targets of efficiency savings were all in place. Table 13.1 shows the results of all these efforts on running costs and on staff numbers.

If we exclude the Ministry of Defence, there were virtually no savings. Because of increases in the volume of work, the Department of Social Security's running costs increased by £500 million or 17.4% and the Home Office by £142 million or 8.8%. Reductions were achieved in the Environment Department (£684 million), Lord Chancellor's department (£129 million), 'other' Chancellor of the Exchequer's departments (£124 million) and Trade and Industry (£87 million). In all of these cases, a proportion of the savings were achieved by cutting functions or transferring them to other bodies.

The government claimed that increases in efficiency resulted in a reduction in the numbers of people employed in the Civil Service, aiming at a target of fewer than half a million home civil servants in 1996/7. If it were the case that improvements in efficiency reduce staff numbers, we might expect staff cuts to be matched by cost savings. However, if we look at the nine departments that spend the most and account for 80% of the total running costs we see a varied pattern of staff and cost changes.

Only the Department of the Environment met the simple interpretation of staff cuts, bringing the same proportionate cost savings: a 56% cut in staffing and a 56% cut in real terms running costs. The other departments produced different results. For example, the Inland Revenue cut its staff by 17% but only managed to reduce its running costs by 2.2% in real terms. Clearly, what happened here was that the budget was switched between direct staff costs and other costs, mainly the costs of contracted services, including computing. The Department for Education and Employment managed to get rid of 13.1% of its staff but only achieved a 0.4% cost reduction. A similar result occurred in the DSS and its agencies: staffing levels increased by 13.1% but costs increased by 17.4%. Only Northern Ireland achieved a combination of staff cuts and cost increase.

Overall, staff was cut by 10% in the nine large departments, achieving a saving of 2.5%. One reason for this result is that staff reductions were achieved in part by contracting work out to the private sector, the cost simply being

Table 13.1 Running costs and employment in central government 1991/2–1995/6

		1991/2	1995/6	% change
DSS	Costs	2869	3369	17.4
	Staff	79.6	90.0	13.1
Inland Revenue	Costs	1842	1801	−2.2
	Staff	68.4	58.6	−17.0
Home Office	Costs	1618	1760	8.8
	Staff	48.6	51.0	4.9
Education and Employment	Costs	1400	1395	−0.4
	Staff	51.1	44.4	−13.1
Environment	Costs	1214	530	−56.0
	Staff	26.7	11.6	−56.0
Lord Chancellor's	Costs	898	769	−14.4
	Staff	30.0	20.6	−31.3
Northern Ireland	Costs	775	803	3.6
	Staff	28.7	26.1	−9.1
Customs and Excise	Costs	775	729	−3.4
	Staff	26.9	23.5	−12.6
Trade and Industry	Costs	575	488	−15.1
	Staff	13.4	9.9	−26.1
Total (above depts)	Costs	11,946	11,644	−2.5
	Staff	373.4	335.7	−10
Other depts	Costs	3002	3282	9.3
	Staff	82.2	101.5	23.5
Total excl. defence	Costs	14,948	14,927	−0.1
	Staff	455.6	437.2	−4.0
Defence	Costs	21,570	17,869	−17.2
	Staff	140.8	100.5	−28.6
Gross Total	**Costs**	**36,518**	**32,796**	**−10.2**
	Staff	**596.4**	**537.7**	**−9.8**

Notes: Gross administrative expenditure adjusted for general inflation to 1994/5 prices (x £1000); numbers of employees (Full-time equivalents x 1000).
Source: HM Treasury (1997) *Public Expenditure Statistical Analyses 1996/7*, Cm 3201. London: HMSO, Tables 3.7 and 3.9

transferred, with a saving in some cases, from the staffing budget to the contracts budget. However, these figures do not take account of the changing volume of work by these departments.

This evidence is not encouraging for the proponents of these changes and perhaps explains the frustration of the incoming 1997 government as it started its own waves of reforms and reorganizations. One target was to improve the responsiveness and popularity of services. An innovation in measuring progress in this direction was an independent assessment of public satisfaction with public services. While public service agreement and Best Value targets included measures of satisfaction, the government took its own measurements of satisfaction through MORI, the polling organization, and its 'people's panel'. Table 13.2 shows the overall results for 1998 and 2000. The

Table 13.2 Consumer satisfaction with public services in 1998 and 2000

How satisfied or dissatisfied are you with the quality of ? People's panel	Wave 1 1998		Wave 2 2000	
	Satisfied %	Dissatisfied %	Satisfied %	Dissatisfied %
Your GP	90	3	90	4
Libraries	87	3	88	3
Local primary schools	88	5	87	4
Refuse/waste collection	86	8	87	8
Local adult education	78	5	84	4
Parks and open spaces	79	10	82	11
Recycling facilities	78	10	81	10
Local secondary schools	82	8	80	10
Local nursery schools/classes	82	4	79	4
NHS hospitals	81	11	78	10
Local sports/leisure facilities	78	6	76	11
Street lighting	76	12	75	12
Museums and art galleries	n/a	n/a	73	2
Passport Agency	n/a	n/a	71	8
Benefits Agency/DSS	n/a	n/a	68	11
Local bus service	62	23	65	21
Police	73	10	63	13
Street cleaning	62	23	62	28
Employment service	n/a	n/a	60	12
Council housing service	73	21	60	30
Fire service	n/a	n/a	58	1
Ambulance services	n/a	n/a	58	2
Train companies	53	21	58	22
Inland Revenue	62	10	56	8
Youth clubs and other facilities for young people	53	12	56	24
Your local council	52	18	51	23
The courts	49	18	49	15
Pavement maintenance	n/a	n/a	41	44
Child Support Agency	n/a	n/a	40	41
Road maintenance and repairs	n/a	n/a	39	46

Source: Cabinet Office (2000) MORI, Consumer Focus for Public Services, People's Panel,
Wave 5, p.12
Base: 5000 in 1998, 1086 in 2000

results are not very encouraging. Satisfaction with some services was improving, including local adult education and, strangely, the train companies.[2] The
big falls in satisfaction were with the police, the Inland Revenue and council
housing, all with net satisfaction levels in the high fifties to low sixties. Despite
the appearance of crisis in the NHS, with myriad special initiatives and a belated
big budget increase, satisfaction with doctors and hospitals remained high.

The government claimed education to be the main priority, the slogan
'education, education, education' having been a feature of the 1997 election
campaign. Almost all the methods of management control had been used on

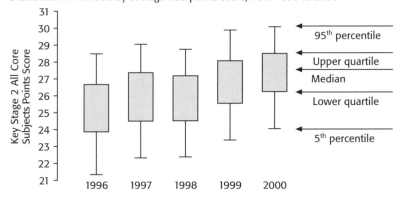

Figure 13.1 Key Stage 2 results
Source: The Annual Report of Her Majesty's Chief Inspector of Schools, February 2001

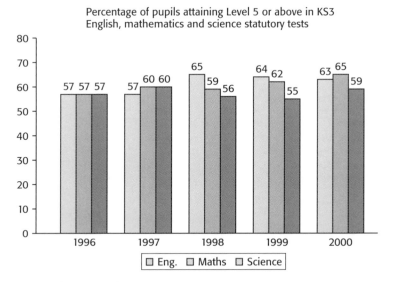

Figure 13.2 Key Stage 3 results
Source: The Annual Report of Her Majesty's Chief Inspector of Schools, February 2001

the education service: targets, national testing, increased use of inspection, intervention in failing schools, performance pay for teachers (eventually). Did educational standards improve? Figure 13.1 shows Key Stage 2 results by school from 1996 to 2000.

Figure 13.2 shows the percentage of pupils attaining Level 5 or above in Key Stage 3 English, mathematics and science tests between 1996 and 2000.

Public examination results in GCSE/GNVQ are also available as a consistent measure of progress in educational attainment, and are shown in Table 13.3.

Table **13.3**   GCSE/GNVQ results

| | Average Total GCSE/GNVQ points score per 15-year-old pupil | | | | | |
	1995	1996	1997	1998	1999	2000
Boys	32.2	32.7	33.3	34.3	35.4	35.8
Girls	37.0	37.4	37.9	39.3	40.6	41.0
All	34.6	35.0	35.5	36.8	38.0	38.4

Source: Department for Education and Employment (2001) *The Annual Report of Her Majesty's Chief Inspector of Schools, 2001*. London: HMSO

Taken together, all the efforts to improve education are producing results. KS 2 and 3 results are slowly improving, as are average scores for GCSE/GNVQ attainment. Of course it is hard to say which of the interventions is responsible for the improvement, but something seems to be working.

The evaluation of the results of the changes in the National Health Service suffers from some of the same methodological problems as other public services. It should be possible to measure efficiency, such as the cost per unit of treatment, and see whether it is improving. Attributing that improvement, or the opposite, to management changes suffers from the problem of the extraneous variables. If technology changes so that procedures become cheaper, the resultant saving cannot be attributed to better organization. The number of hospital beds has declined consistently since the NHS was founded. In 1948[3] there were eleven beds per 1000 population, 6.5 in 1988 and 4.2 in 1999, and bed occupancy stayed at 83%. But as detailed below, the number of 'finished consultant episodes' has risen consistently over that period to reach 14 million a year in 1999.

One thing that did become clear during the period of general management and the internal market in the NHS was that the market required a big increase in the number of administrators and managers, hired at the expense of nursing and midwifery staff numbers. Figure 13.3 shows the changes in staffing numbers in hospitals from 1980 to 1995.

The biggest changes in the management of the NHS came in 1983, with the introduction of general management, and 1990, when the internal market became the main mode of control. If these made a big difference to efficiency we might expect to see step increases in the volume of activity or improvements in efficiency. One measure of volume is the number of 'finished consultant Episodes' (FCEs) in the hospital part of the service. If we look at Figure 13.4 we see a very steady trend increase in activity. There is a 'kink' in the curve at 1987 but that is because before this date the measure of activity was 'discharges and deaths' rather than FCE. The line is a steady upward trend before and after the kink. At the same time, the number of beds as a measure of capacity has been going steadily down, reducing by half between 1970 and 1999. Activity per bed, measured by discharges and deaths or FCEs, has been rising steadily. In 1987–88 there were 23.4 FCEs per bed and in

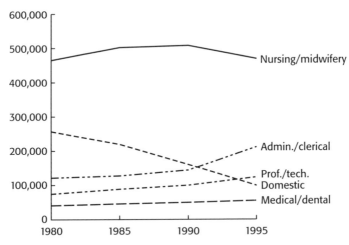

Figure 13.3 Staff employed in NHS hospitals, by category, United Kingdom, 1980–95
Source: Office of Health Economics, 1995, Table 3.5

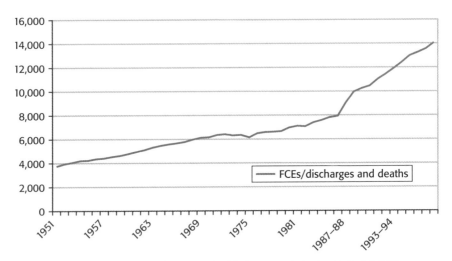

Figure 13.4 NHS finished consultant episodes/discharges and deaths 1951–1998/99
Source: Office of Health Economics (2001) *Compendium of Health Statistics*, 12th edn

1998–99 57.[4] Clearly productivity, at least as measured by 'output' per bed, has risen spectacularly, especially as over the same period the number of nurses also fell.

One of the specific Labour promises was to reduce the size of waiting lists for inpatient surgery and reduce waiting times. Such numbers are easily open to manipulation, as it is possible to keep people off lists if required, but the 'total patients waiting' figure was indeed reduced from 1,239,310 in 1998 to 1,060,356 in 1999 and 1,024,654 in 2000.[5]

It is not easy to attribute improvements to changes in management methods rather than other variables, such as changes in medical technology, that make procedures require a shorter stay in hospital. The crude productivity measures show such a steady increase that it is difficult to tie them to the two main management changes. Of course, the changes may have resulted in other improvements, such as the standard of patient care and relevance of procedures.

The future

The preceding chapters have traced the history of changes in the way in which the public sector is managed and have suggested that there have been efforts to get away from a system of rule by bureaucracy or professional domination. Various alternatives have been tried. Management has been introduced in a variety of forms and styles. Markets and competition were extensively used, mainly in an attempt to get costs down and sometimes to try to improve quality. When these two approaches were seen as not sufficiently successful, other methods of control were devised or developed. Audit, inspection and management through inspection bodies have been strengthened and used to raise standards, to make comparisons and to encourage or impose specific ways of managing. Collaboration has been promoted through exhortation, coercion and incentives. To some degree democratic processes or at least consultation have been introduced to gauge public responses to services and to find out people's preferences.

This process of searching for the right answers to the questions of how to manage services is not a simple technical question of what works best. We have seen Prime Minister Blair's exasperation with those running public services, applied specifically to the British Medical Association but generalized to all services. Even if the solutions were obvious to politicians and their advisers, they had to be implemented in existing organizations with their cultures, power, skills and relationships. Even if new organizations are created, they have to be staffed with people whose experience carries with it expectations about how to work and manage. Previous management changes had required changes in behaviours and attitudes, often accompanied by explicit 'culture change' programmes that assumed that changes to systems and routines may not be sufficient to make services more efficient or of better quality.

'Modernization' was neither universally accepted nor easy to implement after such a long period of initiatives and changes. While the attitudes revealed in the report on the London borough of Hackney that we saw in Chapter 8 were an extreme example, lower levels of cynicism or at least scepticism were apparent in many organizations. At the same time many people were excited in 1997 by the prospect of a new government, less suspicious or hostile to public services, willing to spend money, eventually, on infrastructure and on service improvements.

The context in which changes take place provides explanations for where ideas for change come from, why they arise, how particular solutions are chosen and why some are more easily implemented than others. If we can understand the context we might not only start to explain some of the changes that we have seen but also find some clues as to what changes might happen in the future. The context can be broadly divided into external and internal. External factors include the state of the economy, and the development of the 'supply side' for public services in the voluntary and private sectors. A major factor in the environment is 'events': scandals, disasters and major changes in technology can trigger public alarm or changed expectation that governments judge as requiring some actions to be taken. Sometimes those actions include management changes (or 'reforms') to make sure that disasters do not happen again or that opportunities are seized. In the short-term world of politics, events are often the best explanation for government actions, rather than analysis or ideology.

There is a party political context in which management changes are attempted, including the size of a government's parliamentary majority, which affects how bold it can be. Various political factors are at play within the public services, such as departments in the ascendancy, alliances and coalitions of interests. Alliances with outsiders, such as the information technology and communications industry, arms manufacturers, management consultants and firms of accountants, are also important and can have an influence on what is proposed and implemented. In a more conventional sense of politics, we saw in Chapter 2 that political parties also have positions about how public services are managed, some of which can be traced back to their fundamental view of society.

Internal elements that influence the choice of solution and implementation include the nature of the services and their technologies, the traditions, culture and power relations in the organizations involved, and the capacity of the managers and other employees to make the required or desired changes. These elements could be labelled the 'institutional context'.

Macro-economic conditions

During the 1980s there was a flurry of activity to make changes to and in the public sector that coincided with economic difficulties in many countries. Public spending grew as a proportion of GDP and in many countries there were government spending deficits. The changes included trying to get the state out of some of its activities, especially industries that needed subsidies, and changes in the way the public sector was managed. Not all governments responded in the same way,[6] either in the way the role of government was defined or in the way management changes were made. There was not a universal, automatic response to macro-economic circumstances. In Britain the responses were to privatize the nationalized industries and public utilities (see Chapter 1 for the scale of this) and to try to contain or reduce the costs of public services. For managers in the services that remained in the public sector, cost cutting was the imperative that came before everything else. This led to various contradictions as departments, local authorities and the NHS tried simultaneously to redesign services and improve quality. Quality initiatives that require staff commitment and extra effort are notoriously difficult to manage when staff numbers are being cut and volumes of activity maintained. The extreme was in the schools, in which quality improvement was sought through extra documentation, tighter procedures and testing, while salaries stagnated and staff/pupil ratios deteriorated. The result was disillusion and disaffection leading eventually to a recruitment crisis.

And yet the causes of the growth in spending and the deficits were not to be found in the inefficiencies of the public services. Growth in spending was mainly due to increased transfer payments (benefits, pensions and subsidies), and deficits arose because the volume of taxes collected failed to keep up with that growth. Cutting running costs and improving efficiency might have been useful goals in themselves but they were never going to solve the underlying fiscal problems. Economy and efficiency drives have a symbolic effect, though, as governments presiding over deficits show that they are doing all they can to deal with them. This is especially important in times of relative austerity and unemployment: the public sector can be seen to share the pain of the private sector when times are hard. When times are less hard, such as during the long period of growth from the early 1990s, such drives are less relevant. This does not mean that governments will not be interested in improved productivity and cost reduction but it does mean that other priorities, such as social exclusion or levels of educational attainment, can also be addressed. No doubt the symbolism of 'belt tightening' in future periods of economic downturn will be maintained.

The changed accounting arrangements may make future discussions of public spending more sophisticated, even if the macro-economic circumstances deteriorate. The separation of central government spending into departmental expenditure limits, which are subject to managerial control and to improvements in productivity, and total managed expenditure means that it is harder to make simplistic demands for cost cutting to finance increases in transfer payments. Keeping separate account of capital spending was a useful if long overdue step in linking borrowing and investment, and may make it possible to maintain and improve infrastructure more consistently and less subject to the requirements of macro-economic management. This may be an optimistic view, but the consequences of the twenty years of very low net investment in the public sector that we saw in Chapter 3 were dire and if net investment returns to less than 2% of GDP there will be a return to the decline in the physical infrastructure through which services are delivered.

Individual managers cannot change the macro-economic context but they do have a strong influence on how budgets are made. The distinction between current and capital spending has not always been clear and there have been times during which accounting methods and spending decisions followed political expediency. Strategies to use investment to improve services should in future be easier to implement in line with the high-level aspiration for infrastructure improvement.

Micro-economic conditions

Micro-economic conditions also have an influence on what can be done in the public sector. While a ready market was found for the shares in the nationalized industries and utilities, whether through public offerings or trade sales, it was less easy to create a market in those services that were to be privatized. Where a market was not competitive a regulatory regime was set up to substitute for market forces. As competition developed, regulation could be relaxed. Once that happens, the services are no longer the direct concern of public sector managers or regulators.

Outsourcing is a different matter. If public services are provided by the private or voluntary sector but still financed through taxation they remain a public responsibility. The structure of the markets for those services has a big influence on how the services can be managed. If outsourcing simply meant transferring existing employees and their managers to a new company there was not much genuine benefit. We saw in Chapter 6 that the vacuum was filled partly by new firms, such as Capita, which simply absorbed previous public employees and used them to fulfil their contracts with those people's previous employers. The same was true in the big ICT contracts, where the best source of staff available to contractors was those already in post in the departments and agencies with which they were contracting.

In these and other markets there were few existing or potential suppliers. Mergers and acquisitions to create fewer, bigger companies magnified the problem. As we saw in Chapters 6 and 7, the likely outcome of this is that the department or authority becomes dependent on its contractors and cannot use the market or the threat of switching suppliers to control them. The other solution is to develop a closer working relationship or partnership to try to get out of the contractor what it wants. The structure of the market has an important influence on the nature of the relationships within it. The future of the relationship between government and contractors will be shaped to a large extent by the way the supply side of the various markets develops. If trends continue there will be fewer, bigger players in the market for outsourced services, all of whom will be in potentially powerful bargaining positions.

Controlling a monopoly supplier can be one of the hardest things a manager in the public sector has to do. The tools of adversarial contracting, such as the threat of switching suppliers, withholding payment on failure to comply with the details of specifications, are blunt instruments with which to control a powerful company with a long-term contract. And yet the methods involved in obligational contracting require long periods of subtle work establishing and maintaining relationships and an underlying culture of reliance between commissioner and contractor. In turn this requires continuity of staff in post on both sides of the relationship and a business culture based on long-term mutual benefit.

The other aspect of the supply side that affects how managers can out-source services is the state of the voluntary sector. While Best Value encour-ages managers to look for alternative sources of services, the development of the voluntary sector is uneven by sector and according to geography. The community care legislation accelerated the growth of charities contracting to provide care services, often transforming them from member-run self-help organizations into medium-sized, competitive contractors dependent on work from the local and health authorities for their survival.

'Events'

Periodic scandals have produced statements and actions by governments. Social services departments and their inspectorate have a long history of child deaths, dating back at least to the tragic death of Maria Caldwell in Sussex in 1971. Every year or so there is another tragedy, followed by an inquiry and a set of recommendations to put procedures in place that will stop such a tragedy ever happening again. The procedures become more detailed and prescribed, record keeping more complete and reporting more frequent. The procedures put in place for child protection under 'Quality Protects' are an aggregation of such procedural responses to crises.

There are many other examples. The riots in prisons such as Manchester did more to provoke the search for solutions, including contracting-out and management by detailed objectives, than any number of critical reports by HM Inspector of Prisons. The Macpherson Report on the events following the murder of Stephen Lawrence produced a demand for action in the police forces, not just the Metropolitan Police, to change their procedures of mur-der investigation, treatment of racist incidents and their witnesses and victims. Queues outside the Passport Agency's office because of delays in issuing passports brought the results of the agency's management efforts to public and political attention much more sharply than its annual report on its per-formance targets. Horrendous stories of chronic child abuse in children's homes generate a demand for better regulation. Spectacular overspends on defence equipment generate calls for a reform of the procurement process in defence and other departments.

Positive events can also have an impact on the search for solutions. The development of web-based services is a good example. Once travel agents, banks, stockbrokers and retailers started using the Internet to offer products and services direct to customers, the government thought it had to respond by making a pledge that government services would soon be available on the Internet. The quick development of call centres as a way of dealing with enquiries is another example.

The history of management in the public sector shows that calm and 'rational' analysis has less impact on change than events have. Sensible reports and suggestions can be shelved for years until expediency calls for them to be dusted off and implemented. If managers are wise to this they will take the opportunities for improvement offered by events and have their solutions ready.

By definition such events are unpredictable. What we do know is that they will continue to happen and governments will continue to respond to them, either with initiatives or with new rules and procedures. Response to scandals or disasters is normally a tightening of rules, procedures and scrutiny, and reduction in the discretion of front-line staff. If this is unlikely to produce the desired results, managers have the responsibility to create solutions that will. They need to have a clear view of the risks involved in their services, the skills needed to minimize those risks and the feasible degree of supervision. They also need to be brave enough to make the risks public, including any increased risks that arise from policies adopted by politicians.

Politics

There are two aspects of the influence of politics on management and management changes. The first is the structure of the relationships: the alliances, connections, sources of power and influence within the government system and between it and its constituencies outside. No doubt the close connections between the trade unions and the Labour party in the period up to the mid-1970s had an influence on governments' attitudes to and treatment of the nationalized industries and local authorities. That is not to say that the government did all the unions asked, rather that options that drastically challenged union members' interests would not even surface. The scale and form of the privatization during the Conservative period was no doubt influenced by the close connections between the Party and the merchant banks advising on, organizing and benefiting from the process.

The connections the 1997 Labour government brought with it centred on a select group of business people in banking, insurance, retailing and to a lesser extent manufacturing, who were well represented on publicly announced task forces and working parties and no doubt other informal meetings. Trade unions and the professions working in the public sector are apparently less well connected than this group and are regarded by some ministers and advisers as 'whingers' more likely to point out difficulties than solutions or new ideas.

Within Whitehall the power relationships have remained fairly stable. While new units, usually attached to the Cabinet Office, are established to push forward reforms, there is a big residual power in the Treasury. Departments representing the personnel function have never been very important in Britain as they have in other countries' civil services. Engineers, another professional group important in some governments, have never had much power or status. One consequence of this is that management changes generally have a financial flavour to them: they are more likely to involve costs, efficiency and numerical targets than human resource development. Quality and consultation may be present in the recipes but the main ingredient will be money, in some form. In addition initiatives that have their origins in the Treasury will be pursued relentlessly from a stable and powerful base. Other initiatives arising in special units or weaker departments have a less consistent institutional foundation.

In addition to the connections between politicians, civil servants and business, there are also connections with other governments. Ministers and civil servants have frequent and varied contacts with their counterparts in other countries, sometimes through supra-national government organizations and sometimes through less formal gatherings. Some heads of government and their subordinates feel affinity with each other and are likely to share ideas in their constant search for initiatives.

These connections have an influence on both the expectations about what government can and should do and the way in which it should be managed. Some of these differences can be identified by longstanding differences between Left and Right. Confidence in the ability of the government to affect economic and social development is traditionally higher on the Left than on the Right, while faith in markets has been stronger on the Right. The differences are narrowing. The following quotation could have come from a member of almost any British political party:

> We need to examine and clarify the roles and responsibilities of the state, ensuring it supports, rather than ignores or partly replaces the roles and responsibilities of individuals and families; or in the wider context, the local community, the trade union or the employer. It is a combination of these building blocks which make up our society that form the true welfare state. The Government is the 'enabler', sometimes providing services itself, but increasingly the Government offers a framework for services and support, acting as regulator or information giver or the catalyst for activity. It is not, alone, the 'welfare state'.
>
> State intervention stifled the creativity and innovation that individuals and families craft in finding their own solutions to particular difficulties. Despite the best intentions, the actions of the State ultimately encouraged dependency instead of offering support to those in need while encouraging future independence. It is arguable that at no point in the history of the welfare state did this 'strategy' of rights without responsibility, help without support, prove more disastrous than during the 1980s. In order to develop a welfare state fit for the 21st century, we must recognise the adverse impact of previous policies and learn from the lessons of the past.

The quotation comes from a speech by David Blunkett, Secretary of State for Education, in 2000.[7] While it refers specifically to welfare provision it could be extended to any area of state intervention. Add to that a belief in the 'mixed economy', the idea that even if the state is involved it need not necessarily be directly involved in service provision, and there is apparently an emerging consensus about the big questions of what the state does and how it should do it. The consensus is much closer to the old Right than to the old Left.

Political attitudes to the details of how public services should be run also seem to have converged. The 'public choice' attitude to the motivations of managers and workers seems to have prevailed. All recent schemes of influence and control, as we have seen, contain incentives, whether for individuals or organizations, to meet targets. Competitive bidding for special budgets, extra allocations for complying with Best Value and performance pay for meeting individual targets all assume that people are motivated by personal and organizational advantage.

Political views of the detail of management arrangements encompass a desire to exercise central control through a variety of targets, comparisons and inspections, backed by rewards as well as punitive actions for those who fail. These are rooted in a belief that people working in the public sector will not produce results without these mechanisms. While individual ministers may make speeches about devoted people in particular professions, altruism and duty are concepts that are not recognized in management arrangements.

Institutional context

We saw in Chapter 11 that the technology involved in services varies widely and has a big influence on how management is done. Changes in the technology can lead to changes in management arrangements. Mechanized service delivery is better managed through mechanistic management. Individual response to differentiated service users requires high levels of skill and discretion.

Services generate their own organizational cultures. Sometimes these reinforce values and attitudes that enhance the services and their relationships with service users, while at other times they re-create bad service and a negative relationship. Any management changes have to take account of the existing organizational cultures, how strong they are, whether they are conducive to good service and how they might be changed.

There is also a wider management culture in the society as a whole. Business schools and other training institutions, management consultants, audit and inspection bodies and contacts between politicians and public sector managers and managers in business are all ways in which the general management climate can influence the climate inside the public organizations.

Ways of managing can be very influenced by fashions. The influence of the business schools and management consultants is especially prone to their need to appear innovative and competitive. Wave upon wave of current ideas crash over public sector managers. Sometimes they are small waves, such as different fashions in quality improvement techniques. At other times they are potentially dangerous to the organization, such as the alternative fashions for vertical and horizontal integration. An organization that integrates its supply chain can be dumped by a wave of belief in niche specialism. Centralized and decentralized management are also subject to fashion as much as to relevance.

Periods of decentralization to enhance customer orientation are swamped by waves of standardization and cost reduction. Belief in individualism and individual targets is periodically replaced by a preference for team working and group targets, and vice versa.

The ability of managers and workers to change the way they do things is also influenced by what is sometimes called 'institutional capacity'. Big changes in behaviour may need new skills or new attitudes, whether in budget management, negotiation, collaboration, customer contact, collegiality, respect or competitiveness. Champions of initiatives generally look for fast results, while often the real changes in capacity take a long time.

Diagnoses and proposals

In a world that runs on sequential thinking, proposals for change would be preceded by a diagnosis of the problems. In official documents this sequence is followed, for example in the modernization proposals for central and local government. In practice the diagnoses and prescriptions do not always occur in that order. There is at any time a small number of possible solutions that are applied to the range of problems that arise, and the choice is influenced by the elements we discussed above and carried by the individuals whose job it is to make proposals for change. In principle there might be a wide range of answers but only a narrow range will be politically acceptable, and because of that, the range of problems identified is also restricted. Despite its radical rhetoric the Labour government of 1997–2001 was conservative in its approach. Its ideas about a Third Way were limited to taking the edge off uncritical belief in markets without proposing alternatives, and it has few if any radical ideas about forms of organization or types of ownership. Even when novelty was offered, such as the proposal for a not-for-profit organization owned by the airlines to run Air Traffic Control, it was rejected in favour of the more conservative solution of a contract with a for-profit private company. Ways of getting different people to run or help run schools and education authorities are limited to hiring management consultants and private firms. Changes in ways of motivating public servants are limited to paying them for performance. Even then, the proposals are implemented by an essentially managerial, top-down approach, ideas being generated at the centre and policed through the audit and inspection bodies.

Conclusions

Proactive and innovative public sector managers work out their own solutions and ways of working, rather than always waiting for the next initiative to be handed down. Perhaps this is the most important question of institutional capacity for the future. A likely future is that innovations are generated by the network of business people and management consultants with whom ministers and their advisers talk. The degree to which the innovations are influenced by people working in the public sector will depend on the quality of their own ideas and the skill with which they promote them within such networks.

If there is something distinctive about managing in the public sector, it is important that people who work there develop their own solutions. We have seen the problems that arise when methods are simply imported from the business sector: internal markets generated unforeseen problems; management by objectives and target setting became an elaborate bureaucratic exercise. If the methods developed to replace or supplement these overall approaches are to produce results, they have to be developed with a recognition of the context in which they are being implemented. Inspection takes place within organizational and professional settings that produce very different outcomes in, for example, schools and prisons. Collaboration as a way of working also depends greatly on the institutional context in which it takes place. Evaluation and managing for outcomes has different implications in different settings.

The development of improved management in the public sector requires that people learn from experience. It is not good enough to start each innovation or initiative as if nothing positive had gone before; nor is it good enough to rebrand old initiatives under new names. Each of the main modes of control that we have seen in the public sector has elements that produce positive results in specific circumstances. Bureaucracy provides a protection against arbitrary treatment and corruption in circumstances in which public servants have access to money and patronage. Professionalism can provide motivation and self-regulation in circumstances where rules and supervision can demotivate. Markets can produce efficiency and innovation. Even management by objectives and target setting can produce positive results in circumstances where people do not know the purpose of their work. Audit and inspection can point out inefficiency and corruption and spread good practice. Evaluation can provide a guide to what works and what does not work. Collaboration can create synergies and results unavailable to organizations working on their own.

All the modes of control can also have their negative effects. Bureaucracies can be too rigid. Professionals can be self-interested. Markets generate transaction costs and can become monopolistic. Target setting can become ritualistic and too elaborate to influence behaviour. Inspection with influence can generate reports but no action. Poorly conducted evaluation can produce misleading advice. Collaboration can use up people's energy for no tangible result.

Managers, professionals and other workers in the public sector live in their own context and understand what sort of management is likely to produce results. Initiatives that are invented remotely from the particular contexts are likely to have a poor fit with what works. Eventually the negative effects of many of the initiatives from the period of Conservative rule became apparent, and no doubt the negative effects of more recent initiatives are already apparent.

Of course there are some cynical and even obstructive people working in the public sector, as elsewhere in society. One fundamental question is whether it is desirable or possible to base all the arrangements for managing public services on the premise that the cynics and 'whingers' are in the majority. If so, management has to be based on detailed control and supervision and an atmosphere of low trust.

The other question is whether management solutions that are appropriate for one part of the public sector are likely to work in all the other parts. Public services are produced by about 5 million direct employees and a large range of contractors. The variety of services, from street cleaning to immigration control, from education to surgery, veterinary science to home helps, surely implies a variety of management practices. The choice of management methods must be based on the specific services and organizations and on learning from history and from practice across the sectors. Managers within each sector need to be able to demonstrate the effectiveness of their services and find ways of managing and collaborating with others to get results. If saving money was the absolute priority in the 1990s, making services work is the priority for the 2000s.

Notes and references

[1] See Pollitt, C. (1995) Judgement by works or by faith? *Evaluation* 1 (2).

[2] The interviews were done before the train crisis of 2000/2001.

[3] These figures come from Office of Health Economics (2000) *Compendium of Health Statistics*, 12th edn.

[4] The United Kingdom figures hide country-by-country variations. Scotland has only 27.8 FCEs per bed and Wales 59.9. Scotland has 6.9 hospital beds per 1000 population, while Wales has 3.9 and the UK average is 4.2.

[5] Figures for March each year, from NHS Waiting Times Returns.

[6] For more details of this argument, see Flynn, N. (2000) Managerialism and public services: some international trends in Clarke, J., *et al.* (eds) *New Managerialism, New Welfare?* London: Open University/Sage; Flynn, N. and Strehl, F. (eds) (1996) *Public Sector Management in Europe*. Hemel Hempstead: Harvester Wheatsheaf/Prentice Hall; Pollitt, C. and Bouckaert, G. (2000) *Public Management Reform*. Oxford: Oxford University Press.

[7] 'Enabling government: the welfare state in the 21st century'. David Blunkett, 11 October 2000.

Index

budgets (*continued*)
  inputs-based, 243–4
  management of, 243–51, 275
  national, 9, 246–51
  outcome-based, 116
bureaucracy, 7, 109, 110, 228–9, 267, 276
Business Excellence Model, 186
Butler, Sir Robin, 102

Cabinet Office, 113, 272
Cable and Wireless, 15
call centres, 199, 230, 271
Capita, 169–70, 270
capital expenditure, *see* spending, capital
capital markets, *see* markets
Capital Modernisation Fund, 128
Capstan Northern, 169
Care Standards Act, 175
casualization, *see* employment
central government, 7, 16, 23, 59, 78,
      111, 130, 139
centralization, 27, 67, 79, 187
Challenge Funding, 59, 246
charters, 194–6
Child Care Credit, 62
Child Support Agency, 61
children's services, 78–9, 186, 271
choice, 37, 59, 274
  free, 119, 122
  citizen, 213
  consumer, 121
'Choice and Diversity: A New
      Framework for Schools' White
      Paper (1992), 82
Citizens' Advice Bureaux, 214
Citizen's Charter, 207
citizenship, 8, 192–3
City Academies, 80
City Technology College, 83
civic conservatism, 30, 37
Civil Service, 3, 6, 9, 16, 19, 21–2, 29,
      32, 34, 40, 111, 137, 215, 227,
      232, 236–7, 260, 261
  market testing and, 125
  organizational structure of, 32–3
  pay bargaining in, 232–4
  public spending and, 244, 261
  capital spending in, 127
  contracts in, 144

Clarke, Kenneth, 96
Cockburn, Bill, 137
collaboration, 43, 102–3, 113, 116, 117,
      162–73, 267, 275, 276
  between public and private sectors,
      169–72
  degrees of, 8, 164–6
  health services and, 66
  managerial behaviour and, 86, 102–3,
      163–6
  reduction in, 102–3
collective bargaining, *see* bargaining
Commission for Health Improvement, 68
community care, 38, 63, 75–9, 132,
      149, 150, 165, 192, 205
  management implications of reform
      in, 78
  market for, 126–7
Community Health Councils, 33
competition, 7, 37, 42, 43, 44, 74, 86,
      115, 121, 125, 138, 147, 163,
      169, 175, 190, 210, 267, 275
  in criminal justice system, 91
  in education, 79, 82
  in hospitals, 66, 123, 127
  managerial behaviour and,
  on cost and quality, 117, 135
  'perfect', 119–20
  privatization and, 128, 136–7
  services and, 72–3, 133–4
Competition Act (1982), 144
competitive pressure, 124
competitive spectrum, 129–39
competitive tendering, *see* compulsory
      competitive tendering (CCT)
competitiveness, international, 54
Comprehensive Spending Review, 50,
      111, 215
compulsory competitive tendering
      (CCT), 3, 58, 72–3, 74, 88, 111,
      119, 121, 124–5, 137, 143, 147,
      148, 208, 232, 237, 245, 259
Conservative governments 1979–1997,
      7, 11, 17, 30, 31, 32, 34–9, 41,
      42, 46, 47, 57, 59, 79–80, 95,
      97, 110, 117, 121, 125, 160, 247,
      252, 261
Conservative Party, 13, 17, 31, 43, 47,
      120